The Economic Development of Harlem

 PRAEGER SPECIAL STUDIES IN
U.S. ECONOMIC AND SOCIAL DEVELOPMENT

The Economic Development of Harlem

Thomas Vietorisz
Bennett Harrison

Introduction by
Robert L. Heilbroner

PRAEGER PUBLISHERS
New York • Washington • London

The purpose of Praeger Special Studies is to make specialized research in U.S. and international economics and politics available to the academic, business, and government communities. For further information, write to the Special Projects Division, Praeger Publishers, Inc., 111 Fourth Avenue, New York, N.Y. 10003.

PRAEGER PUBLISHERS
111 Fourth Avenue, New York, N.Y. 10003, U.S.A.
5, Cromwell Place, London S.W.7, England

Published in the United States of America in 1970
by Praeger Publishers, Inc.

Library of Congress Catalog Card Number: 77-83350

Printed in the United States of America

For Toni and Barbara

"We have no adequate idea of . . . the greatness that lies ahead for Harlem."

--Harlem Local Reporter,
April 16, 1890

". . . a nasty, sordid corner into which Black folk are herded. . . . precarious marginal employment, high mortality rates, civil neglect."

--The LaGuardia Papers,
August, 1936

"We went into the kitchen and drank beer from the cans and listened for what seemed like a long time but was only 10 minutes. Then there was this sound in the walls. A scratching sound. The tumbling, scrambling sound when one of the rats moved quickly.
     "It is a sound by itself. And when you are young, and you sleep on the side of the bed next to the wall and the rats scratch against the wall at your ear, you carry the sound with you for the rest of your life."

--Jimmy Breslin
The Washington Post,
July 25, 1967

"It is a waste of time to blame anyone for this state of things. What we must do is restore the economic poten- tial of Harlem which has been so long neglected and abused. . . . to bring back to Harlem that internal economic vitality which is essential to its social development."

--Harlem Commonwealth Council,
Spring, 1968

PREFACE

    This book is based upon a one-year field study
of the Harlem economy and possibilities for its
economic development, undertaken in 1967/68 under
the auspices of the Center for Economic Planning of
the New School for Social Research in New York City.
The study, financed by the Research and Demonstration Division of the U.S. Office of Economic Opportunity, was part of a larger project under Grant
CG-8730 whose components included, among others,
the Development Planning Workshop of Columbia University, the Architects Renewal Committee of Harlem,
and the Harlem Commonwealth Council (HCC), an all-
black community development institution organized
in the first half of 1967. The Harlem project as a
whole was designed in close cooperation with the
black community leaders who became members of the
first Board of Directors of the HCC. They included
Isaiah Robinson of the Harlem Parents' Committee;
Kenneth Marshall of the Metropolitan Applied Research Center; Leo Rolle of the United Block Association; Preston R. Wilcox, Staff Associate of the
Bedford-Stuyvesant Development Service Corporation;
Marshall England of the League of Autonomous Bronx
Organizations for Renewal; Kenneth Simmons of the
Bronx Neighborhood Service Program; Arthur Hill,
Deputy Inspector of the New York City Police De-
partment; and finally, Roy Innis, Chairman of New
York (Harlem) Congress of Racial Equality (CORE)
and later National Director of CORE, the first Ex-
ecutive Director of the Harlem Commonwealth Council.

    Our project component culminated in a report
released in June, 1968. Throughout the study period, we had the privilege of working and exchang-
ing opinions frequently with Roy Innis. We found

this interchange highly stimulating, and we hammered out many of our positions as a result of these discussions. The arguments made in this book are, however, entirely our own and should not be interpreted in any way as reflecting the positions, past or present, of Mr. Innis. Donald Simmons assumed the executive directorship of the HCC while we were engaged in drafting our final report. We are grateful for his comments.

We understand that since the release of our report, individual projects involving support to existing enterprises, and feasibility studies for new ventures that we recommended, have been under active consideration for implementation by the HCC. The underlying premise and unifying theme of our approach--that of planned, comprehensive community development--has, however, not been accepted. The philosophy the HCC has adopted is one of support to and development of black businesses independently of any effort at comprehensive economic development planning.

Members of our own research staff at the center, and consultants who made significant contributions to our field study and project report, included Joyce Dubow, Nathan Ginsburg, Norman Glickman, Jay M. Gould, John Haldi, Thomas Hammer, Helen Kaminsky, Richard Lissak, Stanley Nadel, Phyllis Pinckney, Jeffrey Platt, Thomas Reiner, William Saslow, Sheldon Shreiberg, Edward Tisch, and Edward Wallerstein. At various stages in the project, we received valuable advice from Andrew Bennett, U.S. Economic Development Administration; Fred Bohen, Public Broadcast Laboratory; Leonard Cole, Small Business Administration; Gerson Green, U.S. Office of Economic Opportunity; Howard Samuels, former Director of the Small Business Administration; Henry Sirlin, New York City Planning Commission; and Saul Wallen, Director of the New York Urban Coalition.

In the year following the completion of the Harlem report, we were able to reconsider the specific development recommendations that were made

under the usual pressure of deadlines, develop more
fully the theoretical implications of our operating
approach to urban development project planning, and
lay the basis for generalizing our experience to
the development of other depressed areas. As a result, Chapters 2 and 3, which are concerned with
the strategy of ghetto development and with the
theory of project selection, contain considerably
greater detail than the original discussion found
in the final report of the Center for Economic
Planning. We feel that our comprehensive ghetto
development strategy and our suggested approach to
project evaluation can also be widely applied in
American urban ghetto areas other than Harlem.

Since the Summer of 1968, we were able to undertake a more systematic examination of the structure of the Harlem economy than was feasible during
the earlier field period. This material, contained
in Chapter 1, draws almost entirely on two new primary data sources. The first of these, the Harlem
Business Inventory, was generated by the center's
staff and consultants during the winter of 1967/68,
but was not processed in time for inclusion in the
center's final report. The second source is the
1966 Urban Employment Survey (UES) of ten ghetto
areas in the U.S., undertaken by the Bureau of Labor Statistics (BLS) of the U.S. Department of Labor. We are deeply indebted to BLS officials Jesse
Benjamin, Herbert Bienstock, Sam Ehrenhalt, Susan
Holland, and William Milligan for providing not
only access to the unpublished UES data files but
also invaluable assistance in interpreting the data.
Of course, when the data base of a study is as new
and experimental as this, the authors alone must
bear the responsibility for the uses to which this
material has been put.

Much of the statistical analysis of the Harlem
economy was undertaken by Harrison as part of a
larger dissertation comparing the commercial and
labor force characteristics of eleven urban ghettos.
This effort was financed by a doctoral fellowship
from the U.S. Economic Development Administration.
Additional research support was provided by the

Bureau of Business and Economic Research of the
University of Maryland. All computations were performed at the University of Maryland Computer Science Center.

Our efforts also benefited from conversations
with and criticisms by many academic colleagues at
the New School for Social Research, the University
of Pennsylvania, and the University of Maryland.
We are especially grateful to George Schink of the
Brookings Institution for many helpful comments and
suggestions. The final manuscript was edited and
prepared with the assistance of Irwin L. Kellner
and Burt Weinstein, doctoral candidates in the Department of Economics, the New School for Social
Research. Their energy and generosity were liter-
ally invaluable, and we are very grateful.

Throughout the period beginning with the in-
ception of the Harlem project and ending with the
publication of this book, our wives were closely
associated with our work. They served, at one time
or another, as editors, typists, mimeograph and
telephone operators, and frequently (and effectively) as critics. It is a privilege to dedicate this
book to them.

The Economic Development of Harlem--as well as
the consulting report which preceded it--was written with the strong conviction that, in the present
mood of the country, integration alone is not enough
to solve the problem of urban poverty. In the words
of the Kerner Commission:

> Enrichment must be an important ad-
> junct to integration, for no matter
> how ambitious or energetic the pro-
> gram, few Negroes now living in
> central cities can be quickly inte-
> grated. In the meantime, large-
> scale improvement in the quality of
> ghetto life is essential.[1]

---

[1]Report of the National Advisory Commission on
Civil Disorders (New York: Bantam Books, 1968),
pp. 22-23.

Our commitment to ghetto economic development is based, quite frankly, on what another student of the urban ghetto has called "a sense of kinship with the disadvantaged, belief in their potential, and anger at the condition of their lives."[2]

---

[2]Patricia Cayo Sexton, Spanish Harlem: Anatomy of Poverty (New York: Harper & Row, 1965), p. xiii.

CONTENTS

LIST OF TABLES

TABLES IN THE APPENDIXES

LIST OF FIGURES AND MAPS

INTRODUCTION

by Robert L. Heilbroner

We tend to think of Harlem as a kind of city
within a city--a thousand acres of concentrated
misery that begins north of a vaguely defined fron-
tier along 96th Street and that disappears in the
dreary stretches of the Bronx. What this important
little book makes clear is that we would do much
better to think of it as an underdeveloped country,
transplanted by some cruel joke of geography to the
midst of the richest city in the world. And the
difference is not merely one of metaphor. What is
at stake is the way in which we think about Harlem's
plight, the way we analyze the roots of its poverty,
the way we can best plan for its rescue.

For over the past few decades economics has
made a fundamentally important discovery about the
nature of underdevelopment. It has learned that
we can neither describe its causes, nor plan for
its alleviation, solely in the plusses and minuses
of the traditional economic calculus. Profit and
loss, sound or unsound business projects, the sa-
cred cows of marginal cost and marginal revenue are
all germane to the analysis of underdevelopment--
indeed, indispensable for any successful assault on
underdevelopment--and yet, in themselves, the time-
honored "principles" of economics have failed again
and again to provide the explanations we have needed, much less the guidance we have sought. Instead
a new language of economics has had to be learned
(or more accurately, relearned from the works of
Adam Smith and Karl Marx), a language in which political and social considerations are once again
combined with economic reasoning to provide a new

and very different perspective on the question of how countries move from poverty into affluence.

What Professors Vietorisz and Harrison have given us in The Economic Development of Harlem is an application of developmental thinking to the mini-economy of black New York. They have shown with devastating clarity that we cannot approach the problems of Harlem without bearing in mind, each step along the way, that, in their words, "social externalities are all-important." "A worker cannot be exiled every night to a rat-infested, overcrowded, personally hazardous environment," they write, "while being expected to deliver a high degree of productivity on the job." Nor can projects for Harlem's development be judged by the criteria of market success that would apply only a few blocks away in white New York. Instead, as a central theme of this book, we come to understand that the projects that Harlem needs are those that will provide social cohesion and communal self-esteem and political power just as much as jobs and income.

What sorts of projects can these be? In their detailed inventory of Harlem's lacks and needs-- much of it giving us information that we have never before had--Vietorisz and Harrison lay the groundwork for understanding the kinds of enterprises that are needed. These are "greenhouse" industries --so called because they can provide opportunities for advancement, training grounds for acquiring the skills and attitudes of the developed world, pilot plants for the inculcation of the self-confidence needed to enable Harlem to break out of its crippling backwardness.

These greenhouse industries are not grandiose. In the humble projects the authors have suggested-- repair facilities for automobiles or cooperative supermarkets, for instance--the amounts of capital that will be needed are modest and the organizational requirements within Harlem's reach. But the projects differ from the usual suggestions for ghetto action in two ways. First, these enterprises are

designed as links in what is to be an interlocking
and self-reinforcing structure of commercial and
industrial enterprises that can survive in the
rough competitive struggle that must be waged
against "foreign" enterprises in white New York.
Second, all of them have been chosen with an eye
for their social externalities--that is, for the
career ladders they provide, the foci of social cohesion they offer, the potential bases for political order they create. Hence, for the first time,
we have a blueprint for change that has the consis-
tency and internal logic of a genuine developmental
plan, rather than just a series of projects which,
however excellent one by one, have not been ex-
pressly selected to alter the structure of Harlem's
community as well as to improve its money income.

However humble their dimensions, it will take
a great deal of work to bring these greenhouse
projects into being. The cooperative effort and
support of many agencies will be necessary--that of
white money, white government assistance, and white
business help, as well as that of black organization, black effort, and black entrepreneurship. It
may be that the provision and coordination of all
these agencies will not be forthcoming in the near
future, partly because of white reluctance, and no
less importantly for lack of black leadership. It
may be, as well, that the particular developmental
plan here outlined will have to be amended and re-
directed, or that the projects that have been so
meticulously researched will nevertheless prove to
be impractical.

Yet over the longer run, if Harlem is to be
rescued--or perhaps I should say, when Harlem is
finally launched into a developmental trajectory--
it will surely be because of the kind of research
and analysis for which this book breaks genuinely
new ground. The Economic Development of Harlem is
the most carefully thought out, most hopeful plan
that has yet been offered to white and black New
York alike. I hope it will be more than read--I
hope it will be acted on.

The Economic
Development of Harlem

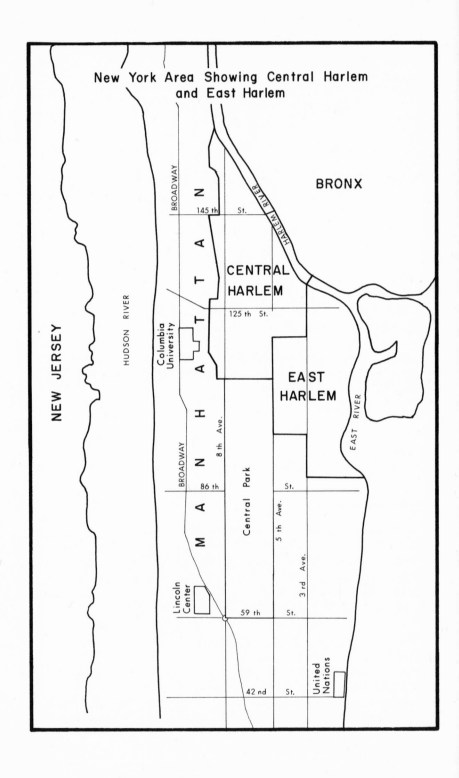

New York Area Showing Central Harlem and East Harlem

CHAPTER **1** A PROFILE OF
THE HARLEM
ECONOMY

A SHORT HISTORY OF HARLEM

Central Harlem is an area of some 1,000 acres
in the north-central part of the Borough of Manhattan in New York City.* Since the early 1900's its
population has been overwhelmingly black. Harlem
was settled by the Dutch in the early seventeenth
century and by the early 1800's was a self-governing
and wealthy rural community. Thirty years later the
land had given out, property values had fallen, and
the New York City Board of Aldermen were referring
to the area as a third- or fourth-rate country vil-
lage."[1]

Harlem's renaissance came during the closing
years of the nineteenth century. New York's population was expanding rapidly, Manhattan passing the
million mark in 1880. Harlem was in the midst of a

---

*The neighboring community of East, or "Spanish,"
Harlem has, since the 1920's, been the principal home
of most of New York City's Puerto Ricans. There are,
of course, many different interpretations of what
should and what should not be included in "Harlem."
The Harlem Development Project took its areal definition from the Harlem Youth Opportunities Unlimited
(HARYOU) study, Youth in the Ghetto (New York:
HARYOU, Inc., 1964), p. 99, largely on pragmatic
(i.e., data-gathering) grounds and at the suggestion of members of the Harlem Commonwealth Council.
The areal names "Harlem" and "Central Harlem" are
used interchangeably in this book.

construction boom and, by 1881, an elevated railroad was extended to 127th Street.   Property values
increased rapidly, and Harlem quickly became one of
Manhattan's most fashionable upper-middle-class
neighborhoods.   Much of Harlem's current housing
stock was built during the period from 1870 through
the first decade of the twentieth century.   In the
late 1890's, Harlem underwent another period of
land speculation and home building--fueled by talk
of a proposed subway line to run from one end of
Manhattan to the other.   This boom finally played
itself out by 1904-05, leaving the area with a glut
of high-rent apartments.   Perpetual vacancies led
to falling prices with banks halting construction
loans and foreclosing mortgages.   This collapse
made it possible for large numbers of blacks then
being displaced from Manhattan's squalid San Juan
Hill and Tenderloin districts to obtain high-quality
housing at relatively low rents in Harlem.*

    The 1907 recession damped the rate at which
blacks were acquiring Harlem property, but, as property ownership returned through defaults to white
realtors, they were forced to retain their black
tenants--whites no longer wanted to live in Harlem.
Attempts by some white landlords to establish re-
strictive covenants were abortive, and by 1914 almost 50,000 blacks were living in the area.   "For
the first and generally the last time in the history

----

    *St. Clair Drake has observed that the disloca-
tion of blacks by urban renewal, which has become
so common in Northern cities (as documented by
Martin Anderson and Robert C. Weaver), was in fact
a "historic accident" where "the decision to check
the expansion of physical deterioration in metropolitan areas came at a time when Negroes were the
main inhabitants of sub-standard housing.   (If urban
redevelopment had been necessary sixty years ago,
immigrants, not Negroes, would have suffered)": St.
Clair Drake, "The Social and Economic Status of
the Negro in the United States," Daedalus, Fall,
1965, p. 780.

of New York City, Negroes were able to live in decent homes in a respectable neighborhood"--Harlem
became a showcase and a magnet for the North's urban
black population. By 1920, 73,000 people--some two
thirds of Manhattan's black population--were living
in the area. Ten years later it had become "the
most incredible slum in the city."

Gilbert Osofsky traces Harlem's transformation
to at least five interrelated factors: (1) the increased rate, and change in origin, of the migration
of Southern blacks; (2) the wholesale exodus of
whites; (3) the settlement of West Indian blacks in
Harlem; (4) the inability of blacks to find employment at wages sufficient to maintain the property;
and (5) the inability and unwillingness of absentee
landlords--white and black alike--to improve or service property which had lost its value.

Between 1920 and 1930, the black population of
New York City grew by 115 per cent. Even as late
as 1930, fewer than 25 per cent of this population
had been born in New York State. While earlier
Southern migrations had originated largely in the
seaboard states (and especially in their urban
areas), these new waves of migrants included an increasingly larger proportion from the Deep South,
a population with virtually no urban experience.
These migrants swamped a community of urbanized New
Yorkers--a community that had just begun to develop
an institutional infrastructure.

By 1930, over 25 per cent of Harlem's population consisted of West Indian blacks. Differences
in life style between this group and the American-
born black population led to internal discord and
occasional intraracial warfare, particularly as the
West Indians quickly came to dominate the political
and commercial life of the ghetto. As a result, "a
divided Harlem confronted major social problems
that desperately called for cooperation."

As more people crowded into Harlem, the demand
for living space outran the area's relatively fixed

housing stock. Blacks found it increasingly more
difficult to find jobs in the urban labor market
which would pay wages sufficient to cover their increasing rents. By 1927, the Urban League estimated
that Harlem residents were paying as much as half of
their incomes in rent. High rents relative to low
salaries--an increasing "cost of living," reinforced
by continued population growth--helped to transform
Harlem into a slum.

New York's blacks moved willingly to Harlem,
and, once there, low salaries and de facto segregation kept them there. Confronted with an ever-
increasing population and stymied in their occasional efforts to find housing elsewhere in the city,
the urban blacks found themselves unable to maintain
the area's physical and social integrity.

To meet high rent bills, blacks were forced to
subdivide their dwelling space. But this process
only accelerated the rate of physical deterioration,
the congestion, and the breakdown of sanitary services. By the early 1930's, Harlem's public health
situation was the worst in the city; its infant mortality rate, for example, was a staggering 98 deaths
per 1,000 births. And the Great Depression made the
amelioration of these conditions a moot issue.

The overwhelming magnitude and compressed time
span of Harlem's population explosion did not enable community development efforts to get off the
ground. An attempt by A. Phillip Randolph and
others to broaden the community's economic base
through the acquisition of existing businesses,
housing reform, and unionism was unsuccessful. A
major housing project initiated in the late 1920's
degenerated into another slum during the depression.
Black migration to Harlem fell off during the 1930's
and the community settled into an uneasy stability.

The economic expansion that World War II
brought to New York City served to improve Harlem's
situation. Many of its workers found good jobs in
the Brooklyn Navy Yard, while others entered

military service. Since that war, however, as
Southern migrants began to turn to newer areas of
the North and as returning black soldiers found
themselves unable to find adequate jobs, the older
urban ghettos like Harlem began to acquire the gray
pall of "permanent poverty." They became places
for whites to avoid. The "two societies" phenomenon
which the Kerner Commission "discovered" in 1968 was
already latent in the postwar evolution of the
American city.

    And yet, somehow, the Harlem community today
is not fully described by an enumeration of its economic and social disabilities. Harlem is more than
the sum total of its troubles. Roy Innis has
(wisely) warned us against subscribing to a seduc-
tive "mystique of the ghetto"; for most of its residents for much of the time, it is a frightening
place to live. And yet

> The "ghettoization" of the Negro has
> resulted in the emergence of a ghetto
> subculture with a distinctive ethos,
> most pronounced, perhaps, in Harlem,
> but recognizable in all Negro neigh-
> borhoods. For the average Negro who
> walks the streets of any American
> Black Ghetto, the smell of barbecued
> ribs, fried shrimps, and chicken
> emanating from numerous restaurants
> give olfactory reinforcement to a
> feeling of "at-homeness." The beat
> of "gut music" spilling into the
> street from ubiquitous tavern juke
> boxes and the sound of tambourines
> and rich harmony behind the crude
> folk art on the windows of store-
> front churches give auditory con-
> firmation to the universal belief
> that "We Negroes have 'soul.'" The
> bedlam of an occasional brawl, the
> shouted obscenities of street corner
> "foul mouths," and the whine of
> police sirens break the monotony of

waiting for the number that never
"falls," the horses that neither win,
place, nor show, and the "good job"
that never materializes. The insouci-
ant swagger of teen-age drop-outs (the
"cats") masks the hurt of their aimless
existence and contrasts sharply with
the ragged clothing and dejected de-
meanor of "skid-row" types who have
long since stopped trying to keep up
appearances and who escape it all by
becoming "winoes." The spontaneous
vigor of the children who crowd streets
and playgrounds (with Cassius Clay,
Ernie Banks, the Harlem Globe Trotters,
and black stars of stage, screen, and
television as their role models) and
the cheerful rushing about of adults,
free from the occupational pressures
of the "white world" in which they
work, create an atmosphere of warmth
and superficial intimacy which ob-
scures the unpleasant facts of life
in the overcrowded rooms behind the
doors, the lack of adequate maintenance standards, and the too prevalent
vermin and rats.

     This is a world whose urban "folk-
ways" the upwardly mobile Negro middle
class deplores as a "drag" on "The
Race," which the upper classes wince
at as an embarrassment, and which race
leaders point to as proof that Negroes
have been victimized. But for the
masses of the ghetto dwellers this is
a warm and familiar milieu, preferable
to the sanitary coldness of middle-
class neighborhoods and a counterpart
of the communities of the foreign-born,
each of which has its own distinctive
subcultural flavor. The arguments in
the barbershop, the gossip in the
beauty parlors, the "jiving" of bar
girls and waitresses, the click of

> poolroom balls, the stomping of feet
> in the dance halls, the shouting in
> the churches are all theirs--and the
> white men who run the pawnshops,
> supermarts, drug stores, and grocery
> stores, the policemen on horseback,
> the teachers in blackboard jungles--
> all these are aliens, conceptualized
> collectively as "The Man," intruders
> on the Black Man's "turf." When an
> occasional riot breaks out, "The Man"
> and his property become targets of
> aggression upon which pent-up frustra-
> tions are vented. When someone dur-
> ing the Harlem riots of 1964 begged
> the street crowds to go home, the cry
> came back, "Baby, we are home!"[2]

Perhaps Claude Brown has said it even more
simply: ". . . despite everything that Harlem did
to our generation, I think it gave something to a
few. It gave them a strength that couldn't be obtained anywhere else."[3]

HOUSING AND LAND USE

The 900-1,000 acres which comprise the community of Central Harlem have traditionally been allocated largely to residential activity. Over two
thirds of the nonstreet area in 1960 was occupied
by residences, principally multiple walk-up dwell-
ings (see Table 1). Exceptionally wide streets and
boulevards--the prevailing style in late Victorian
urban design--still consume over 40 per cent of the
total area. But, while the thoroughfares of the
1890's and early 1900's have been maintained, the
once abundant park space has all but disappeared.
Only 9 per cent of the total nonstreet area of Harlem is presently allocated to park use. It is
scarcely surprising, therefore, that at least some
Harlem residents joined Columbia University students
in 1968 in protesting that university's proposed expansion into adjacent Morningside Park.

TABLE 1

Land Use in Central Harlem, 1960

Use	Acreage	Per Cent		
Total	895.0ᵃ	100.0		
Streets	375.5	41.9		
Nonstreets	519.5	58.1		
Vacant	11.2		2.2	
Residential	352.4		67.8	100.0
1- and 2-family houses	7.8			2.2
Multiple walk-up units	248.9			70.6
Elevator buildings	95.7			27.2
Nonresidential	106.9		20.6	100.0
Commercial offices; retail	25.2			23.6
Light industry	3.4			3.2
Heavy industry	2.5			2.3
Institutional	45.4			42.5
All other	30.4			28.4
Parks	49.0	9.4		

ᵃArea slightly smaller than that defined in this book.

Source: Protestant Council of the City of New York, Harlem-Upper Manhattan (September, 1962), I, pp. 32-33.

Table 2 summarizes 1960 census data on the condition of housing in Central Harlem. Over 10 per
cent of the approximately 76,600 units were considered dilapidated--unfit for human occupancy--while
the rate for Manhattan as a whole was less than 4
per cent. Another 38 per cent were deteriorating,
compared with the Manhattan rate of about 21 per
cent. Closely related to these conditions, and possibly a contributing factor, was the very low incidence of owner-occupied housing. The Harlem rate
of 1.9 per cent was just about half the magnitude
of the borough-wide rate. "At the density rate of
parts of Harlem, the entire United States population could be squeezed into three of New York City's
five boroughs."[4] In fact, Harlem's population density in 1960 (nearly 250,000 persons per square
mile) was more than twice as great as that of Asia's
densest urban areas, including Calcutta.[5] Precise
estimates of the more informative variables--persons
per square foot of floor space or persons per room--
are not available.

TABLE 2

Quality of Housing in Central Harlem, 1960

Rated Quality	Number of Units	Per Cent
Total units	76,585	100.0
Rated sound	39,388	51.4
Rated deteriorating	28,961	37.8
Rated dilapidated	8,236	10.8

Source: Protestant Council of the City of New
York, Harlem-Upper Manhattan (September, 1962),
I, p. 34.

THE HARLEM POPULATION

The U.S. Department of Labor's 1966 Urban Employment Survey estimates the population of Central
Harlem as approximately 200,000 persons.[6] About 85
per cent of this population is black, 10 per cent
Puerto Rican, and 4 per cent white.

Appendix Table 2 shows the distribution of
family size by ethnicity. There is no significant
difference between the median sizes of black and
white families in Central Harlem, and both are surprisingly small--2.9 and 2.7 persons respectively.
Even assuming the existence of a large number of
uncounted husbands, these statistics still indicate
that Harlem families are not as large as is generally supposed. Only 16 per cent of the black family units reported as many as 5 persons; the conventional wisdom apparently requires some modification,
at least for Harlem. Time-series data, evaluated
below, support the Labor Department figures regarding Harlem's relatively small family sizes.

While it is not possible to include pre-World
War II observations in a population series generated specifically for Central Harlem, it is possible
to construct this series for northern Manhattan.
This area includes Central Harlem as well as several
contiguous areas, with an over-all 1960 population
of approximately 500,000 persons.[7] The population
growth path of this area is shown in Figure 1, along
with those of Manhattan and New York City. A more
detailed examination of recent and projected population trends is contained in Tables 3 and 4.

The population of New York City increased until
1950, and resumed this trend after a decade of net
population loss. Harlem, however, has experienced
a secular decrease in population since 1920. Moreover, as the destination of Southern migrants has
shifted away from the older cities of the North, a
growing proportion of Harlem's population could
claim to have been born in New York. Less than 5
per cent of Harlem's 1960 population had lived outside the New York Standard Metropolitan Statistical
Area (SMSA) in 1955 (see Figure 2).

FIGURE I

Population Growth: 1900-60, New York City, Manhattan, Harlem Study Area (Northern Manhattan)[a]

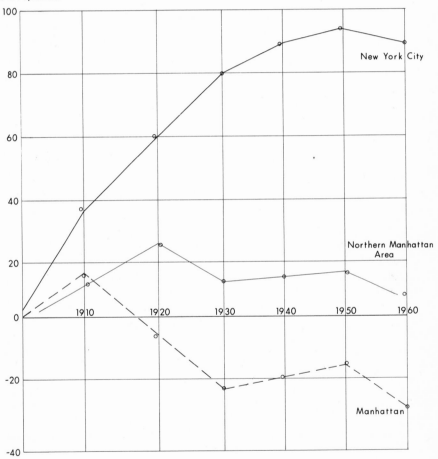

Average Annual Percent
Change in Population

[a]Central Harlem plus several contiguous areas.

Source: Protestant Council of the City of New York, <u>Harlem-Upper Manhattan</u> (September, 1962), I, p. 18.

13

TABLE 3

New York City Population, 1950-70
(thousands)

1950[a] Actual	1960[a] Actual	1965[a] Estimated	1970[b] Forecasted	Average Annual % Change[c] 1950-60	1960-65	1960-70
7,892	7,782	7,993	8,242	-0.2	+0.6	+0.6

[a]First National City Bank, Metropolis New York: An Economic Survey (November, 1966), p. 12.

[b]Port of New York Authority, The Next Twenty Years (August, 1966), Table 5.

[c]$\log_{10}(1+r) = \dfrac{[\log_{10}P_T - \log_{10}P_0]}{\text{number of years}}$

(r = average annual percentage growth rate; P = population).

14

TABLE 4

Population of Central Harlem, 1950-66
(thousands)

1950[a] Adjusted	1960[a] Adjusted	1966[b] Estimated	Average Annual Per Cent Change[c]	
			1950-60	1960-66
277	244	198	-1.3	-3.6

[a]Census data adjusted for the probable non-white undercount by Andrea Beller, "Demographic Trends," in The Economy of Harlem, Final Report of the Development Planning Workshop (New York: Columbia University, 1968) (Grant No. CG-8730, U.S. Office of Economic Opportunity), I, p. 20. (Mimeographed.)

[b]In 1960, about 23.8 per cent of the Central Harlem population was under 14 years of age; see Protestant Council of the City of New York, Harlem-Upper Manhattan (September, 1962), I, p. 29. The Bureau of Labor Statistics (BLS) estimated the 1966 population aged 14 and up at about 150,000 (1966 Urban Employment Survey, unpublished summary sheets). The BLS areal definition is somewhat larger than that used by Beller. These (obviously crude) figures then yield a 1966 total population estimate of

$$(1 - .238)x = 150,000$$
$$x = 198,000$$

This is unadjusted for a probable male nonwhite undercount, and may therefore be an underestimate.

[c]$$\log_{10}(1 + r) = \frac{\log_{10} P_T - \log_{10} P_0}{\text{number of years}}$$

(r = average annual percentage growth rate; P = population).

FIGURE 2

Distribution of 1960 Population by Place of Residence in 1955: Central Harlem and New York City

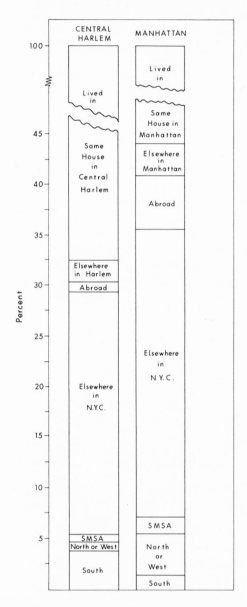

Source: Protestant Council of the City of New York, Harlem-Upper Manhattan (September, 1962) I, p.19.

16

The 1950 median age of Harlem's population was 32.7 years; by 1960 it had increased to 34.4, and by 1966 to 40.7. This trend suggests that a significant number of relatively young married couples and families have been able to move out of Harlem--leaving behind a population skewed toward the very young and the very old. The dispersion of a significant number of ghetto residents--a pronounced objective of many urban planners--has apparently been under way for some time. If this explanation has any validity, the proportions of both younger and older population groups should be increasing over time. This is indicated in Figure 3 and Appendix Table 2.

The 1950 and 1960 population shares of persons 15 years and younger were 19 per cent and 23.8 per cent respectively. The population share of persons 45 years and older in 1950 was 24.9 per cent; by 1960 this proportion had increased to 32.9 per cent, and, in 1966, persons 45 years and older accounted for 41.2 per cent of Harlem's population. These general demographic patterns are summarized in Table 5.

TABLE 5

The Changing Structure of Harlem's Population

Variable	1950	1960	1966
Total population	277,000	244,000	198,000
Median age (yrs)	32.7	34.4	40.7
Proportion married (%)	60.2	55.9	32.0-43.0
Proportion in age group:			
1-14 (%)	19.0	23.8	(a)
45 and up (%)	24.9	32.9	41.2

[a]No information available. The 198,000 total population estimate assumes the 1966 proportion aged 1-14 to be equal to the 1960 proportion.

Source: Authors' computations.

FIGURE 3

Age Distribution of the Central Harlem
Population, 1950 and 1960

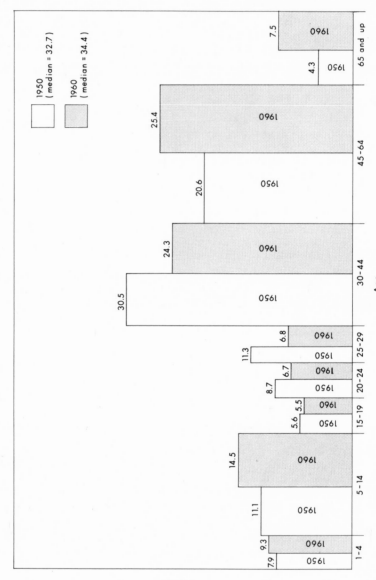

1950
(median = 32.7)

1960
(median = 34.4)

Percent

Age

Source: Protestant Council of the City of New York, Harlem-Upper Manhattan
(September, 1962), I, p. 21.

18

Available data indicate that Harlem's population is surprisingly well-educated, at least in
terms of hours spent in the classroom. According
to the 1960 census, some 40 per cent of Harlem's
adult population had completed at least some high
school.[8] Six years later, the Labor Department's
Urban Employment Survey indicated that--even including teen-agers--this proportion had increased to
64.1 per cent (Appendix Table 2). Yet Harlem's
labor force has, for the most part, not been able
to translate its formal education into job creden-
tials. The educational attainment of those Harlem
residents unemployed during the 1966 urban survey
week was, if anything, greater than that of Harlem
workers who were employed. The pattern breaks only
at the college level.

TABLE 6

Education and Employment Status in Harlem in 1966

Highest Grade- Years Attended	Employed[a]	Unemployed[a]	Total[b]
	%	%	%
8 years or less	25.8	18.1	28.0
9-11 years	26.7	36.1	28.9
12 years	38.1	39.8	35.2
13 years or more	9.4	6.0	11.5
	(100.0)	(100.0)	(100.0)

[a]During the survey week in November, 1966.

[b]Includes the employed, unemployed, those not
in the labor force at all, and those not reporting
employment status.

Source: Authors' computations from U.S. Department of Labor, Urban Employment Survey (unpublished files).

Is it possible that the short-run effect of
education on the employment status of ghetto workers
is--at least over some critical interval--relatively
insignificant? Economists generally believe that
few issues are as certain as the positive wage and
employment effects of additional schooling, and insofar as the over-all urban labor force is concerned,
they are probably correct. In a comprehensive cross-
sectional analysis of various types and sizes of
population centers in the United States, Jeffrey K.
Hadden and Edgar F. Borgatta correlated the median
school years of urban populations with their unemployment rates.[9] The results, shown in Table 7,
strongly supported the maintained hypothesis of a
strong inverse relationship between education and
unemployment. This relationship is also thought to
hold for nonwhites in general and slum-dwellers in
particular. For example, a study of the South Bronx
impacted area cites national statistics in conclud-
ing that "as with estimates of weekly earnings, the
relationship between unemployment and educational
achievement attests to the crucial economic significance of education to the individual."[10]

TABLE 7

Urbanization and Education/Employment
Coefficients, United States

City Type	Correlation Coefficient for Median School Years and Unemployment Rate
Towns	-.54
Small cities	-.45
Intermediate cities	-.53
Large cities	-.39
All cities	-.51
Central cities only	-.40
Suburban rings only	-.59
Independent (isolated) cities	-.42

Source: Jeffrey K. Hadden and Edgar F.
Borgatta, American Cities: Their Social Characteristics (Chicago: Rand McNally, 1965), pp.
138-40.

Presidential advisor Daniel P. Moynihan also observes that, "In the familiar pattern, wages of white and non-white workers tend to increase as the amount of education completed rises [although] the gain for non-white men is much less than for white men."[11]

Perhaps the absence of the expected effect in Harlem is but another manifestation of job discrimination, wherein ghetto workers are limited to blue-collar jobs where physical strength and repetitive procedures are more important than formal education beyond, of course, functional literacy. In any case, the education-employment-wage nexus will be explored more thoroughly below, where the labor force itself becomes the focus of our attention.

THE HARLEM LABOR FORCE

In November, 1966, the U.S. Department of Labor conducted interviews in Central Harlem and in nine other urban ghettos.[12] The Harlem interviews yielded information on 3,581 residents--a sample large enough to permit a detailed analysis of the area's income and employment.

The straightforward problem of finding a job-- any job--is a serious one for Harlem workers. Calculations from the unpublished Urban Employment Survey data files show that the over-all Harlem unemployment rate in November, 1966, was about 8.3 per cent, contrasted with the New York SMSA rate of 3.4 per cent.[13] Unemployment in Harlem ranged from a low of 7 per cent, for males aged 20-44, to a high of 30 per cent, for males aged 16-19. Again (as Table 8 indicates) the unemployment situation in Harlem was considerably more serious than would have been inferred from the national averages.

Unemployment is most serious among Harlem's teen-age males. This is doubly distressing because fully 52 per cent were labor force participants in November, 1966, i.e., they were working or looking

for work. This rate is well above the national
average of 42 per cent for nonwhite teen-agers.[14]
Apparently, relatively more Harlem teen-agers tried
to find work than their peers elsewhere in the country, but relatively fewer were able to find work.
This is particularly significant when one of the
signal characteristics of the "typical" participant
in the urban riots of 1967 was found to be relative
youth.[15]

TABLE 8

Unemployment Rates, United States and
Harlem, November, 1966

	Harlem	Total U.S.	U.S. Nonwhite
	%	%	%
Males, 20-44	7.0	2.7	5.4
Males, 16-19	30.0	10.4	18.1

Source: U.S. Department of Labor, Urban Employment Survey (unpublished files) and Bureau of
Labor Statistics, Handbook of Labor Statistics,
1967, Bulletin No. 1555 (1968), Tables 51 and 52.

Of those Harlem residents who do work, many
hold marginal jobs, are employed only part-time but
would prefer full-time work, or earn poverty wages.
The Labor Department's "subemployment rate" for Harlem, a measure designed to capture these hidden aspects of the unemployment problem in a single index,
was estimated at 28.6 per cent.[16] This means that
nearly 3 out of every 10 members of the Harlem
labor force manifested a substandard employment
status in 1966.

Appendix Table 1 indicates that the median
weekly wage of individuals able to find work was
only $74, with well over a quarter of the sample
earning less than $60 a week--a wage considerably

below the current "poverty threshhold." Median annual income of Harlem families, even after including
welfare payments and all other reported nonwage income, was only about $3,566. This is some $2,500
below the Bureau of Labor Statistics' estimated subsistence budget for New York City as of mid-1967.
At the recommended nutritionally minimal level of
$6,021, a New York family is assumed--at best--to
live in rented quarters, own an eight-year-old automobile, and consume a diet consisting largely of
dried beans.[17] By our calculations, almost three
quarters of Harlem's families were unable to achieve
even this standard of living.

The dimensions and implications of subemployment are pervasive in Appendix Table 1. The median
annual income of families containing part-time workers was nearly $1,000 less than that of families
whose wage-earners were fully employed (i.e., worked
35 hours or more per week on a regular basis). Moreover, about 35 per cent of the families with part-
time workers had annual incomes under $3,000, while
for those with full-time workers the corresponding
proportion was about 15 per cent.

The occupational distribution of Harlem's work
force conforms fully to the findings of the U.S.
Equal Employment Opportunity Commission (EEOC), according to which minority workers tend to be found
primarily in the lower-paying occupations and--when
they are able to obtain "better" jobs--they tend to
be hired at the lowest wage scales.[18] Of 3,489
Harlem individuals reporting occupation and family
income, only 13 per cent of the area's labor force
were professionals or craftsmen, the remainder being distributed among the blue-collar and clerical
occupations. Family incomes for the two groups
ranged from $4,500-$6,900 to $2,800-$5,800 respectively. Removing clerical and sales workers from
the second group reduces the upper end of the blue-
collar family income distribution to $5,000. Thus
a partial explanation of Harlem poverty is the high
incidence of low-grade and low-wage employment.

But this is hardly a complete explanation. As
"predicted" by the EEOC's national study, even those
few Harlem workers who do manage to obtain relatively well-paying jobs are nonetheless relegated to the
lowest-level positions in their respective firms or
agencies. Of Harlem's reporting professionals (doc-
tors, teachers, managers, proprietors, and so forth),
97 per cent earned a weekly salary under $100.
Furthermore, none of the craftsmen (carpenters,
plumbers, and so forth) earned even this much.

This, then, is the nature of the "employment
problem" in Harlem: Too many people who are looking for work cannot find it, and too many of those
who are working are earning wages which are totally
inadequate to support their families at even a nutritionally adequate level.

Much has been written about the need for "disadvantaged" persons to "get themselves a good education" as a means of procuring decent employment.
In the previous section of this chapter, we saw
that Harlem's residents have as a body acquired
close to a full high school education. The data in
Table 6 fail to disclose the expected inverse relationship between unemployment rates and education.
In our attempt to "explain" the high incidence of
unemployment and subemployment in Harlem, we return
to this line of investigation.

Table 9 takes the previous analysis one step
further by grouping the observations into age strata.
Thus, the youngest group observed (those aged 20-24)
will have received their education in the late 1950's
and early 1960's, while those in the older age groups
will have been educated during successively earlier
periods. If there is, over time, any increasing payoff to increased educational investment in human
capital--or rather, if the usual payoff is not offset by such factors as racial discrimination--then
we should expect to find within each age stratum an
inverse relationship between education and unemployment rates which grows stronger in successively
lower age groups.

Clearly, Table 9 shows no such relationship, either for the unemployment rate or for the labor force participation rate (which reflects, among other things, the worker's expectations about the probable success or futility of job search). The most conservative interpretation to be put on this finding is that, in Harlem, there is no evidence for the hypothesis that unemployment rates decline with increased education within any given age bracket, or that the strength of the relationship is itself inversely related to age.

Perhaps ghetto workers with a high school education (or close to it) will not accept poverty wages and/or semimenial labor with equanimity. Or perhaps employers in low-wage industries do not choose to confront their regular white workers with well-educated or otherwise professionally competent blacks.[19]

Having looked at the relationship between education and employment status, the next logical step is to investigate the ability of education to explain the interpersonal variation in wage rates, controlling for such theoretically relevant correlates as age, family size, and eligibility for welfare (as measured by the actual incidence of welfare receipts). In the first of two models, we decided to restrict our attention to what must presumably be the most favored group within the Harlem labor force: male household heads, aged 20 or over, employed full-time (i.e., at least 35 hours per week), and with a wife present at home. There were 551 such individuals in our Harlem sample, earning an average wage of $82 per week.* In repeated sampling from the same population, 95 per cent of the families of such workers would range in size from a little under 2 to about 6 persons; that is, a maximum of 4 children. The mean educational attainment of these fully employed workers was 10.2 years, but this

_____

*A 95 per cent confidence interval about this mean is $58-$106 per week.

TABLE 9

Unemployment and Labor Force Participation Rates in Harlem
by Age, Sex, and Education

No. of Years of School, by Age	Males			Females		
	N	Unemployment Rates %	Labor Force Participation Rates %	N	Unemployment Rates %	Labor Force Participation Rates %
Age 20-24						
8 or less	8	0.0	100.0	12	0.0	66.7
9-11	36	9.7	86.1	34	30.0	29.4
12	49	12.8	95.9	108	15.5	69.7
13 or more	19	23.1	68.4	13	0.0	53.8
Age 25-44						
8 or less	96	9.3	89.6	133	8.8	51.1
9-11	166	11.0	92.8	218	5.7	56.4
12	206	6.6	95.1	353	5.8	58.9
13 or more	60	7.1	93.3	61	6.7	73.8

26

Age 45-54

8 or less	105	0.0	85.7	118	4.1	62.7
9-11	61	1.8	93.4	92	3.4	64.1
12	72	3.0	91.7	111	5.9	61.3
13 or more	33	0.0	93.9	15	0.0	46.7

Age 55 and over

8 or less	91	9.5	23.1	123	11.5	21.1
9-11	16	28.6	43.8	25	0.0	12.0
12	36	0.0	30.6	39	0.0	7.7
13 or more	191	6.8	77.5	261	6.8	45.2

Source: Authors' calculations from the 1966 Urban Employment Survey, U.S. Department of Labor (unpublished); sample size for Harlem = 3581. The Department of Labor projections for the entire Harlem labor force, applying appropriate weights to this sample, were 8.3 per cent for the unemployment rate and about 50.0 per cent for the labor force participation rate.

does not reflect the exceptionally great variation
in this statistic; a 95 per cent confidence interval
for mean years of school is 4-16 years. This vari-
ability, of course, recommends multiple regression
analysis as an appropriate tool for exploring the
problem further.

The strongest link between wages and education
was found in the regression for the youngest men;
i.e., those most recently educated. This in itself
was a source of some optimism; perhaps things were
improving over time. But if so, then the pace was
surely far too slow, for this strongest of marginal
education effects amounted to only about $1.74 a
week in higher wages for each additional year of
school, or about $87 a year. For the sample as a
whole (N = 551), the marginal payoff was only $0.77
a week. At a 5 per cent rate of discount and under
the assumption of a 50-year working life, the present value of the lifetime return for an extra year
of schooling for the elite subsample of Harlem workers amounts to only about $1,500. This is several
orders of magnitude below the present values calcu-
lated from similar cross-section microdata on nonghetto samples.[20] Of considerably greater importance, it is below the earnings available to ghetto
youth in narcotics, prostitution, the "numbers,"
and other illegal activities.

The hourly wage rate tells us more than any
other measure of employment status about the kind
of employer a worker has. The weekly rate may reflect absenteeism, the occurrence of holidays during the survey week when the worker was interviewed,
and so on. Therefore, it seemed worthwhile to develop an hourly wage rate series.

In the second of our models, this hourly wage
rate was used, together with a nonlinear step function, using dummy variables.[21] In particular, completion of each additional year (or group of years)
of school was permitted to register its own independent effect on wages. Additional variables,
for whose effects we hoped to control, were also
specified, including race, age, family size,

relationship to household head, presence or absence
of spouse, and sex. This model, which turned out
to be considerably more satisfactory than the earlier continuous specification, was fit to the sample
of all employed Harlem adults. Their mean hourly
wage rate was $1.82. We found that no step up to
and including eight years (representing completion
of grammar school), was statistically significant.
Completion of some high school short of a diploma
showed a marginal payoff of only about $0.10 an
hour. Graduation added another $0.17 to the hourly
rate. Most surprising of all, college experience
raised the over-all expected wage rate by only another $0.29 an hour.[22]

Thus, for example, the model predicted that of
two 45-year-old black craftsmen (e.g., carpenters)
with a wife and two children at home, the man with
some college behind him would be expected to earn
$2.38 an hour, as compared with the $1.82 wage of
the man who never got beyond the eighth grade. At
a 5 per cent discount rate, and this time assuming
a 40-year earning lifetime, this differential of
$0.56 an hour, or about $1,120 a year, has a present
value of less than $20,000. Confronted with such
information, and with the knowledge that well-paying
(albeit risky and short-term) alternatives to school
are readily available out in "the street," a seventh-
grader in Harlem might well decide that the opportunity cost of investing in at least six additional
years of school exceeds $20,000--perhaps by a sub-
stantial margin.*

----

*Using a sample of nearly 12,000 interviews, sub-
sequent examination of the marginal returns to nonwhite
education in the core and in the suburban rings of twelve
large metropolitan areas in 1966 displayed similar results, regardless of where in the SMSA the nonwhite
worker resided. Moreover, of 7,200 ghetto families re-
interviewed by the Bureau of Labor Statistics over a
twelve-month period in 1968-69 (a period of exceptionally high mobility nationally), only 900 had moved from
one residence to another. And of these 900 families,
only 60 had moved out of the ghetto; all of the rest
were either intraghetto moves (750) or involuntary re-
locations, e.g., to jail or into the armed forces (90).

What now can we make of all this? For ghetto
workers, increased education (at least in the short
run, i.e., while labor markets are adjusting to the
newly emerging militancy of young urban blacks) is
not likely to be the panacea that many professional
educators, sociologists, and economists frequently
assume it to be. In particular, increased schooling does not appear to be of much assistance in
finding or holding a job--probably because the majority of jobs open to ghetto residents are still largely semi-skilled, unskilled, or routine clerical
positions for which relatively little education is
needed or expected. Once the ghetto worker is employed, weekly wage earnings are positively related
to education, at least for fully-employed adult
males. But the marginal expected payoff to staying
in school another year, in terms of extra wages,
never reaches as much as $100 per year.

Harlem's workers face serious employment problems. These will require direct solutions: more
and--what now seems to be far more important--
higher paying jobs. In the face of the minimal influence of years of education on wage levels--even
allowing for the substandard schooling society im-
poses on ghetto residents--the proposition is surely
not tenable that blacks are merely paid the wages
they deserve on account of their low productivity.
While staying in school is marginally desirable for
those to whom the loss of currently forgone income
is not deemed critical,* at the level of social
policy the education of ghetto youth may simply not
be an applicable short-term policy instrument for
improving future employment status and wage levels
as long as racial discrimination continues.

Thus, the findings reported in the text are probably
not biased by virtue of having concentrated exclusive
on the ghetto. See Bennett Harrison, "Studies in the
Structure of the Ghetto Economy" (unpublished Ph.D.
dissertation, Department of Economics, University of
Pennsylvania, in preparation).

*For many, the loss of present income is criti-
cal; the poor are probably quite rational in having
high rates of time preference.

BUSINESS AND INDUSTRY IN HARLEM

This examination of Harlem's commercial base rests upon a telephone survey of 2,690 Harlem firms, conducted during the winter of 1967/68 by the Center for Economic Planning. Subsequent analysis of the data, supplemented by Dun and Bradstreet credit reports and by New York City Planning Commission interviews, indicated that the survey probably covered 80 to 90 per cent of the relevant universe. The information is summarized in Appendix Tables 3, 4, and 5.

The total number of jobs provided by business and industry in Harlem in 1966 was 11,000 to 14,000. This is a minimum estimate obtained by projecting the survey data (presented in aggregated form in Appendix Table 3) on the assumption that nonreporting firms have the same average employment as reporting firms. However, consider an alternative hypothesis: Assume the nonreporting firms to have been relatively larger, predominantly white-owned businesses. We know that the average size of the reporting white firms was 8+. We also know that not all of the nonreporting firms are white. If, therefore, we assign an average of 7 employees (rather than the over-all mean of 5+) to all nonreporting firms plus the "missing" 20 per cent, we arrive at the estimate of 21,288 jobs shown in Table 10.

TABLE 10

High Estimate of Number of Jobs
Held in Harlem, 1966

No. of Establishments	Average No. of Employees		Estimate
	Measured	Assumed	
983	5.7		5,573
1,707		7	11,949
(2,690)			17,522
538		7	3,766
			21,288

Source: Authors' computations.

Harlem's economy is dominated by small firms. Two thirds of all its businesses reported an employment size of fewer than 4 workers.* The smallest Harlem firms surveyed employed only one owner-manager, while the largest firm surveyed had 325 full-time equivalent employees. Modal employment size was 2.0 workers.

Harlem's manufacturing sector, comprising 103 of 2,690 firms surveyed, is small and extremely fragmented. It supports perhaps 2,500 workers.** Its largest manufacturing activities are in printing, women's ready-to-wear clothing, and the game-toy-novelty industry. This activity mix is not surprising in view of the high concentration of these same activities in the over-all city-wide manufacturing sector.

"Urban" industries generally thought to be capable of generating the greatest social benefits in terms of upgrading the skills of their work force--industries such as metalworking and food processing--are of marginal importance in the Harlem area. With the exception of one dairy-products firm employing 325 workers, none of the other establishments reporting their employment were carrying as many as 10 full-time workers at the time of their interview. Pervasive small firm size makes it virtually impossible for individual firms, or firm groups, to exploit any potential internal or external economies of scale.

----

*A two-tailed 95 per cent confidence level for the mean employment size of Harlem establishments is 3.2 to 6.3 workers.

**Assume that the number of employees in each firm of those manufacturing industries classified by 4-digit Standard Industrial Classification code in which no firms reported employment is equal to the minimum mean estimate of $2117/103 = 20$. There are 15 such industries, containing 19 firms. Then an estimate of total manufacturing employment is given by $2,117 + 19(20) = 2,497$.

TABLE 11

Size of Harlem Businesses by Number of Employees

Sector	Total Establishments	Number Reporting Employment	Total Reporting Employment[a]	Distribution by Number of Employees			
				1-3	4-9	10-19	20 or more
Construction	88	29	229	11	11	2	5
Manufacturing	103	64	1,517	20	14	12	18
Infrastructure[b]	50	17	53	11	6	0	0
Wholesale trade	28	12	166	4	2	2	4
Retail trade	1,409	554	2,628	372	138	29	15
Financial	140	27	97	21	3	2	1
Services	871	280	883	220	49	9	2
Total	2,690	983	5,573	659	223	56	45

[a]Measured in full-time equivalents, assumed to equal one full-time employee or two part-time employees.

[b]Transportation, communications, and utilities.

Source: Center for Economic Planning, Harlem Business Inventory.

We were able to identify 88 construction firms
in Central Harlem, of which 29 reported their employment. Of these, 7 employed ten or more men at
the time of their interview. As the level of construction activity, and therefore employment, tends
to be minimal during the winter--when this survey
was conducted--these figures probably understate
the total annual employment generated by Central
Harlem construction firms. Assuming that employment in nonreporting firms is distributed in a
fashion similar to employment in those firms who
answered this question, it may be inferred that
Harlem's construction sector employs between 700
and 900 workers at any particular time. An employment of this magnitude represents a substantial
community capability of carrying out local improvement projects, the ability to subcontract from
larger firms, and the ability to perform moderate-
scale independent construction or urban renewal
projects.

The percentages of total Harlem employment
found in manufacturing and construction--activities
which must form the base of any long-range development program--are similar to the corresponding percentages within the city-wide economy, as shown in
Table 12. The data indicate, however, that Harlem
lacks the infrastructure and financial activities
of the city as a whole. Its disproportionately
large retail sector is inadequately supported by a
wholesaling base--a base less than one third of the
relative size of this activity in similar areas
throughout the city. This activity mix cannot be
explained simply by referring to the area as a residential neighborhood. Harlem's economic development has been a process whereby a mixed industrial-
residential neighborhood has deteriorated through
the inability of its residents to command the resources necessary to implement a balanced type of
growth. Businessmen have established themselves
in the retail market because they have been excluded from entry into more capital-intensive wholesale and other infrastructural support activities.

TABLE 12

Percentages of Employment by Industry
Sectors, Harlem and New York City

Sector	Central Harlem[a] (1967-68)	New York City[b] (1966)
Construction	4.1	3.4
Manufacturing	27.2	27.7
Infrastructure	1.0	10.2
Wholesale trade	3.0	9.9
Retail trade	47.2	13.9
Finance	1.7	12.7
Services	15.8	22.2
	(100.0)	(100.0)

[a]Center for Economic Planning, Harlem Business Inventory.

[b]New York State Department of Labor, Employment Review (August, 1967), pp. 17-22.

Ownership of Business Properties

The great majority of Harlem businessmen do not own their premises. Almost 90 per cent of the entrepreneurs responding to this question in the survey indicated that they rented their establishments. Ownership of business establishments appears to be concentrated in those activities having only a single representative firm in the Harlem area. Although there is no inexpensive short cut to determining who holds the titles to Harlem's commercial

properties, it does appear that they are not held by
the business community, black or white, inside the
ghetto itself:

Total number of establishments: 2,690

Number reporting on ownership: 1,001
   no. of owners   113 (11%)
   no. of renters   888 (89%)

Age of Harlem Businesses

It is reasonable to suppose that differences
in the size and efficiency of firms may depend to
some extent on their age. More precisely, it is
often hypothesized that older establishments are
generally small and, by implication, not very efficient. New firms, however, are supposed to be larger and more modern in terms of their embodied technologies.

Almost 970 firms responded to our question regarding how long they have been doing business at
their present site. The mean number of years at
the present location for the reporting sample was
16 years;* however, there were significant devia-
tions within the sample--the youngest establishment
was a year old, while the oldest had been operating
in the same location for 80 years. One hundred and
ninety individual firms had been operating for 30
years or more, and nearly 3 per cent of the reporting businesses were at least a half-century old.
In general the industrial businesses were older
than those in commercial or financial activities,
with the oldest in structural steel construction,
wholesale machinery, and wholesale plumbing and
heating supplies.

The age distribution of Harlem businesses may
be typical of center-city neighborhoods in older

-----

*With a two-tailed 95 per cent confidence in-
terval of 15 to 17-1/2 years.

metropolitan areas. The structure of local consumer
demand is undoubtedly more variable over time than
the metropolitan demand for intermediate industrial
products. This, coupled with a relatively higher
degree of mobility in the commercial than in the industrial activities, has left Harlem's economy with
a residual of industrial firms that have failed to
move along with city-wide shifts in the location of
commercial and financial activity.

In an attempt to confirm the relationship between the size of ghetto establishments and their
age, a series of regression analyses were conducted
on the maintained hypothesis that old establishments will be smaller.

The formal model was: $S = \alpha_0 + \alpha_1 A + \varepsilon$, where
S is firm size by number of employees, A is age of
firm, ε is a random disturbance term. The maintained hypothesis is: $\alpha_1 < 0$.

Result: $S = 4.5947 - 0.0081 A$
Std. error   (0.9674) (0.0446)

While the negative sign of the age coefficient
was as expected, the coefficient itself had no
statistical significance. Subsequent analysis
performed by regrouping establishments by race and
by type of industrial activity yielded similar results. In Harlem there is no simple and easily
identified relationship between the employment size
of a firm and its age.

Ownership and Race of Harlem Businesses

Approximately 1,075 firms reported on the ethnicity of the owner or, in some cases, of the manager of the firm. Of these, 50 per cent were black-
owned, 37 per cent white-owned, and 4 per cent owned
by Spanish-speaking persons, virtually all Puerto
Rican. Assuming that these data are reliable--that
is, assuming away the all-too-realistic possibility
that blacks are employed as front men by white absentee owners--we are still left with the problem

of determining whether or not the sample is representative. It is our belief that a large majority
of the 1,600 firms that did not report their ownership ethnicity were owned by whites who did not
wish to have this fact known--at least to us.

In most of the activities where a majority of
the firms did report the ethnicity of their owner,
blacks fared rather well. Black-owned or black-
managed firms dominated trucking, dry-cleaning, and
service-station activities. They also accounted
for a substantial share of liquor-store and drugstore ownership; they do not, however, own much of
the area's manufacturing activities.*

A summary of the distribution of number of employees of Harlem businesses tabulated by ownership
ethnicity is presented in Table 13 and Figures 4
and 5.

The distribution of number of employees in Harlem firms owned by whites (Figure 4) reflects the
existence of a number of fairly large outliers. To
assess the relevance of ownership ethnicity as a de-
terminant of firm size, we ran regressions of firm
size (measured by number of employees) on ownership
ethnicity. The model specified was:

$$S = \alpha_0 + \sum_{i=1}^{4} \alpha_i X_i + \varepsilon$$

where

S = Firm size by number of employees

$$X_1 = \begin{cases} 1 \text{ if black owner} \\ 0 \text{ otherwise} \end{cases}$$

---

*In an attempt to ameliorate this situation
somewhat, the Harlem Commonwealth Council recently
purchased the area's largest metalworking operation, the Acme Foundry.

TABLE 13

Employment in Harlem Businesses by Race of Owner

Race	Total Establishments Reporting Race	Number Reporting Employment	Total Employment Reported	Distribution by Number of Employees							
				1 - 3		4 - 9		10 - 19		20 or more	
				No.	%	No.	%	No.	%	No.	%
Black	629	505	1,566	400	79.2	83	16.4	14	2.7	8	1.7
White	397	339	2,802	181	53.3	106	31.3	26	7.7	26	7.7
Spanish	44	32	231	18	56.3	5	15.6	4	12.5	5	15.6
Chinese	8	7	22	4	57.1	3	42.9	0	0.0	0	0.0

Source: Center for Economic Planning, Harlem Business Inventory.

FIGURE 4

Distribution of Number of Employees in White-Owned
Establishments in Central Harlem, Winter 1967 / 68

sample = 339

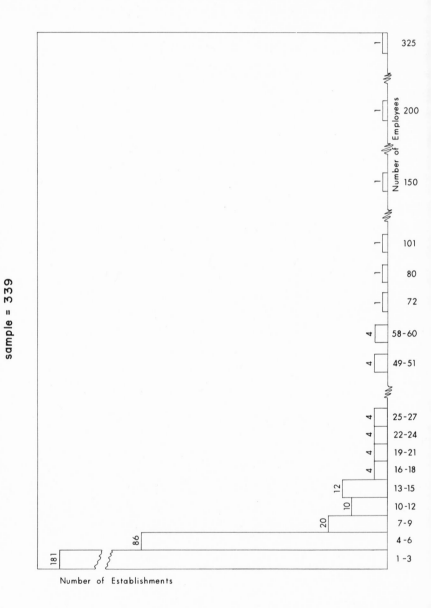

Number of Establishments

FIGURE 5

Distribution of Number of Employees in Black-Owned
Establishments in Central Harlem, Winter 1967/68

sample = 505

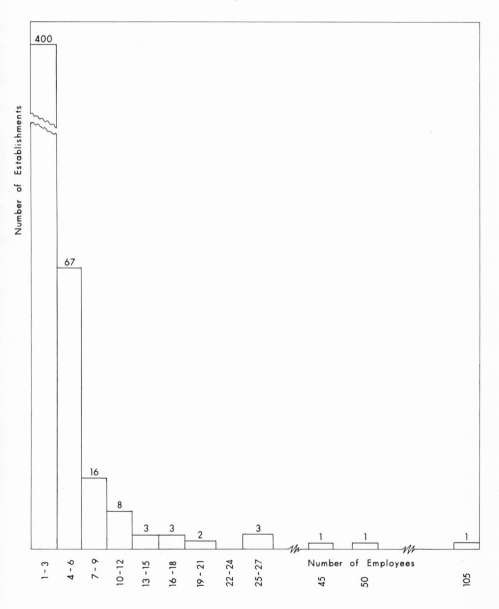

41

$$X_2 = \begin{cases} 1 \text{ if white owner} \\ 0 \text{ otherwise} \end{cases}$$

$$X_3 = \begin{cases} 1 \text{ if Spanish-speaking owner} \\ 0 \text{ otherwise} \end{cases}$$

$$X_4 = \begin{cases} 1 \text{ if Chinese owner} \\ 0 \text{ otherwise} \end{cases}$$

The X_4 dummy variable was excluded to avoid singularity in the moments matrix. The fitted regression equation (with standard errors in parentheses) was:

$$S = 2.9380 + 0.0983 \ X_1 - 3.9370 \ X_2 + 1.4906 \ X_3$$
$$(0.8002) \ (0.1050) \qquad (1.3536) \qquad (4.0382)$$

The $\underline{t}$ value of the X_2 variable (race-white) is 2.91 and is significant at the 99 per cent confidence level. Clearly there is some tendency for white-owned firms to be larger than those owned by blacks or Puerto Ricans.

Two variables previously discussed--ownership of business property and age of the business--are tabulated again by race in Tables 14 and 15. These tables lead to the conclusion that more whites own their premises than do blacks, but the differences are not large. Harlem entrepreneurs, black and white, are paying rent to someone else. Insofar as the age-of-business variable is concerned, however, there is a significant difference in ownership ethnicity. White-owned Harlem businesses are, on the average, almost twice as old as those owned by blacks (22 years as against 13.5 years). A very substantial proportion (one third) of the white businesses were established prior to World War II. Over three quarters of the white-owned businesses are at least 10 years old, whereas only one half of the black-owned businesses are at least 10 years old.

Beyond these differences, the general impression is one of substantial age. Harlem's business base is relatively old--carrying with it various implications regarding the probable quality of its capital stock and state of technology.

TABLE 14

Distribution of Harlem Businesses by Ownership and Race

Race of Owner	Total Establishments Reporting Race	Ownership of Business Property			
		Number Reporting	Rent Premises No.	%	Own Premises No.	%
Black	629	515	474	92.0	41	8.0
White	397	330	275	83.3	55	16.7
Spanish	44	35	34	97.1	1	2.9
Chinese	8	7	6	85.7	1	14.3

Source: Center for Economic Planning, Harlem Business Inventory.

43

TABLE 15

Distribution of Harlem Businesses by Age and Race

Race of Owner	Total Establishments Reporting Race	Number Reporting	Mean Years	Age Distribution of Establishment							
				1 - 2		3 - 9		10 - 29		30 or more	
				No.	%	No.	%	No.	%	No.	%
Black	629	482	13.4	73	15.1	154	32.0	200	41.5	55	11.4
White	397	330	22.0	15	4.5	63	19.1	144	43.6	108	32.7
Spanish	44	35	11.7	6	17.1	15	42.9	11	31.4	3	8.6
Chinese	8	7	8.1	1	14.3	3	42.9	3	42.9	0	0.0

Source: Center for Economic Planning, Harlem Business Inventory.

The 1965-67 period saw little new business investment in Central Harlem. The investment that
took place was predominantly black. More than
three quarters of the new businesses reporting
their ownership ethnicity were owned by black entrepreneurs.

Business Conditions

During a period (1967/68) characterized by
high rates of national economic growth, less than
20 per cent of Harlem firms responding to our question regarding their individual business conditions
reported that they were "doing better." Firms reporting black ownership were, in general, more op-
timistic regarding their present situation, while
relatively more of those owned by whites felt that
their business position had deteriorated compared
with the previous year. (See Table 16.)

TABLE 16

Reported Business Conditions in Harlem

Race of Owner	No. of Responses	Doing Better	Doing Worse	Doing the Same
Black-owned	393	84	167	142
	100.0%	21.4%	42.5%	36.1%
White-owned	205	27	102	76
	100.0%	13.2%	49.8%	37.0%
Total	598	111	269	218
	100.0%	18.5%	45.0%	36.5%

Source: Center for Economic Planning, Harlem
Business Inventory.

When these responses are disaggregated into
Standard Industrial Classification (SIC) groups it
is clear that, within a general framework of blacks
responding "better" somewhat more than whites,
there were significant differences in the outlook
of specific business groups (see Table 17). Among
the SIC classes with a high incidence of "better"
responses are food and furniture manufacturing,
transportation services, and insurance agents;
among those with a high incidence of "worse" are
building materials dealers, retail furniture and
appliances, eating places, banking, real estate,
and miscellaneous business services.

Conducting a business in Harlem confronts an
entrepreneur with difficulties that may or may not
be encountered by firms in general. Although many
firms face one or another operating difficulty, in
Harlem, as in other slum areas, these factors may
all be present simultaneously. From our survey, we
have selected sample indicators of the types and
magnitudes of the problems that Harlem entrepre-
neurs--both black and white--must face in the course
of their daily operations; these are shown in Table
18.

As firm size in Harlem tends to be small, difficulties in running a business are often faced by
individuals--and not by impersonal corporate structures. The candid responses of these individuals
provide an insight into their problems--an insight
which strongly complements the findings shown in
Table 18.

On police protection:
-Pilferage is tremendous
-Because I'm black, I can't get police pro-
 tection
-Drug addiction is a hazard
-Put plainclothes Negro cops on the beat
 rather than white cops
-The precinct is down the street--but I don't
 get any help

TABLE 17

Reported Harlem Business Conditions
by Selected Industries

Standard Industrial Classification		No. of Firms	Per Cent of Responses		
			"Better"	"Worse"	"Same"
	Contract Construction				
15	General building contractors	37	0	33	67
17	Special trade contractors	51	0	46	54
	Manufacturing				
20	Food and kindred	6	66	0	34
23	Apparel and other textile products	23	33	22	44
25	Furniture and fixtures	6	60	40	0
27	Printing and publishing	27	40	20	40
34	Fabricated metal products	8	0	50	50
35	Machinery (exc. electrical)	6	50	50	0
39	Miscellaneous manufacturing	11	0	100	0
	Transportation & Utilities				
42	Trucking and warehousing	30	36	18	46
47	Transportation services	11	100	0	0
	Wholesale and retail trade				
50	Wholesale trade	28	13	37	50
52	Building materials	39	0	60	40
53	General merchandise, retail	51	43	36	21

(continued)

TABLE 17 (continued)

Standard Industrial Classification	No. of Firms	Per Cent of Responses		
		"Better"	"Worse"	"Same"
54 Food stores	325	13	46	40
55 Automotive dealers and service stations	34	36	27	36
56 Apparel and accessory stores	161	20	46	34
57 Furniture and home furnishings	108	24	52	24
58 Eating and drinking places	332	16	50	40
59 Miscellaneous retail stores	358	16	46	37
Finance, Insurance, Real Estate				
60 Banking	10	0	67	33
64 Insurance agents, brokers and service	30	100	0	0
65 Real estate	88	14	79	7
Services				
72 Personal services	660	17	46	37
73 Miscellaneous business services	56	20	60	20
75 Auto repair, services, and garages	35	37	13	50
76 Miscellaneous repair services	61	21	22	57
		19%	45%	36%

Source: Authors' computations.

TABLE 18

Operating Difficulties Reported by Harlem Businesses

Type of Difficulty	Per Cent
Lack of adequate police protection	33.3
Difficulty in obtaining commercial insurance	22.4
Difficulty in securing various types of credit	15.7
General lack of skilled help in the area	7.7
High costs of doing business	6.7
Poorly maintained physical plant and area	5.3
Unable to compete with larger firms	3.9
Secular shift in population and consumer tastes	3.6
"Brand name" syndrome and lack of trust in black-owned business	.7
Poor market location	.5
Admitted entrepreneurial failure	.2

49

On insurance and credit:
-Can't get an FHA loan
-Getting credit is a racial problem
-I need $2,000, and can't get it
-I am interested in any kind of financial aid

On the general lack of skilled help:
-Skilled help is impossible to find unless you
 go outside the area
-Impossible to get qualified help in the area--
 someone has to do the training
-Skilled help refuses to work for Negro employers
-My help quits after a few months

On entrepreneurial failures:
-People lack confidence in the Negro's ability,
 and buy from white-owned business
-Negroes go to whites for their larger purchases
-I'm open only for specific customers
-I used to have six stores--now I've only got
 two

On the area and physical plant:
-The neighborhood is absolutely deteriorating
-If I institute legal action to get the place
 repaired, the landlord pays off the lawyer
-The general appearance of the area is the
 major problem
-The area has been burnt out
-I made a wrong decision when I moved to this
 area
-I'm closing not because of money but the in-
 sanity of the area

Summary

The business sector of the Harlem economy probably provides a minimum of between 11,000 and 14,000
and perhaps as many as 21,000 jobs in the area.

It is presently not possible to determine how
many of these jobs are (or might conceivably be)
filled by Harlem residents. In any case, they constitute a potential base for a local economic

development program. The construction industry,
while fragmented, could provide (under suitable organizational arrangements) a core of project development and renewal workers. The dominance of retail and service activities suggests that a development program ought to pay special attention to problems of distribution and the possibilities for backward linkage into wholesaling and manufacturing.

NOTES

1. This history draws principally upon Gilbert
Osofsky, Harlem: The Making of a Ghetto (New York:
Harper and Row, 1967), and Kenneth Clark, Dark
Ghetto (New York: Harper and Row, 1965). The
direct quotations are from Osofsky, unless noted
otherwise.

2. St. Clair Drake, "The Social and Economic
Status of the Negro in the United States," Daedalus,
Fall, 1965, p. 780.

3. Claude Brown, Manchild in the Promised
Land (New York: Signet, 1965), p. 421.

4. Newsweek, November 20, 1967, cited in
Bennett Harrison, "A Pilot Project for the Economic
Development Planning of American Urban Slums," In-
ternational Development Review, March, 1968. The
Manhattan housing statistics are from Protestant
Council of the City of New York, Harlem-Upper Man-
hattan (September, 1962), I, p. 34.

5. T. G. McGee, The Southeast Asian City:
A Social Geography of the Primate Cities of Southeast Asia (London and New York: Bell and Sons,
Ltd., and Frederick A. Praeger, Inc., 1967), Chapter 9.

6. U.S. Department of Labor, 1966 Urban Employment Survey, unpublished data files (hereafter
cited as UES); see also Tables 3 and 4.

7. Protestant Council, op. cit.

8. Ibid., Chart VII.

9. Jeffrey K. Hadden and Edgar F. Borgatta, American Cities: Their Social Characteristics (Chicago: Rand McNally, 1965); the intercorrelation tables are on pp. 138-40.

10. Fordham University, Institute for Urban Studies, A Profile of the Bronx Economy (New York: 1967), p. 37.

11. Daniel P. Moynihan, "Employment, Income, and the Ordeal of the Negro Family," Daedalus, Fall, 1965, p. 756.

12. UES; the entire ten-area sample is examined in Bennett Harrison, "Studies in the Structure of the Ghetto Economy" (unpublished Ph.D. dissertation, Department of Economics, University of Pennsylvania). (Hereafter cited as "Studies.")

13. U.S. Department of Labor, Bureau of Labor Statistics, Handbook of Labor Statistics, 1967, Bulletin No. 1555 (1968), Tables 51 and 52. The national nonwhite rate was 6.7 per cent during this period.

14. Ibid., Table 2.

15. Report of the National Advisory Commission on Civil Disorders (New York: Bantam Books, 1968), p. 128.

16. U.S. Department of Labor, Subemployment in the Slums of New York, 1967 (1967), p. 5.

17. U.S. Department of Labor, Bureau of Labor Statistics, Three Standards of Living for an Urban Family of Four Persons: Spring, 1967, Bulletin 1570-5 (1967).

18. U.S. Equal Employment Opportunity Commission, Job Patterns for Minorities and Women in Private Industry, 1966, Equal Employment Opportunity
Report No. 1 (3 volumes; 1969), I, p. 2.

19. "The director of finance for the city of
Baton Rouge, when asked if he would hire a Negro
certified as qualified by his city's civil service
commission, replied: 'Would you steal a million
dollars?'": U.S. Civil Rights Commission, For All
the People, by All the People (Washington, D.C.:
Government Printing Office, 1969), p. 5.

20. Hirsch and Segelhorst estimated that the
present value of the extra male lifetime income
attributable to one additional year of school in a
St. Louis suburb was equal to $3,621, at a 5 per
cent discount rate; see Werner Z. Hirsch and Elbert
W. Segelhorst, "Incremental Income Benefits of Public Education," Review of Economics and Statistics,
November, 1965, pp. 392-99. According to Herman P.
Miller, "additional schooling is associated with a
very substantial increase in lifetime income. On
the basis of conditions in 1958 . . . the average
[male] elementary school graduate could expect a
lifetime income of about $182,000 as compared with
about $258,000 for the average high school gradu-
ate"; see Herman P. Miller, "Annual and Lifetime Income in Relation to Education," American Economic
Review, December, 1960, p. 982. Assuming a 50-year
earning lifetime, a crude estimate of the payoff
per annum of starting and completing high school
(i.e., an estimate which assumes a rectangular lifetime income distribution) is $76,000/4/50 = $380.
At a 5 per cent rate of discount, the present value
of $380 received annually for 50 years is roughly
$6,840. Using the 1950 census, W. Lee Hansen's cal-
culations imply a present value of about $2,500 for
annual male income per year of school over the
range 8-16 years (this figure assumes a discount
rate of 5 per cent; Hansen's tables show only the
present values at 6 per cent and 10 per cent); see
W. Lee Hansen, "Total and Private Rates of Return
on Investment in Schooling," Journal of Political

Economy, April, 1963, Table 6. Finally, Hendrik S. Houthakker has published results (also based on the 1950 census) which, at 5 per cent, imply an incremental male present value of at least $2,800 ($2,560 at the 6 per cent rate used by Houthakker) for the range 8-16 years of school completed; see H. S. Houthakker, "Education and Income," Review of Economics and Statistics, February, 1959, Table 3.

The wide variation in these estimates is the result of using different samples and, more important, different methodologies. In particular, Houthakker and Hansen seem to have included in their samples people who reported no earnings, while Hirsch and Miller (and we) did not. But in any case, all of these estimates for the nonghetto population are substantially above the figure reported for Harlem in the text.

21. See Daniel P. Suits, "Use of Dummy Variables in Regression Equations," Journal of the American Statistical Association, LII (December, 1957), pp. 548-51.

22. For further experiments in explaining wage variation in ten urban ghettos including Harlem, see Harrison, "Studies," op. cit.

CHAPTER **2** THE NEED
FOR GHETTO
DEVELOPMENT

The construction of a viable investment program for a developing region or subarea requires the
definition of a development strategy and the translation of this strategy into project selection criteria and recommendations. In the course of our
economic development study of Harlem,[1] we became
progressively more aware of the limitations of conventional project selection criteria--limitations
which forced us to seek more generally applicable
criteria of our own. Since ghetto development problems are dominated by social, psychological, and
political considerations, the economist's narrow
focus on resource allocation is too confining and
serves, in fact, to wish away the substantive issues. Whereas the economist is traditionally accustomed to formulating economic policy subject to
political constraints, we have found it necessary
to focus on political policy-making subject to economic constraints.[2] This reversal in emphasis leads
us to replace the customary maximization of a material payoff with a qualitative priority ordering of
major project alternatives. Resource allocation
remains a valid concern, but is reduced to a subsidiary role. It helps to choose between alternative variants of major projects, sets time schedules
for implementation, and tests the sensitivity of the
development program to changes in the definition of
project priorities.

This chapter is addressed to the need for a
ghetto development strategy. In Chapter 3, a development strategy is defined in terms of qualitative
ranking criteria for determining project priorities,

and a conceptual framework is established for working with such priority rankings in the construction
of a development program.

THE MAGNITUDE OF THE JOB PROBLEM

We originally viewed the selection of projects
for Harlem as a development problem similar to that
of an underdeveloped nation, the essential difference being that a ghetto has a more restricted
range of autonomous policy options.[3] Yet as the
investigation proceeded, it became obvious that the
major symptom of underlying economic and social
distress--pervasive employment and income deficits
--could not be dealt with exclusively within the
geographical confines of the ghetto. In attempting
to outline a program of job-creating investments,
we came to realize that ghetto-based economic activities could not yield, apart from the most ex-
ceptional cases, the 10-15 per cent net return which
characterizes the major investments of large American corporations.[4]

High rents and the initial low productivity of
the ghetto unemployed serve to handicap any attempt
to find commercially attractive investments in a
ghetto like Harlem. At best, feasible activities
can probably do little more than break even or return modest profits.* The usual profit motive,

----

*The New York Times, May 4, 1969, "Economic
Development of Blighted Inner-City Areas Is Running
Into Snags." A Center of Manpower Policy Study of
George Washington University by S. Levitan and R.
Taggert is cited to the effect that the experiences
of industries that have established subsidiaries in
central cities "generally have not been favorable
and the business environment of ghetto areas does
not seem to be profitable." The Aerojet-General
plant in Watts had been losing money despite very
heavy labor training subsidies, and the IBM plant
in Bedford-Stuyvesant has higher production costs

then, cannot generate the investment activity required for ghetto development. Yet, unless massive
investment activity is forthcoming, ghetto development cannot take place. The magnitude of the job
deficit in the Harlem ghetto is such that small-
scale investments--either public or private, from
within the ghetto or from the outside--will be of
little help. There are some 200,000 persons living
in Central Harlem, with an over-all labor force
participation rate of about 50 per cent (as shown
in Tables 4 and 9). Of the 100,000 in the Harlem
labor force, close to 30 per cent can be classified
as "subemployed," an index comprising the conventional measurement of those not working but active-
ly seeking jobs, and expanded to include those who
have given up, those who are working part-time but
would like to work full-time, and those who earn so
little at full-time jobs that they cannot support a
family at minimum standards exceeding government
definitions of poverty.[5]

It is this concept of subemployment, rather
than the customary unemployment norm, which is the
relevant analytical tool for the analysis of labor
market failures in the ghetto. During the winter
of 1966/67, the conventional unemployment rate for
Harlem workers was a little over twice the over-all
city average. In terms of subemployment, however,
the Harlem rate was at least five times the city
average.

----

than other comparable company facilities. In a recent symposium, "Business in the Ghetto," sponsored
in Chicago by the American Bar Association, Eugene
L. Conroy, Senior Vice President and General Counsel of the Prudential Insurance Company, said that
investments undertaken by life insurance companies
in housing and businesses in the slums had been
found to be, "almost without exception, high risk
and low yield."

The true dimensions of Harlem's labor market
failure can be identified by applying this subemployment rate to the labor force participants--a
process which yields a deficit of almost 30,000
jobs.* Estimates of capital-to-labor ratios in manufacturing and service industries indicate that it
requires at least $10,000 to equip a work-place.[6]
This figure, combined with Harlem's job deficit, indicates that the absorption of the Harlem labor
force into the mainstream of the U.S. economy could
cost some $300 million.

SOCIAL AND ECONOMIC ASPECTS OF THE
GHETTO DEVELOPMENT PROBLEM

It is clear that the magnitude of the ghetto
problem, both in the number of adequate jobs which
must be created and in the size of the required investment, forces a solution on a much grander scale
than even the most ambitious development policy can
hope to muster from within the ghetto itself, especially if a breakthrough is to be achieved in the
near future. We recognize this fact, but we do not
discount the importance of internal ghetto development. For even though this may be insufficient as
a strategy for eliminating poverty in Harlem, it is
surely necessary. Indeed, the absorption of the
ghetto labor force into outside jobs and attempts
at the internal development of the ghetto are complementary. The dimensions of the problem to be
dealt with make a purely internal solution immense-
ly difficult, but any attempt at a purely outside
solution is certainly an illusion.

We are convinced that without the development
of the ghetto by and for its residents--reflected

---

*That is, work must be found for those present-
ly unemployed, and better jobs must be found for
those who presently work for a living but do not
earn a living wage.

by, but by no means restricted to, the creation of
more and better jobs in the ghetto--even a concerted
effort to attack urban poverty will fail. Such an
effort will fail because it is simply not possible
to transport large numbers of ghetto workers to an
outside work-place without transporting, as a part
of the workers' psychological baggage, the total
demoralization that the ghetto breeds into its inhabitants. Workers are hired for what they contrib-
ute to a firm's output and profit--they are hired,
in short, for their productivity. A worker cannot
be exiled every night to a rat-infested, overcrowded,
personally hazardous, and miserably serviced environment while being expected to deliver a high degree of productivity on the job.

A maximal effort to disperse the present racial
concentration of the ghetto to integrated communities located outside of the urban core will, of necessity, be a gradual and lengthy process. Ghetto
residents, in the meantime, can entertain little
real hope of escaping from their intolerable environment. According to the Bureau of the Census,

> residential segregation was increasing
> in most large cities of the United
> States between 1940 and 1950. . . .
> During the 1950's, residential segre-
> gation continued to increase in South-
> ern cities, whereas it generally
> registered modest declines in Northern
> cities. Data for selected cities
> based on special censuses taken since
> 1960 suggest that there has been an
> increase in residential segregation
> in Southern and Northern cities dur-
> ing the past few years.[7]

This has been true in both absolute and relative terms. "The [absolute] number of Negroes residing in poverty areas in most of the places for
which such data are available increased since 1960."
("Poverty areas" are census tracts with high proportions of families earning under $3,000 a year,

with young children present but without one parent
present, with adult males who have received less
than eight years of education, with unskilled males,
or with dilapidated housing or housing which lacks
some or all plumbing facilities.)[8] In relative
terms, "a greater proportion of the poverty areas
were Negro when the special census was taken [1964-
67] than had been the case in 1960."[9] In New Haven,
for example, the Negro population in slum neighborhoods grew by nearly 30 per cent between 1960 and
mid-decade, while the remainder of the slum population fell by nearly the same percentage. In Louis-
ville, the rates were +12 per cent and -15 per cent
respectively.[10]

    Development within the ghetto itself therefore
constitutes an indispensable and direct attack on
the immediate problems that plague the ghetto community. In its absence, everything else, including
the promise of outside job opportunities, becomes
meaningless in all but the very long term. Yet this
development, if properly undertaken, can result in
breaking the cycle of hopelessness, stimulate and
focus community participation, and create essential
and salable job skills.

    The crucial part that economic development must
play in a comprehensive attack on urban poverty cannot be appreciated as a purely economic exercise.
Oscar Lewis, a cultural anthropologist, has conducted major field studies among the urban poor in Mexico
City and San Juan.[11] Lewis argues that the problems
of ghettos must be interpreted as manifestations of
a self-contained cultural system. In a recent article, "The Culture of Poverty," he has identified
four main dimensions of the cultural system characteristic of modern poverty areas:

    1. The relationship between the subculture and
the larger society, characterized by disengagement
and nonintegration of the poor with respect to the
major institutions of society.

    2. The nature of the slum community, which
is high in gregariousness but has a minimum of

sociocultural organization--less, in fact, than that
of most primitive peoples.

3. The nature of the family, centered on the
mother and tied to her extended family, with an
authoritarian atmosphere, a short period of protected childhood, intense sibling rivalry, and little
privacy.

4. The attitudes, values, and character structure of the individual, with strong feelings of
helplessness, fatalism, dependence, and inferiority;
a high incidence of weak ego, orality, and confusion
of sexual identification; a strong present-time orientation; and a high tolerance for psychopathology
of all kinds.[12]

Lewis draws a sharp distinction between the
material manifestations of poverty and the culture
of poverty. He offers examples of poor but relatively integrated, satisfying, and self-sufficient
cultures with a high degree of social organization,
including primitive and preliterate societies, some
lower-caste peoples in India, and traditional east-
ern European Jewish culture. He includes among
these a case of special significance to us: that
of a transformed modern urban slum:

> In 1947 I undertook a study of a slum
> in Havana. Recently I had an opportu-
> nity to revisit the same slum and some
> of the same families. The physical
> aspect of the place had changed little,
> except for a beautiful new nursery
> school. The people were as poor as
> before, but I was impressed to find
> much less of the feelings of despair
> and apathy, so symptomatic of the cul-
> ture of poverty in the urban slums of
> the U.S. The slum was now highly orga-
> nized, with block committees, educa-
> tional committees, and party committees.
> The people had found a new sense of
> power and importance.[13]

If the helplessness of the poor in the face of
abominable living conditions and major labor market
failures is the root cause of social and psychological morbidity in the ghetto, then it is crucial to
combine sociopolitical and economic approaches to
the material problems of depressed urban areas—to
create a strategy for local control over the local
economy which can begin to alleviate the ghettos'
severe employment problem.

A modern private enterprise society offers the
individual no means for attacking his employment
problem directly. If the economy as a whole is ex-
periencing a given level of unemployment, the job-
seeking efforts of a determined and intelligent
worker can bear fruit only by displacing some less
fortunate worker and not by adding an extra unit to
total employment. His chances of entering the economy as an independent entrepreneur, thereby creating
a new job for himself, are virtually nil, except at
the fringes, where he could offer some small-time
services. Even there, if successful, he encroaches
on total effective demand and again displaces someone else.

This analysis remains valid when cast in terms
of the earnings structure of the labor force rather
than the level of unemployment. Our survey of
ghetto employment and earnings in Chapter 1 indicated that, even for those Harlem workers who are
employed, many jobs fall well below the subsistence
threshold in terms of wages. These are jobs in
name only, for they leave their holders unable to
function even at the lowest level of organized family life—that is, they do not assure the minimum
economic condition for reproducing the labor force.
Workers with such earnings levels are subject to the
very same pressures as the unemployed in attempting
to find jobs that pay living wages. In a modern
private-enterprise economy one of the key functions
of unemployment, quantified by the Phillips curve,
is to hold down inflationary pressures. Jobs that
pay less than subsistence wages can substitute for
unemployment in fulfilling this function.

The existence of excess workers relative to
the number of jobs that pay a living wage creates
an impersonal sort of game which leaves some workers
out. Those who have drawn a blank in this lottery
are no longer protected by the social web of a traditional society. On the contrary, our surviving
puritanical mores equate their unemployment and
poverty with idleness. We punish these people
through contempt and rejection and--because these
values are unfortunately internalized--they punish
themselves through self-hate and self-rejection as
well.

In an attempt to soften the indictment of our
culture's impersonal morality, the concept of structural unemployment has been used as an explanation
of ghetto poverty. In this view the persistent unemployment in poverty areas results largely from a
mismatch between job skills in short supply in the
economy at large and the skills possessed by the
ghetto unemployed.* Education and training are
posed as remedies. But, as shown in Chapter 1,
major differences in years of schooling have but
minimal impact on the employment and earnings prospects of ghetto residents. The inescapable conclusion is that the conventional rules of the game
lead to an impasse.

Thus, we have come to view economic development in the ghetto both as a tool that allows its
residents to collectively attack their economic

---

*The notion of structural unemployment goes
back to the problem of factor proportions first discussed by Richard Eckaus in "The Factor Proportions
Problem in Underdeveloped Areas," American Economic
Review, September, 1955, pp. 539-65. The analysis
of mathematical programming models of resource allocation has revealed that the existence of an optimal solution is compatible with a less than full
utilization of all resources. Surplus resources
are free goods in such a system; their price in the
optimal solution must therefore be zero.

problems where isolated individual efforts could
not work, and as a catalyst that will help to transform an urban slum such as Harlem from a culture of
poverty to an initially poor but integrated, satisfying, and organized social system. Economic development is viewed by the black ghetto leadership
in this context of self-determination and political
power--and it is desired as a symbol and instrument
of this power as much as for its material payoff.
The creation of jobs in the ghetto is only one component of this development. Management of ghetto
enterprises and ownership in private or cooperative
forms is another essential component, emphasized
even more strongly than job creation and skill
training in the aspirations of the Harlem community.

What can a community do in terms of economic
self-determination that an individual cannot? Developing countries use a planned effort to build up
their national income within the world economy.
This involves putting their slack resources--pri-
marily labor--to productive use, and generating new
resources: savings, skills, and technological know-
how. They achieve this by means of import substi-
tution, the generation of new exports, and broad
productive investments. Urban ghettos can, and
must, follow a similar planned development strategy.
In this they are aided by free access to the broader economy of which they are a part, e.g., they obtain a large fraction of their area income by ex-
porting labor power, and can sell locally produced
commodities in outside markets with no hindrance.
At the same time, their efforts are hampered by a
lack of the usual development instruments: a separate currency, taxing, and tariff powers. Ghetto
communities must therefore depend on social and political organization to achieve collective economic
objectives. Local income multipliers can, for example, be raised through "buy-local" campaigns and
by a restructuring of consumption in favor of locally producible services--an extension of taking
in each other's wash--provided that a community consensus can be reached on questions of equity and
the enforcement of cooperation. This entails a

degree of isolation between the local community and
the mainstream of the U.S. economy, and raises the
well-known issues in international economics concerning the advantages and drawbacks of a protec-
tionist policy toward domestic industries from the
point of view of economic development. Yet in the
face of persistent, overwhelming differences in
standards of living, enforced through the artificial
isolation of the black ghetto community on the basis of race, who can credibly argue that "business
as usual" is a solution to the problems of the
ghetto?

   Many critics have argued recently that it is
costly and wasteful to attempt to reverse existing
trends toward the suburbanization of economic activity.* Others base their opposition to ghetto
development on projected comparative returns to investments inside and outside the ghetto, especially
in terms of the number of jobs created per dollar
of expenditure. And still others fault a ghetto
development strategy because of supposed "negative
feedback effects," e.g., new inmigrants from the
South--attracted to the city by its slum development programs--creating an excess supply of labor
relative to those jobs which are open to the urban
poor and an excess demand for the available stock
of slum housing, thus forcing wages down, rents up,
and generally making the urban poverty problem even
worse than it had been before the "development"
program began.** A common attitude seems to

----

   *The suburbanization of jobs, industry, and
population in the New York metropolitan area is
discussed in Chapter 6.

   **The "negative feedback" argument implicitly
assumes that ghetto organizations--not to mention
city managers--will be no better prepared to absorb
and accommodate new inmigrants after undertaking
planned community development than they were before-
hand. In other words, those who criticize ghetto

underlie all of these critiques; it is the belief--
the value judgment--that the function of the ghetto
(and indeed perhaps of the city itself) is primarily
to prepare its current residents for the fastest
possible assimilation into suburban life.[14] That
the residents of the central city may not share
this preference is seldom taken into account.

But economic development is far more than a
mechanism for allocating resources efficiently,
organizing production, generating profit streams,
or creating jobs. Moreover, jobs created outside
the ghetto are incommensurable in their over-all
social welfare effects with jobs created inside the
ghetto as part of an over-all development effort.
Economic development, wherever it takes place, acts
as a catalyst of social and political change. Jobs
created inside the ghetto are the instruments as
well as the objects of this change, contributing to
a reduction in psychological and social pathology,
an improvement in the "technology" of community organization, increased skill levels, and the re-
enforcement of the community's political base and
potential. Conventional economic analysis treats
these social effects as external--incidental to,
and not very important in light of, the over-all
economic infrastructure. We believe, however, that
economic development of the ghetto is vital because
of the social externalities that it can generate--
social benefits far in excess of the mere creation
of even a considerable number of sterile work-
places.

----

development on these grounds must maintain the static view that planned economic change will not be
accompanied by political maturation of the agents
of change. All the historical experience of other
urban ethnic minorities argues against such an
assumption.

ELEMENTS OF A GHETTO DEVELOPMENT STRATEGY

Community-Owned Industries

The new activities which we suggest as the key to a development strategy in the ghetto will be referred to as "greenhouse industries." We define these as community-owned or sponsored manufacturing, commercial, and service enterprises whose main function is the upgrading of the area's labor force and economic base. They are designed to create new jobs in the familiar local environment, and perform systematic skill-training functions that are coordinated with the productive operations of each establishment. Training may take several complementary forms, the most important of which is structured on-the-job training, supplemented by formal remedial classroom instruction, and followed by a period of practical job experience in surroundings conducive to the deepening of newly acquired skills. After a time spent in this protective environment, workers will be ready to compete in the urban labor market.

To qualify as a greenhouse industry, an activity must offer the proper level and mix of skills; in addition, it must also fit into the developing economic base of the ghetto. The upgrading of service to the local consumer, the filling of gaps in the area's economic base, and the production of commodities and services both for local use and for outside sale are some of the requirements that greenhouse industries must meet. The general need for community ownership or sponsorship of such industries is a pragmatic consequence of our expectation that most greenhouse industries will be commercially unattractive, and will therefore not be undertaken by outside business interests except as showpieces. Black community leaders attach a high value to local ownership or control of ghetto businesses; this characteristic of typical greenhouse industries is therefore part of the social and political benefits to the community.

We expect that firms will be reimbursed from public funds to whatever extent is possible under existing programs in order to compensate them for undertaking the training functions referred to earlier. Private training that receives reimbursement from public funds is often criticized as providing de facto subsidies to the productive activities of individual firms. This form of subsidy can be turned into a strategic asset in the development process. Any institutional device which can supplement the cash flow of a ghetto enterprise serves to enhance the ability of the activity to survive and thereby increases the scope of feasible development projects.

Training activities and work in greenhouse industries should be organized into a hierarchy of skills which constitute the rungs of a career ladder,[15] so that no workers will be trained for dead-end jobs. Jobs that cannot offer at least some degree of insulation from the business cycle are also to be avoided.

A greenhouse industry must be designed to accommodate a steady flow of workers through both the labor training functions and productive jobs. As workers complete their training period and initial work experience, they can be placed in jobs outside the ghetto. By this time they will have acquired not only the technical skill necessary for competing on more equal terms in the metropolitan labor market but also the confidence and working habits that are needed, even beyond technical competence, to hold jobs in a middle-class white environment.

In addition to the creation of new greenhouse activities, an economic development strategy for the ghetto involves the upgrading of enterprises through technical assistance and the rationalization of purchasing and marketing functions.

The Profitability of Ghetto Investments

When emphasis is placed on economic development as a catalyst of social and political change,

project recommendations cannot be made primarily on
the basis of commercial profitability. Yet it is
impossible to disregard profit considerations altogether, since activities or enterprises that cannot
break even (allowing for the receipt of labor training reimbursements) will be unable to survive unless
they receive a constant financial subsidy. "Breaking even" in this context means more than merely
meeting costs, since bank loans have to be amortized
on schedule out of profits if the enterprise is to
avoid bankruptcy. Financial and profit considerations therefore play the role of a constraint in
ghetto economic development. This constraint is
fortunately not very strong: it is far easier to
find ghetto investment projects that are capable of
earning a few percentage points of profit than, e.g.,
meeting the 10-15 per cent after-tax profit objective of the large corporations.

     If a project whose equity is locally owned is
capable of earning more profit than the minimum
necessary for survival, then profit becomes an independent project selection consideration: This
profit adds to the community's income and reinvestment potential. In choosing among alternative
projects, some of which are more profitable than
others, profits have to be traded off against other
community benefits. Highly profitable locally
owned enterprises will, however, be the exception
rather than the rule. We have formulated our ghetto development strategy on the conservative assumption that most projects will barely break even.

     On this point our judgment differs from that
of black ghetto leaders in the Harlem Commonwealth
Council (HCC) who have acted throughout the Harlem
Project on the assumption that highly profitable
ghetto investments could be identified. This is
attested, for example, by the close association between some of these leaders and the Community Self-
Determination Bill submitted to the U.S. Congress
in 1968.[16] In the main, the bill sought to stimulate large U.S. corporations to undertake massive,
profitable ghetto investments whose equity, after

the investments were paid off, was to be transferred
to community-owned or controlled ghetto development
corporations.

It is our conviction that there are few such
investment opportunities in the ghetto. If we are
wrong, then the tasks of ghetto development could
be greatly simplified. We do not, of course, con-
test that the exploitation of the ghetto through
extralegal or illicit activities can yield substantial profits. Indeed, black leaders see these
profits made in the ghetto, and apparently assume
that their communities can support highly profitable
ventures. If, however, we restrict ourselves to
those profit-making ventures that will develop the
ghetto instead of exploiting it, we will not find
many. A few profitable ones undoubtedly exist; we
have attempted to identify some of these for Harlem.
Such projects can be expected to be among the first
to be implemented, and may then raise the illusion
of great potentialities. Yet once these unique opportunities have been exhausted, continued ghetto
development will have to fall back on projects offering a much lower level of profitability.

Thus, we advocate a strategy of selecting development projects with high social, political, and
other community benefits, and generally hope for no
more than breaking even. Project selection criteria
prevailing elsewhere in the American economy would
label such projects as high-cost, poorly located,
and apparently irrational. Were it not for the
vast irrationality of the existence of slums in the
world's richest society, we would agree. If slums
and poverty did not exist, one would indeed never
recommend the location of a food-canning factory in
the core of a metropolitan area.

Yet, if the only feasible way of achieving an
acceptable rate of ghetto development is to include
projects of this kind in the development program,
it makes sense to tolerate waste in the economy-wide
allocation of material resources in order to break
out of the social irrationality that the ghetto

represents. The social benefits of ghetto development are so great that they easily override inferior
and second-best patterns of resource allocation.

Our "greenhouse industry" argument differs
from the "infant industry" argument often used to
justify the protection of domestic industries in
underdeveloped countries. Some ghetto industries,
such as food canning, will never mature to the
point of acquiring a comparative advantage in a
ghetto location. The parallel is closer--again referring to international economics--with the protection of the merchant marine by the United States,
in spite of resource allocation considerations.
Yet the strategy we propose does have elements in
common with the "infant industry" or "young economy"
arguments. As the labor force of the ghetto is upgraded and its economic base is strengthened, relatively more sophisticated activities become possible
candidates for ghetto investments, and the comparative advantage of the newer ghetto industries will
gradually improve. The least viable of the original
activities can then be gradually abandoned, further
strengthening the comparative advantage of the re-
maining ghetto industries. This process of gradual
transformation can be expected to narrow down and
eventually eliminate differentials between the material productivities of ghetto and nonghetto industries.

The Financing of Ghetto Investments

The shift from purely commercial profit motivation forces the development of new forms of control institutions. Paramount among these is the
locally based ghetto development corporation--in
our case, the HCC--which serves as the focus of all
development efforts. This corporation will own,
sponsor, and control ghetto investments, and will
exert influence on existing ghetto businesses
through technical assistance and affiliation programs.

Perhaps the key question in a ghetto development strategy concerns the origin of investment

funds. Who will finance the ghetto development
corporation, given that most of its ventures will
just break even? Two simple answers are the federal government and the ghetto community itself. The
required resources are there in either case, but
political problems stand in the way. For the federal government, a revision of national priorities
would be implied; for the Harlem community, a rec-
ognition that an annual per capita income level of
over $1,000 places it on a par with several western
European countries would be required. If the ghetto were able to act socially and politically as a
unit, it could afford a high rate of savings and
reinvestment.

We do not wish to pursue these superficially
simple yet politically difficult extreme solutions,
since at the present writing they appear unattain-
able, even though--with the pace of change that is
all around us--a re-evaluation may be necessary
within a short time. Instead, we will discuss a
financing mechanism which we have pieced together
from existing institutional structures (with slight
additions) during the course of the Harlem Project
itself. As our recommended approach to the question of financing, it offered some hope of immediate realization, given the mid-1968 time frame. We
regarded this mechanism--to be referred to hereafter as the "short-term financing mechanism"--as
suitable for supporting a demonstration effort such
as the Harlem Project was meant to be. The social
and political problems that come to a head over the
issue of ghetto development financing are discussed
in Chapter 7.

Our short-term financing mechanism was designed
to create black equity in new or expanded Harlem
enterprises. It was based on the establishment of
a three-layer revolving trust fund that would enable HCC to finance particular development activities while replenishing the fund from project earnings. The need for such a fund arises from our
premise that none of the required general-purpose
development capital would be raised in the ghetto

community itself. While this does not exclude the
possibility that some local equity capital could be
raised for specific ventures, especially the expansion and upgrading of existing businesses, it still
represents a highly conservative assumption; if it
should turn out to be overly pessimistic, the financing task will be that much easier.

The main function of such a trust fund would
be to enable a community development organization
to undertake development ventures with virtually
all of the required capital coming from the outside,
while retaining equity in these ventures. The development organization would draw on the trust fund
to obtain the initial capitalization--a minimum of
10 per cent--which has to be provided for individual projects in order to activate a number of existing government programs that provide development
loans on terms more favorable than those commercially available from banks and other lending institutions. Some of the Small Business Administration
and Economic Development Administration (U.S. Department of Commerce) programs are shown in Figure
6, together with other relevant sources of funding
administered by the Department of Labor and the Department of Health, Education and Welfare. Commercial loans could be built on top of this financial
base for a given project.

When we designed this short-term financing
mechanism in 1968, consortia of local banks, insurance companies, and other business firms appeared
to be promising sources of ghetto development trust
funds large enough to set in motion a meaningful
demonstration program for Harlem. Yet the control
of a potential trust fund posed a most delicate
problem whose resolution, we felt, was the key to
the success of this financing strategy.

An organizational structure used elsewhere in
which a "white" corporation exercises control and
a "black" corporation is placed in the position of
permanent petitioner was rejected out of hand.
Large corporations, however, are accustomed to

FIGURE 6

Prototypical Flow of Governmental
and Private Financing
for Ghetto Development

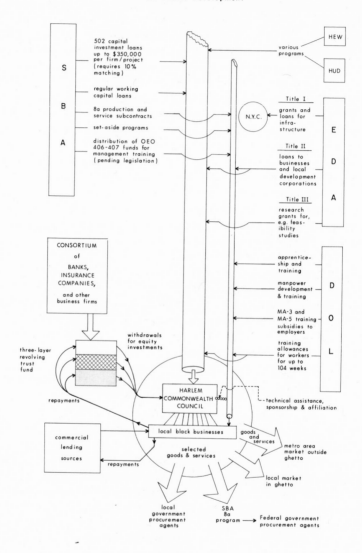

LEGEND

SBA   Small Business Administration

HEW   U.S. Department of Health, Education and Welfare

HUD   U.S. Department of Housing and Urban Development

EDA   Economic Development Administration, U.S. Department of Commerce

DOL   U.S. Department of Labor

MA-3
MA-5   Manpower Assistance Act, Sections 3 and 5

OEO   Office of Economic Opportunity

tight, centralized control over all investment de-
cisions--we felt sure they were not going to place
a large fund in the hands of an independent black
group. This control issue might be resolved by establishing the fund in three parts, or "layers."

Drawings on a "black" layer would be controlled
fully and exclusively by the ghetto development corporation, while drawings on a "white" layer, together with conditions of repayment, would be subject
to full approval by the consortium that established
the fund. There would also be an intermediate, or
"gray" layer, on which drawings for specific projects could be held up by the consortium for a fixed
period of time, after which the community development corporation would be free to go ahead with the
project whether approved by the consortium or not.
The exact apportionment of the fund among the three
layers and the maximum time delay affecting the
gray layer for each of several classes of projects
would be determined by negotiation and incorporated
in the bylaws governing the fund.

While this scheme places two of the three fund
layers under ultimate black control, it also encour-
ages extensive consultations. Whenever a new project is proposed the ghetto development corporation
will find it attractive to secure the full approval
of the consortium. This will permit the development
corporation to draw on the white layer while retaining a maximum share of uncommitted funds under its
own control. With meaningful consultation on all
projects, the consortium will be able to exercise a
considerable influence on the technical level of
decisions--provided that it accepts the aspirations
of the black community leadership. Out of these
consultations can grow a relationship of mutual respect that will be the best guarantee of the stability and future expansion of the arrangement. Specifically, if the process of consultations results
in the white layer being fully committed well ahead
of the gray and black layers, this will enable the
consortium to expand the white layer progressively
at a minimum of risk, while the gray and black

layers continue to safeguard the autonomy of the
community development organization. From the point
of view of this organization, the arrangement is a
device to expand the funds under its management.
If such an organization insisted on full control of
the entire trust fund, it would probably end by re-
stricting the size of the fund as a whole to that
of the black layer within a three-layer fund. From
the point of view of a community development organization, then, the gray and white layers represent
additional financial leverage that does not diminish
the amount of financial resources under its own autonomous control.

Figure 6 presents the details of the financial
strategy built around the three-layer revolving
trust fund. It shows the major government programs
that may provide financial resources either directly to the HCC, or to local black businesses assisted,
sponsored, or affiliated with HCC.

The identification and selection of concrete
development projects involving both new and expanded
ghetto enterprises is the key task in implementing
a ghetto development and financing strategy. In
confronting this task, we had to develop a set of
criteria for evaluating project benefits and setting
project priorities. We now turn to these criteria
and to a discussion of a general approach to project
selection that is workable in the context of urban
ghetto development.

NOTES

1. A Proposed Investment Program for the Economic Development of Central Harlem; Final Report of the Center for Economic Planning (New York: The New School for Social Research, 1968) (Grant No. CG-8730, U.S. Office of Economic Opportunity). (Mimeographed.) (Hereafter cited as A Proposed Investment Program.)

2. We owe this concise description of our approach to Dr. Dudley Seers, Director of the Institute for Development Studies, University of Sussex, England.

3. Thomas Vietorisz, "Developing Countries and Black Ghettos: Parallels and Differences," Conference on the Economics of Growth and Development, University of Akron, March 22-23, 1968; Bennett Harrison, "A Pilot Project for the Economic Development Planning of American Urban Slums," International Development Review, March, 1968.

4. Fortune, June 15, 1968, p. 205. Net income on invested capital for all industry in 1967 was approximately 11.5 per cent.

5. U.S. Department of Labor, Subemployment in the Slums of New York, 1967 (1967).

6. A Proposed Investment Program, op. cit., Table 7.6.

7. Bureau of the Census, Current Population Reports, Series P-20, No. 168, "Negro Population: March, 1966" (Washington, D.C., 1967), p. 1.

8. Ibid., Series P-23, No. 19, "Characteristics of Families Residing in 'Poverty Areas': March, 1966" (Washington, D.C., 1966), p. 3.

9. Ibid., Series P-60, No. 61, "Characteristics of Families and Persons Living in Metropolitan Poverty Areas: 1967" (Washington, D.C., 1969), p. 4.

10. Ibid., Table E.

11. Oscar Lewis, The Children of Sanchez (New
York: Knopf, 1961); and La Vida (New York: Random
House, 1966).

12. Oscar Lewis, "The Culture of Poverty,"
Scientific American, October, 1966, pp. 19-25.

13. Ibid.

14. For example, see: John F. Kain and Joseph
J. Persky, "Alternatives to the Guilded Ghetto,"
The Public Interest, Winter, 1969, pp. 74-87; John
F. Kain, "Coping with Ghetto Unemployment," Journal
of the American Institute of Planners, March, 1969,
pp. 80-83; National Industrial Conference Board,
Education, Training, and Employment of the Disadvantaged, Studies in Public Affairs No. 4 (1968),
pp. 42-44 ("Ghetto Development vs. Beltway"). The
feedback effects associated with urban job develop-
ment--especially the interactions between investments in urban jobs and housing and inmigration of
poor people from outside the city--are considerably
more complex and more poorly understood than the
advocates of "ghetto dispersal" would have us believe. This is amply demonstrated by recent computer simulations conducted at M.I.T.; see Jay M.
Forrester, Urban Dynamics (Cambridge: The M.I.T.
Press, 1969). For a comprehensive review of the
"ghetto development" versus "ghetto dispersal" debate, and a powerful and comprehensive attack on
the latter, see Gerson Green and Geoffrey Faux,
"The Social Utility of Black Enterprise," in William
F. Haddad and G. Douglas Pugh, eds., Black Economic
Development (New York: Spectrum, 1969), pp. 21-37.

15. Arthur Pearl and Frank Riessman, New Careers for the Poor (New York: Free Press, 1965);
see also Sidney A. Fine, Guidelines for the Design
of New Careers, W. E. Upjohn Institute Staff Paper
(September, 1967).

16. The genesis of the proposed legislation,
which has lain in the Congressional hoppers for over

a year awaiting presidential support, is described
in detail by John McClaughry, "Black Ownership and
National Politics," in William F. Haddad and G.
Douglas Pugh, eds., <u>Black Economic Development</u>, <u>op.
cit</u>., pp. 38-49. The opinion of both the Harlem
Commonwealth Council and the Congress of Racial
Equality on this position is defended by Roy Innis
in the same volume; see "Separatist Economics: A
New Social Contract," pp. 50-59.

CHAPTER **3** PROBLEMS OF
PROJECT
SELECTION

The economic literature abounds with discussions of criteria to be used in the selection of
economic development projects.[1] Some of these are
based on simple methods--such as the determination
of the relative labor or capital intensities of
candidate projects--while others are derived from
sophisticated mathematical programming models.
However, they all have in common a central concern
with problems of resource allocation. Since we
have already indicated in Chapter 2 that in our
view the heart of the ghetto development problem
consists of social and political considerations
rather than of resource allocation, our task in
this chapter will be to translate our general ghetto development strategy into practical guides for
the selection of individual development projects.

The major part of this chapter is devoted to
five qualitative ranking criteria that can be used
to establish priorities among competing projects.
Each of these five criteria captures some essential
feature of ghetto development that escapes conventional resource allocation models.

In the closing part of the chapter, we briefly
indicate the manner in which such an approach,
which puts noneconomic and/or nonquantifiable considerations at center stage, can be reconciled with
a proper degree of attention to inescapable resource
scarcities.

QUALITATIVE CRITERIA FOR PROJECT RANKING

The elements of ghetto development strategy spelled out in Chapter 2 must be translated into project selection criteria before they can be implemented. This translation cannot be done in a strictly quantitative manner, because some of the most important kinds of information on which key development decisions inevitably hinge--for example, factors influencing future changes in technology and organization, or external economies and diseconomies of particular projects that manifest themselves by influencing the morale and productivity of ghetto workers--are impossible to estimate precisely.

The best that can be done is to specify such information by means of verbal description, in as specific a form as circumstances permit. The same holds for social, psychological, or political considerations that affect the course of development when given projects are or are not adopted. The weighting of these incommensurable qualitative considerations then becomes a matter of informed value judgment, expressed through a priority ordering of the relevant development projects.

Project priorities have a long history of successful use in planning. Operational priority orderings of major developmental alternatives have been a prominent feature of Soviet plans beginning with the first five-year plan, and production targets for some more restricted branches or key products, referred to as "leading links," have been given overriding priority.[2] An allocation of key materials based on a hierarchy of priorities has also been the fundamental organizing principle of U.S. wartime planning.[3] Such priority orderings, by their very nature, are simple, effective, and easy to work with. In this they differ markedly from certain abstract analytical concepts used in economic theory for expressing planners' preferences, such as "indifference maps," which have never been made operational. The relationship of project

priorities to these abstract concepts is briefly
indicated in the closing part of this chapter.

Ultimate judgments on project selection and
program definition must always be made, or at least
sanctioned, by the political decision-maker. Experience, however, shows that politicians are not
aware, in the abstract, of all the dimensions that
may affect their choice. This results in a need
for successive plan revisions as policy-makers pass
judgment on concrete features of proposed trial
plans.[4]

In this section we offer five qualitative criteria for the definition of project priorities in
urban ghetto development, with the aim of clarifying the issues involved in ranking projects by priorities. The better we succeed in clarifying these
issues, the likelier it is that policy-makers will
be able to set firm preliminary priorities that will
require only slight modifications after trial programs become available in the course of development
planning. These criteria are (a) the dynamics of
technology, training, and growth; (b) distribution
and marketing considerations; (c) balance in the
economic base of the area; (d) labor intensity in
relation to project profitability; and (e) other
external economies and diseconomies.

Technology, Training, and Growth

There is a continuing debate among theoretical
development economists concerning the proper level
of technology that should be introduced in a developing area.[5] The traditional argument favors a
labor-intensive technology, since this will ensure
the optimal utilization of scarce investment resources.[6] At the other extreme is the argument that
favors the introduction of a high-level, capital-
intensive technology for at least three reasons.
First, this argument asserts that labor-intensive
technologies in practice tend to be archaic; second,
it contends that once a labor-intensive technology
is adopted, this freezes the structure of production

into a pattern of low labor productivity which pre-
vents growth; and finally, it advocates rapid growth
by means of a high rate of saving and reinvestment
which is adversely affected when labor-intensive
activities create large payrolls that are then
translated into massive increases in popular consumption.[7]

The traditional position reflects a static
view of economic development, since it is primarily
in such a static context that a capital shortage
appears to be a fixed and immutable fact of life.
With a shift in point of view to that of a dynamic,
growing system, capital changes its aspect and
comes to be seen as a by-product of growth, since
the more growth there is, the more income will be
generated, out of which additional savings and
capital formation can take place.[8] Moreover, this
position assumes that capital is the controlling
factor in growth, and greatly underplays the importance of the formation of new skills and of
technological change. If the selection of labor-
intensive activities is prejudicial to the formation of higher skills and to technological and organizational progress, then in spite of an apparent
short-term superiority of labor-intensive technology, long-term growth will be stifled.

Yet, it is not possible to totally agree with
the contrary position either. It is futile to argue
--for example, in the ghetto development context--
that the hard-core unemployed can be channeled in
short order into the most sophisticated, leading-
edge technology of which the American economy is
capable. Training activities have time lags which
can be severe, and the upgrading of workers in middle life cannot span orders of magnitude in skill
levels. As an extreme example, one typically cannot train a forty-year-old hard-core unemployed
worker to become a computer engineer. By and large,
the fundamental changes in the educational and
skill levels of entire populations take place by
virtue of the fact that young people who are entering the labor force for the first time have skill

levels--especially prevocational skills that place
them in a position to absorb specific job skills as
they advance in their careers--that are considerably higher than those of the retiring older workers, whom they replace. Retraining in midcareer,
although very important, can achieve only smaller
adjustments. This is of course not to deny that
even modest increases in the average skill levels
of the hard-core unemployed could have dramatic
benefits and could break them free of the poverty
in which they are trapped.

A recent trend in the debate concerning a proper choice of techniques has been to adopt a compro-
mise between the two extreme arguments. Much of the
literature on such "intermediate-level" technology
is pragmatic rather than theoretical, and is oriented to the application of abstract concepts to particular cases in economic development.[9]

Our position rests on the assertion that this
entire debate is somewhat beside the point, since
it has a hopelessly static cast even when the argument is conducted in terms of growth models. We
start from the premise that a "high" or "low" level
of technology, or capital intensity, in relation to
a major project--which, as we shall argue in the
next section, must always be viewed as a complex of
complementary activities--cannot be measured by a
single parameter, since it is apt to change dras-
tically over time. One of the striking phenomena
associated with some development projects is their
ability to take on an independent life of their own
and undergo broad transformations which were not
foreseen by the planners when the project was first
started. For example, the product assortment of a
new metalworking project may experience a large
shift over a period of a few years; the project may
stimulate the appearance of subsidiary or feeder enterprises; new designs may open up new markets and
fields of application; in sum, then, the level of
skills and technology may rise spontaneously and
dramatically over the life of the project. The vehicles of this change may be, among others, formal

labor training activities, on-the-job training, or
just "learning by doing"; the successful encouragement of innovations on the part of blue-collar, technical, and management personnel; or the strengthening of the project's infrastructure through better
education and morale in the developing economy.

If major projects differ strikingly in their
potential for such spontaneous self-upgrading--and
we assert that they do--this changes the whole frame
of reference in which project selection must be approached. What will matter most in evaluating a
major project is then no longer the initial level
of technical sophistication or capital-labor intensity, but the expected rate of advance in these
characteristics over the life of the project. Given
a goal of rapid economic growth, a high priority
should be attached to those branches of economic
activity that are capable of powerful advances in
technology, skills, and organization, even if it
should be necessary to start projects with relatively low levels of the above characteristics.

At the focus of growth in skills, technology,
and organization is the individual productive enterprise, to be regarded as a bundle of actual and
potential production and training activities. At
each point of time only a limited set of activities
will be in actual operation. Some activities--
rudimentary techniques, crude products, basic skill
training--may already have been left behind, while
others--pioneering designs, not-yet-invented adap-
tations--may still be in the future. The activities
within the bundle are characterized by (a) mutual
support; (b) a prescribed sequencing: higher-level
activities preceded by a learning period involving
lower-level activities; and (c) open-endedness:
the planner can foresee at best only the approximate
range of improvements, and not their exact detail,
and he must be prepared for major surprises in the
direction of future development.

It should be clear from the above discussion
why project selection criteria are hard to quantify.

We are dealing with learning behavior[10] reflected
not in the deterministic coefficients of an individual activity, but in the expected organic self-
upgrading process of an entire bundle of production
and training activities, where the identity of those
activities in use is undergoing a progressive change,
and where actual (as distinguished from potential)
advances depend not only on economic, but also on
social, cultural, and political factors.

The qualitative project selection criteria derived from these considerations place primary emphasis on the potential of a candidate project to
support formal and on-the-job labor training rather
than on the technological and skill level at which
workers enter. We have attempted to select projects
containing a broad range of labor skills that permit
the construction of a career ladder, so that workers
will have the opportunity to advance from one rung
of the ladder to another; i.e., from one skill level
to a higher one.[11] It is also considered an advantage if on-the-job training can be combined with
prevocational courses and formal classroom instruc-
tion--to open up opportunities for highly motivated
individuals that will encourage them to put an extra effort into their own education and training.

We specifically reject activities that offer
low-grade, poorly paying, dead-end jobs, no matter
how large the number.

Our project selection criteria tie in closely
with the greenhouse industry strategy discussed in
Chapter 2. Effective training, especially when the
hard-core unemployed initially enter the labor force,
requires a sheltered environment and supportive,
morale-building functions that are best provided
under the sponsorship of a local ghetto development
organization. In order to provide opportunities
for training the largest possible number of individuals, however, the training period cannot be
overly protracted, and an effort has to be made to
create a flow of trainees through these industries
who are then placed in other jobs, both within and

outside the ghetto. This strategy is also prescribed by the fact that public funds are available
for formal and on-the-job training only for limited
periods of time for each worker; therefore, the
flow of public funds will cease if workers remain
in the greenhouse industries indefinitely.

The need to keep a flow of workers moving
through the greenhouse industries appears to be in
conflict with an effective application of the career ladder concept, in that a worker cannot be
held long enough to advance by several skill rungs.
This apparent conflict can, perhaps, be resolved by
a recycling strategy which might work as follows:
A hard-core unemployed worker enters a greenhouse
activity and leaves after a year for an outside job,
having had the benefit of considerable skill and
prevocational upgrading. This represents the first
rung of a career ladder. After a couple of years on
an outside job, he returns to this or another greenhouse activity and a year later leaves with skills
corresponding to the second rung of the ladder; and
so forth. In this way, skill upgrading can take
place simultaneously and at all levels, and individuals will advance from rung to rung of the skill
ladder by multiple passes through the greenhouse
training system, interspersed with stretches in outside jobs. Experience with the application of the
career ladder concept indicates that the majority
of individuals will advance by only one or two rungs
over a period of several years, but it is important
to ensure that the opportunity of advancing through
all rungs be provided to highly motivated individuals. The existence of such a system may also motivate outside employers to provide training and other
benefits to workers in their own firms, in order to
induce their black employees to remain on the payroll. In other words, such a system increases the
competitiveness of the urban black labor market.

Distribution and Marketing Considerations

While the former project selection criterion
focused on the payoff to the ghetto community in
terms of increased job skills and improved ability

to compete in the market for outside jobs, the
present section aims at developing a criterion concerning the ability of projects to survive in the
market.

The central economic function around which
much of the present American productive structure
is organized is distribution and marketing. In the
nineteenth century, the ability to produce was the
key to industrial success; at the turn of the century, this role shifted to finance. While finance
is still important, especially for the largest ventures, most large firms retain sufficient earnings
to cover major portions of their own expansion
needs, and this downgrades the role of institutional financial considerations. The organizing role
has now shifted to distribution and marketing, and
most recently, especially in the military and space
sectors, to research and development. We shall,
however, not be concerned with the latter.

In most industries it is still true that who-
ever controls distribution and marketing will be
able to capture the major share of available profits. Under oligopoly, the ability of a firm to
capture profits depends on its ability to maintain
--together with other oligopolistic producers--
effective barriers to new entry. Economies of
scale in production are no longer the dominant barrier: among U.S. industries with the most pronounced oligopolistic structures, economies of
scale in establishing and maintaining a dealership
network or economies of scale in advertising function as key barriers.[12] Production can be largely
taken for granted in many lines: given a distribution system, there are always sources from which
a supply of merchandise can be readily procured.[13]
Finance is a problem only for smaller or for rapidly expanding enterprises. Given these institutional conditions, one way of identifying ghetto development projects with a reasonable profit potential, or at least a survival ability, is to focus
on the role of the distribution system. Some examples will illustrate this point.

We have found that a cooperative supermarket
project is an attractive venture for ghetto areas
for a number of independent reasons (see Chapter 5).
Once such a supermarket, or network of supermarkets,
is established in ghetto areas under the control of
a ghetto development organization, an entirely new
realm of industrial development possibilities
through backward integration into food manufacturing is opened up. Standing alone, such manufacturing operations would be desperately weak--they would
have to compete with well-established firms for access to supermarket shelf space. Once control of a
large number of supermarket shelves is secured, however, the prospects of such manufacturing activities
become substantially better. While they may not be
particularly profitable, their probable survival is
greatly enhanced by the assured market, and they
need to concentrate simply on achieving a degree of
customer acceptance once their products are placed
on the shelves. While the price at which these
products can be sold to the supermarkets is largely
fixed by the competition of established brands, the
mere fact of meeting their price (and the standard
quality) would not assure the new food manufacturing
firms access to shelf space in open competition,
since they would have to break through a great many
advantages enjoyed by established producers. These
advantages include long-standing relationships with
persons controlling supermarket purchasing, en-
trenched advertising positions, and an existing
consumer acceptance that assures the supermarket of
rapid stock turnover. These advantages cannot be
neutralized by simply meeting the prevailing price
and quality standards. Given control of supermarket
shelves, however, the picture changes radically.
Purchasing relationships cease to matter; advertising can be offset in part or in whole by emphasizing
sales under a house brand--this is done by all supermarkets in regard to many categories of merchandise, but in the case of ghetto supermarkets, the
house brand could easily emphasize the sponsorship
of the manufacturing operation by the ghetto development corporation--and customer acceptance could
be further enhanced by preferential display (a matter

of life-and-death competition between commercial
brands) and special promotion throughout the ghetto
community through low-cost, informal campaigns.

The same principle of control of the distribution system is applicable to nonfood items sold in
supermarkets; to automotive products tied in with a
distribution system through gas stations, garages,
and repair shops (recapped tires, minor products
such as window cleaners, radiator compounds, anti-
freezes and the like), and to many other categories
of merchandise sold at retail or to small commercial
or service establishments. Further examples are:
supplies for barbershops and beauty parlors; hardware; paper and stationery products; children's
clothes; restaurant supplies.

In order to translate this background information into a project selection criterion, the following specific conditions must be met:

1. There must be control over a distribution
network--single outlets have only minimal impact.
Suitable networks can be developed by cooperative
projects (e.g., food co-ops); the affiliation of independent retailers and service establishments to
an affiliating institution controlled by the ghetto
development corporation (the best nonghetto parallel
is the spectacular success of affiliated independent
grocery stores); or the establishment of a sufficient number of new ventures under the control of a
ghetto development corporation. The last route may
be the most difficult one for individual ghettos,
but could be successful if ghetto development in a
number of areas could be coordinated.

2. The manufacturing operation should not be
subject to strong economies of scale in the range
of demand that is of interest. In other words, the
market provided by the distributive outlets should
be sufficient to run the manufacturing operation at
a reasonable commercial scale. This consideration
rules out the manufacture of such items as refrig-
erators or television sets even if several dozen
retail outlets are available.

The product should be characterized by heavy
advertising promotion. To the extent that such
promotion can be neutralized by the "house brand"
approach or low-cost promotional campaigns within
the ghetto community, the advertising expenditures
of commercial brands offer a margin of safety for
the attainment of profits, or at least a break-even
position.

A Balanced Economic Base

A useful, though limited, project selection
criterion concerns a balance in the economic base
of an area. If a survey reveals important gaps in
this base, this constitutes prima facie evidence in
favor of supplying the missing activities. For example, our Harlem Business Inventory discloses that
the area is badly underserviced in regard to food
stores (see Chapter 5) and is lacking in wholesaling
and large service activities capable of supplying
local institutional demands. If such activities
are distributed in a reasonably regular manner over
the rest of the central city area, the extent of
the gap in the ghetto's economic base can be readily
quantified. The distribution of food stores can,
for example, be statistically related to population
density and income. The difference between what
might under this statistical relationship be called
the "expected" employment in Harlem food stores and
the actual employment is a measure of the gap.[14]

Having identified such a gap (in the above
sense), we can state with a fair degree of confidence that the activity in question has a reasonable
prospect of success--provided that we can identify
and remove the social and economic factors that
have given rise to the gap in the first place. In
the case of small businesses, support by a community
organization such as HCC might make the difference
between success and failure.

The probable success of various lines of economic activity, based on the identification of gaps
in the area's economic base, has to be translated

into a priority ranking of potential projects on
the basis of the contributions such projects might
make to the over-all development of the area.

Labor Intensity and
Project Profitability

Projects that generate large amounts of employment are favored for ghetto development if
their skill distribution and training adaptability
are suitable, following the first criterion developed above. It is, however, necessary to consider
the particular question of labor-intensive project
planning in greater detail. The reason is that
highly labor-intensive activities are shunned by
large industrial and commercial firms, since these
firms are not able to make what they consider adequate profits on such activities. Two cases in
point are automotive diagnostic clinics and maintenance services on consumer durable products. Why
profits cannot be adequate has no explanation in
terms of the conventional economic theory of the
firm, but can be interpreted in terms of the dynamic relationship between technological innovations
and general advances in wage scales. If we posit,
following Joseph Schumpeter, that the profits of
large industrial corporations depend on the maintenance of temporary monopoly positions through a
stream of innovations, we can identify two forces
which steadily erode these monopoly profits.[15] One
is the market force of competition which, in spite
of the barriers to the entry of new market participants, forces the monopolistic competitors to
progressively narrow the spread between their costs
and prices. This is manifested, for example, in
the well-known life-cycle pricing of new products.
The other force tending to erode profits is the
general advance in wage levels. With a steady rate
of wage-level increases per unit time, the higher
the proportion of wage costs in total costs, the
faster the spread between costs and prices will be
cut down. The total benefit to the firm over time
from an innovation producing a given initial spread
between costs and prices per unit investment will,

therefore, vary inversely with the degree of labor
intensity of the new activity; i.e., with the proportion of labor costs in total costs. Although potential innovations may be just as likely to have a
high labor intensity as a low one, profit maximization will lead the firm to give preference to innovations that happen to have a low degree of labor
intensity.

FIGURE 7

The Dynamic Relationship Between Profits,
Innovation, and Labor Intensity

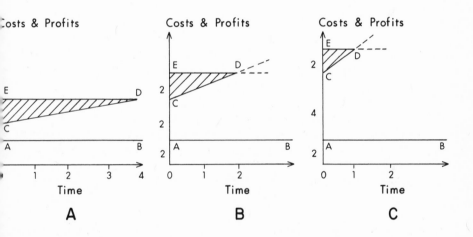

Figure 7 gives a simple illustration of this
phenomenon for three different potential innovations: A, B, and C, with identical capital investments and initial profit rates but differing labor
requirements. In each diagram in the figure, line
AB represents capital charges including normal
profits; the level of line CD above that of AB represents labor costs; and the level of line ED above
that of CD represents temporary monopoly profits.
Wages are assumed to rise in a linear fashion, by

50 per cent of the initial wage level per period.
The shaded area in each diagram represents total
(undiscounted) temporary monopoly profits resulting
from each potential innovation A, B, or C, which
are clearly most favorable for the least labor-
intensive innovation, A.

The inherently limited profits associated with
labor-intensive projects are less of a barrier to
community-sponsored ghetto development institutions
than they are for large commercial corporations
since, in the case of the former, the largest part
of the payoff does not (or should not) come from
profits but from external effects such as the creation of large amounts of employment with proper
skill-level distributions and training opportunities.
Therefore highly labor-intensive activities, ceteris
paribus, are good candidates for ghetto industries.
Due to the bias of large companies, the economy as
a whole is underserviced with regard to the outputs
of activities that are inherently labor-intensive;
therefore such activities might open up significant
opportunities for the sale of ghetto-produced commodities and services to outside areas, without being exposed to strong competition from powerful and
well-established enterprises.

Other External Economies and Diseconomies

Our qualitative project selection criteria are
all aimed at capturing community benefits that are
not reflected in terms of conventional resource-
allocation criteria. In this sense they can be regarded as external economies or (if projects have
harmful side effects) as external diseconomies. In
this section we survey three additional classes of
externalities having to do with employment, community service, and pollution.

Employment

The generation of new ghetto jobs is a community benefit in its own right. In evaluating this
benefit, the following considerations arise.

The Kind of Employment Generated. Under purely
commercial criteria, this is a matter of indifference as long as the activity is profitable. We
have already stressed that, as far as the kind of
employment is concerned, we favor projects with as-
sorted skill levels that lend themselves to the
establishment of training activities linked to career ladders, and we specifically reject projects
that offer low-grade, poorly paying, dead-end jobs,
in whatever number.

For Whom the Employment Is Generated. A project
rates low if there is an expectation that the jobs
will not accrue primarily to ghetto residents but
to outsiders who commute into the ghetto.

Community Service

     Raising the quality and reducing the prices of
locally consumed commodities and services results
in important community benefits. For example, food
co-op and automotive projects are capable of creating external economies insofar as they aim at raising quality and reducing the excessive price levels
that prevail, especially in food retailing. It de-
serves emphasis that in the last case--the reduction of the price level--the criterion of generating
"external" community benefits goes directly counter
to profit maximization, since every cent in price
concessions is taken out of profits when the demand,
as for food, is largely inelastic. The same goes
also for quality--except for the fact that at times
the quality of service can be raised at little or
no cost, with just a little more attention to the
needs of the consumers. The criterion of external
effects is also relied upon when profitable activities, such as the operation of slum housing for
profit, are rejected.

Pollution and Crowding

     Air pollution, noise, and the generation of
toxic wastes are clear cases of external diseconomies that should be scored against a given project.

Closely related to pollution are the effects of
crowding, particularly in regard to transport.
Projects that lead to large shipments and time-
consuming loading and unloading operations are likely to create traffic jams and are thus rated lower
than their commercial profitability would otherwise
suggest.

This completes our discussion of qualitative
criteria for determining project priorities, and
we turn to the question of how these qualitative
criteria relate to the conventional project selection criteria based on resource allocation.

THE RECONCILIATION OF PROJECT PRIORITIES
WITH RESOURCE ALLOCATION

The emphasis placed on qualitative project
evaluation criteria, which has been characteristic
of our discussion heretofore, does not mean that we
propose to neglect legitimate concern with questions
of resource allocation. In the urban ghetto context, financial resources of several classes--in-
ternally generated by the community itself, available through private channels, city funds, state
funds, federal funds--are of key importance. Land
area available for residential, commercial, and industrial purposes also limits the kind of activities that may be undertaken, and there are constraints on the availabilities of labor skills.
All of these play an important role in the formulation of a ghetto development program, in spite of
the fact that they do not merit exclusive attention.

Project evaluation criteria of the kind most
frequently applied by the professional economist
are intimately related to resource allocation models, usually of the mathematical programming type.
In our opinion, no quantitative model, be it of the
mathematical programming or any other variety, is
ready for implementation in the ghetto development
context. While resource scarcities can be set out
in general terms, it is very hard to specify precisely what the relevant scarce resources are in a

ghetto such as Harlem--for example, how many kinds
of public funds, under individual programs or con-
solidated program categories, should be regarded as
separate constraints, or how their supply levels
could be anticipated. Moreover, even if a quantitative model could clearly specify project priorities,
actual implementation may depend on concrete opportunities rather than theoretical preferences; the
first project to be implemented is often the one
for which a sponsor can be found immediately. Nor
are resource supplies in practice independent of
project selection; certain funds may be tied to the
execution of specific projects. The best that can
be hoped for from project selection criteria at
this stage, whether they be based on rigorous mathematical analysis or on a qualitative appraisal, as
we propose, is that they will provide a conceptual
framework for a pragmatic decision-making process.
Theoretical rigor is thus of no immediate practical
consequence.

Nonetheless, the theoretical foundations of
the proposed new approach to project selection have
to be explored, since the analytical framework with
which practical problems are approached underlies
the judgment of whether given development policies
and programs appear reasonable or not. In economic
analysis, conceptual model-building traditionally
outruns quantitative implementation. We shall thus
attempt to at least sketch out the theoretical bases
of our proposed approach. A detailed analysis can
be found elsewhere.[16]

We assume, first of all, that the decision
process is quantized. This means that we are not
concerned with marginal decisions but with choosing
between major developmental alternatives. In most
development programming work, "linkages"[17] between
individual economic activities have to be taken into account. Production processes use common inputs,
provide raw materials and markets for each other,
and are related by a host of other threads that the
economist usually refers to as "external economies
and diseconomies." In the urban ghetto context,

the most important of these are labor training, the
interaction, of production and distribution activities, and costs due to crowding and pollution. Activities that are subject to strong economies of
scale or all-or-nothing decisions also lead to similar interconnections between individual investments. As a result of such linkages, the logical
unit of development programming is not the individual activity, but a complex (or group) of interrelated activities.[18] The complex acts as a module
or quantum in the course of decision-making. Development programs are best constructed from such
modules, which play the role of building blocks in
piecing together a comprehensive ghetto development
program. Each module is either included in a program or not; it cannot be used at half scale or at
other partial scales. This is the sense in which
we assert that the decision-making process is quantized. From this point on, in referring to development projects, we shall have in mind such activity complexes or modules.

     In order to connect up the quantized decision
process with the usual kind of resource allocation
model, we assume that each project (complex, module)
exists in several secondary variants that may differ among themselves in regard to such resource-
bound characteristics as intensity of space use,
labor use, the use of specific kinds of funds, the
degree of mechanization or automation, and so forth.
Ordinary resource allocation models select both
major projects and their secondary variants at the
same time, in such a way as to make most efficient
use of the available scarce resources. What we
propose is to introduce just one major modification
into this approach. We associate a rank with each
major project (complex, module), designating the
relative priority of the project in such a way that
this rank is identical for all secondary variants.
We then insist that major projects be executed in
the order of their externally imposed priority
ranking, regardless of considerations of resource
allocation. Yet at the same time we permit the efficient use of resources to guide the selection of

secondary project variants. If the range of such
variants is sufficiently broad, this leaves a great
deal of leeway in organizing a development program.
The efficiency with which resource allocation is
undertaken at the level of the secondary project
variants sets the calendar times at which projects
further down the priority lists are executed. If
the selection is efficient, higher-priority projects
will leave more resources for the rapid execution
of lower-priority projects; if the selection is inefficient, higher-priority projects will pre-empt
excessive amounts of resources and will delay the
implementation of lower-priority projects until additional resources can be accumulated.

When the resource inputs required for execut-
ing alternative project variants of major projects
down the priority list are graphically represented,
they lead to a family of nested curves which the
professional economist immediately recognizes as a
quantized version of one of his standard theoretical
constructs, the so-called indifference curves.
While indifference curves play a crucial role in
received economic doctrine, their empirical determination has so far run into almost insuperable obstacles. Since our proposed approach to project
selection succeeds in deriving such curves from much
simpler information on the priority ranking and on
the secondary technical variants of major projects,
this approach not only connects up with standard
economic theory in an acceptable manner, but it
also provides the theory with a new tool for the
empirical investigation of decision processes.
Apart from decisions in development planning that
are naturally quantized, we believe that our approach can be generalized to the decisions of households and enterprises, insofar as these decisions
can also be broken down into self-contained modules
whose priority ordering and technical variants are
then open to empirical investigation.

SUMMARY

Some of the issues we have been concerned with in this chapter are of interest in their own right to the theoretical economist. Yet we have not set out to look for new analytical insights, only to try to make sense out of the development problem of the Harlem economy. We have been forced into experimenting with new approaches to project evaluation and selection because we became convinced that the problem would not fit into the most widely used categories of theoretical economics. Nevertheless, we were reluctant to work on a purely ad hoc basis, trusting that our intuition would lead us to more valuable results if disciplined by a continuous attempt to bridge the gap between reality and the standard approaches of economic theory.

This chapter has been a record of our attempt at such a reconciliation. We started out by systematizing those noneconomic, or at least nonquantitative, considerations that give the Harlem development problem far more depth than is available to simple resource allocation models. We then went on to establish the modular structure of development projects that results from the web of interrelations between individual candidate activities involved in development programming and showed that a priority ordering of these development modules or activity complexes which is formally suitable for expressing the effects of extra-economic or nonquantitative considerations is also closely related to standard tools of economic theory such as indifference curves.

We now proceed to discuss some of the concrete development projects--projects that support existing Harlem enterprises (Chapter 4) and new ventures (Chapter 5)--that resulted from our over-all approach. Some of these projects involved the organization and presentation of a large bulk of operational detail. The next two chapters emphasize the practical side of development programming problems rather than the general questions of strategy and

method that have been dealt with up to now. We
pass on to these more mundane matters in the conviction that effective work on new models of development programming problems will inevitably proceed
at two levels--the theoretical and the practical.
The tension between these levels will, it is hoped,
provide the stimulus for further efforts in the
theory of ghetto development.

NOTES

1.   Standard references concerning such models
of the mathematical programming type are R. Dorfman,
P. A. Samuelson, and R. Solow, Linear Programming
and Economic Analysis (New York: McGraw-Hill, 1958);
H. B. Chenery and P. G. Clark, Interindustry Economics (New York: Wiley, 1959).

2.   A comprehensive survey of Soviet and East
European economic planning by the U.N. Economic
Commission for Europe (Economic Planning in Europe,
Economic Survey of Europe in 1967, Part 2, Geneva,
1965) describes this as follows (pp. 15-16):

> The division of the first Soviet Five-
> Year Plan document, the prototype--in
> many respects--of succeeding Soviet
> and Eastern European plans . . . pro-
> vides an outline of the order of
> priority attached by the planning
> authorities to the various quantita-
> tive targets falling under each head-
> ing. . . . It . . . provides guide-
> lines for the priority allocation of
> capital and manpower to heavy indus-
> try, within the industrial sector,
> and to industry as a whole in relation
> to other sectors of the economy . . .
> in practice, production targets for
> still more restricted branches or key
> items within this sector ('leading
> links') have been given an overriding
> priority.

3. For the use of priorities in U.S. wartime planning, see T. Scitovsky, E. Shaw, and L. Tarshis, <u>Mobilizing Resources for War</u> (New York: McGraw-Hill, 1951); and D. Novick, M. Anshen, and W. C. Truppner, <u>War Time Production Controls</u> (New York: Columbia University Press, 1959).

4. The issue of policy-makers' value judgments has an ample theoretical literature, most of which is couched in terms of estimating a preference function whose existence is taken for granted. More instructive is a pragmatic discussion of the ways in which policy-makers communicate their desires and judgments and the extent to which they are aware of these at various stages of planning, in P. Davidoff and T. Reiner, "A Choice Theory of Planning," <u>Journal of the American Institute of Planners</u>, May, 1962.

5. A simple discursive survey of the principal issues is found in G. M. Meier, <u>Leading Issues in Economic Development</u> (New York: Oxford University Press, 1964), pp. 231-50. An excellent brief analytical survey is given by A. K. Sen in <u>Choice of Technology: A Critical Survey of a Class of Debates</u>, U.N. ADHOC Meeting of Experts on the Role of Advanced Skills and Technologies in Industrial Development, New York, Document No. ID/WG. 3/DP. 7 (May, 1967); see also A. K. Sen, <u>Choice of Techniques: An Aspect of the Theory of Planned Economic Development</u> (2d ed.; Oxford: Blackwell, 1962).

6. This line of argument goes back to J. J. Polak, "Balance of Payments Problems of Countries Reconstructing With the Help of Foreign Loans," <u>Quarterly Journal of Economics</u>, February, 1943, pp. 208-40, reprinted in American Economics Association, <u>Readings in the Theory of International Trade</u> (Homewood, Ill.: Irwin, 1949), pp. 459-93. Polak presented the argument in terms of a low capital-output ratio. A formal version requires the equalization of the marginal product of labor in all uses. More sophisticated restatements in terms of the social marginal productivity of factors

are A. E. Kahn, "Investment Criteria in Development Programmes," Quarterly Journal of Economics, February, 1951, pp. 38-61, and H. B. Chenery, "The Application of Investment Criteria," Quarterly Journal of Economics, February, 1953, pp. 76-96.

7. See W. Galenson and H. Leibenstein, "Investment Criteria, Productivity, and Economic Development," Quarterly Journal of Economics, August, 1955, pp. 343-70. This argument has been introduced into economic growth models with many variations, specifying differential saving rates for wage and profit-income receivers. For a survey of such models, see F. H. Hahn and R. C. O. Matthews, "The Theory of Economic Growth: A Survey," Economic Journal, 74 (December, 1964), pp. 779-902, reprinted in Surveys of Economic Theory (New York: St. Martin's Press, 1967), II.

8. The argument for regarding capital as a by-product of growth has been put most forcefully by Branko Horvat in "The Optimum Rate of Investment," Economic Journal, December, 1958, pp. 747-67; also "Methodological Problems in Long-Term Economic Development Programming," Industrialization and Productivity, Bulletin 5 (New York: United Nations, 1962), pp. 37-51.

9. This literature has been surveyed by Jack Baranson in Industrial Technologies for Developing Economies (New York: Praeger, 1969); see also Baranson's annotated bibliography, Technology for Underdeveloped Areas (New York: Pergamon, 1967).

10. Learning models in modern resource allocation theory go back to H. Asher, Cost-Quantity Relationships in the Airframe Industry, Report PR 191 (Santa Monica: The Rand Corp., July, 1956); the major contribution has been by K. Arrow, "The Economic Implications of Learning by Doing," Review of Economic Studies, 29 (June, 1962), pp. 155-73, which led to a family of economic growth models built on its premises. These are described in Hahn and Matthews, op. cit. To our knowledge, learning

phenomena have not been considered as project selection criteria.

11. See Arthur Pearl and Frank Riessman, New
Careers for the Poor (New York: Free Press, 1965).

12. Franco Modigliani, "New Developments on
the Oligopoly Front," Journal of Political Economy,
June, 1958, pp. 215-32.

13. Mail-order houses often act as organizers
of production, marketing, and output of many independent producers under their own labels. U.S.
distribution firms such as Sears Roebuck have had
a stimulating effect on the development of domestic
lines of manufacture in a number of developing
countries. For example, see John F. Gallagher,
"Markets as A Basis for Industrial Development:
Sears Roebuck in Peru," in Richard J. Ward, ed.,
The Challenge of Development (Chicago: Aldine,
1967), pp. 310-18.

14. These measures are quantitatively explored for a number of lines of activity in Bennett
Harrison, "Studies in the Structure of the Ghetto
Economy" (unpublished Ph.D. dissertation, Department of Economics, University of Pennsylvania).

15. Joseph Schumpeter, The Theory of Economic
Development (New York: Oxford University Press,
1934); and Business Cycles (1939).

16. Thomas Vietorisz, "Quantized Preferences
and Planning by Priorities," American Economic Review, May, 1970 (forthcoming).

17. Forward and backward linkages have been
defined and extensively discussed by A. O. Hirschman
in The Strategy of Economic Development (New Haven:
Yale University Press, 1958), Chapters 6-8.

18. For problems of project evaluation and
program formulation under economies of scale, indivisibilities, and external economies and diseconomies,

see Thomas Vietorisz, "Decentralization and Project
Evaluation in the Presence of Economies of Scale
and Indivisibilities," Industrialization and Pro-
ductivity, Bulletin 12 (New York: United Nations,
1968), pp. 25-58; T. Vietorisz, "Industrial Devel-
opment Planning Models with Economies of Scale and
Indivisibilities," Regional Science Association
Papers, XII (1964), pp. 157-92; T. Vietorisz and
A. S. Manne, "Chemical Processes, Plant Location,
and Economies of Scale," in A. S. Manne and H. M.
Markowitz, eds., Studies in Process Analysis:
Economy-Wide Production Capabilities, Cowles Foundation Monograph No. 18 (New York: Wiley, 1963),
Chapter 6, pp. 136-58.

CHAPTER **4** THE SUPPORT AND
UPGRADING OF
EXISTING ENTERPRISES

A development strategy for an urban ghetto
area is translated into action along two fronts.
The first, entailing the effective use and upgrading of the area's existing economic base, is the
subject of this chapter. The second, promotion and
implementation of new economic activities, is discussed in Chapter 5.

This chapter explores potential new markets
for local businesses, identifies gaps in Harlem's
economic base, and discusses ways of organizing
the scatter of existing Harlem businesses into more
efficient distribution and service networks. This
will improve the quality of services rendered to
the community and increase the incomes of local
entrepreneurs and workers. It will also create a
potential for the procurement of contracts from
local institutions and federal agencies. Moreover,
it will demonstrate to the community that the notion of black entrepreneurship is valid.

POTENTIAL NEW MARKETS FOR
HARLEM BUSINESSES

In the early part of 1968, officers of many of
the largest institutions located in the Harlem area
--Columbia University, Barnard College, the Union
and Jewish Theological Seminaries, St. Luke's Hospital, and the Julliard School of Music--met to
consider ways in which their institutional purchasing from Harlem businesses could be expanded. Participants drew up a list of those activities in

which Harlem businessmen could increase their sales
to institutional customers. We have expanded this
list to embrace a broad range of relevant activities. These activities are presented in Table 19,
classified by 4-digit SIC code, together with an
estimate of existing black and nonblack Harlem
businesses in each class. When this list was established, only three Harlem businesses--a black-
owned stationery and printing firm, a black-owned
pharmacy, and a linen supply company with ownership
unreported--were identified as institutional suppliers. Harlem's business community, as shown in
Table 19, is, however, in a relatively good position to supply at least some of the institutional
demands revealed by these purchasing agents. Within the 45 lines of activity that are of primary
interest to us, nearly 700 establishments are now
operating in Central Harlem, of which almost 200
reported black ownership. Sixteen of the activities listed were not represented by a single establishment in the Harlem area. Of these, we recommended that 8 activities (noted in Table 19) be
given priority as potential new projects, because
they involve goods and services which other New
York City institutions, including city, state, and
federal governmental units, could be persuaded to
purchase from Harlem firms. Filling these gaps in
the area's economic base would provide direct service to the community as well as outside sales.
The two functions are in fact complementary. For
example, firms engaged in the sale and repair of
air-conditioning equipment should serve the household and business demands of the local community as
well as the demands of Morningside Heights and outside institutional clients. Harlem's food whole-
salers should service the various institutional
cafeterias, as well as the 200 retail grocers already located in Central Harlem.

New wholesale and service activities established in areas where Harlem is particularly deficient can best fulfill this dual function if they
are set up as affiliating institutions which can
combine the existing small retail and service establishments into networks of more efficient, more
specialized, and more complementary units.

TABLE 19

Institutional Demand and Potential Supply in Harlem[a]

Standard Industrial Classification	Total Number	Number Reporting Ownership		
		Total	Black	Nonblack
1721 Painting, paper hanging, decorating	2			
2396 Printing & embossing on plastic or fabric	0			
2731 Printing books & pamphlets	1			
2751 Job printing	17	9	5	4
2752 Lithography; offset printing	3	2	2	
3069 Manufacture of rubber stamps	0			
322x Pressed or blown glass and glassware[b]	0			
421x Trucking, local and long distance	24	15	14	1
5013 Wholesale automotive equipment	0			
5022 Wholesale drugs and supplies	1			
5028 Wholesale paints	0			
5041 Wholesale groceries, general[b]	0			
5042 Wholesale frozen foods[b]	0			
5043 Wholesale dairy products[b]	0			
5072 Wholesale hardware	0			
5077 Wholesale air conditioning, refrigeration equipment & supplies[b]	0			
5081 Wholesale food warming equipment	1			
5084 Wholesale industrial machinery, equipment & supplies	0			
5086 Wholesale surgical equipment & supplies	2	2	1	1
5096 Wholesale stationery supplies	1	1	1	
5097 Wholesale linen and mattress purchases	1			
5099 Wholesale photographic supplies	10	5	3	2
5221 Retail plumbing, heating and air-conditioning equipment[b]	0			
5231 Paint, glass and wallpaper stores	7	3	1	2
5251 Hardware stores	25	12	4	8

SIC	Industrial group				
5411	Grocery stores	199	98	49	49
5712	New & reconditioned mattresses; other furniture	56	27	5	22
5719	Venetian blinds	3	3		
5912	Drugstores	51	27	10	17
5943	Stationery stores	94	37	32	5
5971	Jewelry stores	29	14	6	8
5996	Camera & photographic supply stores	1	1	1	
7213	Linen supply services	2	1		1
7216	Linen cleaning	104	59	39	20
7217	Rug & carpet cleaning	0			
7341	Window cleaning[b]	0			
7349	Venetian blind cleaning & repair	5			
7394	Equipment rental & leasing	0			
7622	Radio & television repair shops	31	12	11	1
7623	Refrigerator & air-conditioning repair shops[b]	0			
7629	Electrical repair shops	4			
7631	Watch, clock & jewelry repair shops	2	1		
7641	Reupholstery & furniture repair	9	4	4	
7694	Electric motor repairs	1			
7699	Instrument & tool sharpening & repair; repair of surgical instruments	11	4	3	1
45 SIC Classes	Totals	697	337	191	146
	Percentages	100.0	48.3	27.4	20.9

[a] The industrial groups listed in this table are those from which Morningside Heights institutions currently purchase goods and services. The numerical entries indicate the existence or nonexistence of such businesses in Harlem. Information on race of owners is reported where available.

[b] Recommended for priority as new projects, as explained in the text.

Source: Center for Economic Planning, Harlem Business Inventory.

ALLIANCES OF INDEPENDENT BUSINESSES

Organizations of affiliated independent businesses are a form of producers' cooperative built
around the function of joint purchasing. They differ from the traditional U.S. producer's co-op
which emphasized joint marketing (particularly the
restriction of supply in inelastic farm commodity
markets) in order to increase sales revenues. These
co-ops were never very successful, for they were
bedeviled by perverse incentives: If ninety-nine
farmers joined together to restrict output and one
did not, the hold-out reaped the double benefits of
higher prices and larger sales. In a producer's
co-op organized around the purchasing function,
however, the benefits received from large-scale
purchasing can be readily restricted to member
firms.

The modern affiliated independents' organization originated in food retailing and is one of the
little-known success stories of the last few years.
It is not the large food chains that have made
spectacular recent market advances--their share
hovered around 40 per cent in the last decade--but
the affiliated independents, whose share advanced
from 8 per cent to 55 per cent by signing up new
members. This success was built on a combination
of the economies of large-scale purchases characteristic of the chain stores, and the high motivation and flexible adaptation to local conditions
characteristic of the independent entrepreneurs.

We have recommended the use of the affiliation
strategy as a general approach to the upgrading of
Harlem's existing businesses not only in food retailing but also in other lines of activity. Beside their purchasing function, affiliating institutions can provide technical and business assistance, negotiate contracts, and assist in expansion
and specialization plans.

Our survey of potential institutional demand
led us to the conclusion that, in the absence of an

affiliation system, Harlem firms will not be able
to fill sizable institutional contracts. It is not
that these firms have a lack of entrepreneurial
talent; rather, their apparent inability to handle
large volumes stems from a lack of proper equipment,
overly restricted inventories, and a lack of experience in large-volume selling.

By increasing the efficiency of the small
firms, it is possible to raise their profitability.
If the affiliating organization is under community
control, it can enforce higher quality, lower
prices, and improved wages, under threat of exclusion from the affiliation network.

The major features of an affiliation strategy
can be systematically set out as follows:

1. Pooled purchases create the basis for adequate economies of scale in supply operations at
the wholesale level. The affiliating organization
acts as a wholesaler for the group; but its functions extend beyond a simple commercial wholesaling
enterprise. It may be fully owned by the affiliates, or if not (if the affiliating organization is
sponsored and established by a community development organization such as HCC), the affiliates can
still have an important element of control over its
operations.

2. Affiliation will operate best when there
is not only pooling but also standardization of
purchases, and coordination of the operations and
policies of the affiliates. In this context, it is
possible to provide business assistance--legal, accounting, technical, management consulting--at a
much lower average cost than that at which such
services would be commercially available to an
isolated enterprise.

3. The affiliating organizations, in addition
to supplying merchandise, can also act as a broker
for affiliates in negotiating for credit, insurance,
trucking services, or other input items.

4. Some inputs may be secured at lower cost
through backward integration. A medium-load truck
fleet which could not operate at a break-even scale
by supplying services to a number of separate firms
may become feasible when the activities of the
firms are coordinated. Such a service could be
maintained by a community-controlled auto service
center and pass along its lower maintenance costs
in the form of lower transport charges to the firms
that it services.

5. The affiliating organization can assist
member firms in the preparation of formal bids
where this is required, and in the negotiation of
supply contracts with the government or large private institutional clients.

6. This marketing function, moreover, can extend beyond assistance to the individual affiliate
into the area of the negotiation of supply contracts
on behalf of the group as a whole, where individual
affiliates supply portions of the over-all contract.

7. The former function leads naturally to the
possibility for progressive specialization within
the affiliated group, encouraged, planned, and coordinated by the affiliating organization.

8. The affiliating organization may assist
in the planning and implementation of the expansion
plans of individual affiliates and may set up new
businesses that are affiliated from the beginning.
In this regard, it may assist through expansion
loans and the negotiation of financial assistance
from government agencies. These functions offer
the sponsoring community organization an opportunity
to acquire equity holdings in individual businesses,
with a consequent improvement in potential control
and coordination.

9. The affiliating organization may offer assistance in labor and management training and may
help to arrange government or other support for
formal or on-the-job training programs run either
by itself or by its affiliates.

10.   The control over distribution made possible by the affiliated independent mode forms an
excellent basis for backward integration into manufacturing. In this connection it should be noted
that, since the same manufacturing activities can
supply both distributive modes, no conflict exists
between a community-sponsored group of affiliated
independent food retailers and a parallel community-
sponsored retail food co-op structure. In fact,
the broader distribution structure inherent in the
parallel use of the two modes makes the outlook for
the manufacturing operations that much more favorable.

11.   The affiliation approach is the most effective way of protecting small independent businesses from the catastrophic consequences that may
follow the establishment of large and efficient
community-sponsored units in the same lines of
business. As the aim of such units will be community service through quality and low prices, the
relatively inefficient small stores will bear intolerable competitive pressures. Affiliation is
then a means of resolving the inherent conflict between community service and small-business survival.

The black community organization that promotes
and coordinates these affiliation activities must
recognize the de facto existence of a considerable
white ownership of ghetto-located businesses. It
is our impression that many of these would be willing to join groups of community-sponsored affiliated
independents. The inclusion of white-owned enterprises in over-all development or support strategies
may be advantageous to the black community--the
community would be trading off the continued existence of the white-owned firm's markets for a
greater degree of control over the local economy
and a broader economic base. As it is cheaper to
rehabilitate and expand existing enterprises than
to devise, establish, and run new ones, such a
strategy could result in bringing large segments of
the local economy under some measure of community
influence. Moreover, the probability of success

increases with the number of firms and activities
in the affiliation network. The inclusion of white-
owned firms would thus help to form organizations of
the required minimum economical scale.

Firms in Harlem that reported black ownership
supply 18 out of the 45 classes of institutional
demand listed in Table 19. The inclusion of white
firms would add 11 more classes, for a total of 29.
We do not want to overemphasize this recommendation;
fundamentally, it is a political decision. Nonetheless, we wish to point out that the economic implications for the black community are likely to be
positive.

Of the black-owned activities which do exist,
which ought to be given priority in an affiliation/
expansion program? Table 20 indicates our choices
for further (feasibility) study; it is apparent
that these shops are far too small to be able to
manage any kind of significant contracts with the
quality control and punctuality required by institutional purchasers. Even treated collectively,
some of the groups are still too small--with a combined employment of under 10 persons. In these
cases, the basis of an affiliation/expansion program cannot be found in existing staff or equipment
only the existing entrepreneurial experience is
relevant. The generally small size of black-owned
business does not indicate a lack of entrepreneurial talent, given the externally imposed constraints within which blacks must operate. In any
event, the existing black managerial experience
should be exploited by HCC as fully as possible in
the recommended affiliation/training programs.

A successful affiliation strategy will permit
member firms to appraise and enter new markets,
some of which may be quite distant. Among these
are the procurement markets of the federal govern-
ment--markets that have never been adequately exploited for the development of economically depressed areas.

TABLE 20

Black-Owned Activities Recommended for Affiliation/Expansion Studies

Standard Industrial Classification	Existing Number	Total Est. Employment	Mean Empl. Per Firm
2751 Job printing	5	6	1.2
2752 Lithography; offset	2	4	2.0
421x Trucking; movers	14	38	2.7
5912 Drugstores	10	32	3.2
5943 Stationers	32	41	1.3
7216 Cleaners	39	83	2.1
7622 Radio & TV repairs	11	11	1.0
7641 Reupholstery; furniture repairs	4	4	1.0

SELLING TO THE FEDERAL GOVERNMENT

The securing of government contracts is a useful device in over-all ghetto development strategy. The considerations mentioned below, while hardly exhaustive, serve to indicate the ways in which a general strategy for selling to the federal government may be devised and implemented.

Federal contracts may be large enough and stable enough to allow small establishments to develop the necessary production potential to compete in the private sector on a more equal basis with other established manufacturers. Yet a heavy reliance on federal contracting is a double-edged weapon for ghetto development, since it makes the black community vulnerable to political pressures. Such sales should, therefore, be held to a small proportion of total sales--a maximum of some 25-30 per cent--in the same way that businesses in general maintain a similar ratio between their export sales, which may be subject to unpredictable policy shifts by foreign governments, and their more stable domestic sales. In the immediate future, this consideration is unlikely to act as a constraint because it will be hard enough to secure any federal contracts at all.

Federal contracting is in many ways a closed world. The most important single factor in developing a strategy for selling to the federal government is an understanding of the system's present bias toward the acquisition of the best deal for the government rather than the accomplishment of socially desirable secondary goals. This bias is reflected in the various codes and regulations which structure the procurement system but, most importantly, it is embodied in the attitudes and motivations of many procurement officials.

The development of a successful strategy to secure government contracts will depend primarily on the establishment of lines of communication between ghetto developers and government officials.

When a firm approaches governmental procurement agencies it must have well-defined objectives with respect to the goods that it wishes to sell.   In Harlem's case it is necessary to identify those goods which confer the most direct benefits on the community; these, however, are not necessarily the goods currently in short supply.   To get the best reception from procurement officers, then, it may well be necessary to trade off community benefits for salable goods.   Informal and statistical techniques can identify those goods whose inventory levels are (or are expected to be) low relative to demand.   Once these are identified, a selection can then be made between the particular goods which would have the optimum impact on Harlem's development while still being within the present and projected production resources of the community.

The Government Procurement Process

Government buying programs can be divided into three broad categories:

1.   Military procurements: each branch of the armed forces buys products and contracts for services which are peculiar to its own needs.

2.   General Services Administration (GSA) procurements: the commodities and services common to many civilian agencies are generally bought through GSA.

3.   Specialized civil agency procurements: supply activities for products and services peculiar to one agency usually involve open market purchases by that agency.

Procurement in each of these categories is conducted in accordance with federal procurement regulations and under the requirements pertaining to the particular procuring agency.   Generally, goods and services are purchased through competitive bidding, although there are certain conditions under which direct negotiations may be undertaken.

No attempt will be made here to describe the
complex organizational structure of government purchasing agencies. However, GSA warrants special
attention since it is responsible for the centralized procurement, storage, and distribution of most
of the nonmilitary items purchased by the government. This agency operates under five major programs: (a) Defense Materials Service, which buys
strategic and critical materials for the national
stockpile; (b) Transportation and Communication
Service, which negotiates and contracts for transportation, public utility, and communication services for federal agencies; (c) Federal Supply Service, which buys supplies and contracts for services
for the common needs of all government agencies;
(d) Public Buildings Service, which acquires real
estate and constructs buildings for government use;
(e) Utilization and Disposal Service, which over-
sees the sale of surplus real and personal property,
administers contracts for services on in-use and
excess personal property for all government agencies.

GSA, like most other agencies, has a complete regional network of field offices which exe-
cute and administer contracts locally. It will be
virtually impossible for a relatively inexperienced
ghetto firm or organization to penetrate this decentralized organizational maze without a well-
thought-out strategy. When considering the potential of government procurement as a development
tool, it is impossible to ignore the system of administrative and legal safeguards established to
insure that the government gets the best possible
deal for each procurement dollar. Procurement officers are concerned with securing a thousand screwdrivers of standard specifications for the lowest
dollar prices, not with who made them or what benefits might accrue to the manufacturer or community
that produced them.

Although the objectives of the federal government include promoting high employment and eliminating pockets of long-term unemployment, its procurement offices can defeat this policy in their daily

operations. Most procurement officials are concerned with negotiating contracts at lowest possible
costs. It is our contention, however, that the government might well be better off when it buys from
the ghetto firm--even if it must pay a 10-20 per cent
differential in the process. For when the government buys a thousand screwdrivers from a ghetto
company, it may receive not only screwdrivers, but
also some job training, a reduction in welfare payments, greater community pride, fewer riots, and
other benefits. Bidding forms, however, do not
provide space for calculating and presenting these
or other social benefits. Unfortunately most federal procurement policies have not reached this
level of economic and social sophistication.

Most procurement activity consists in publi-
cizing the government's needs to established lists
of bidders--manufacturers and dealers who have indicated an interest in doing business with the government and have furnished evidence of their ability to carry out contractual obligations. Here as
in many other areas, a government policy of strict
neutrality may work against minority-owned ghetto
establishments.

There are exceptions to the standard bidding
procedures; for instance (a) emergency situations
where there is no time for the formal bidding procedures to be followed; (b) purchases under a certain dollar amount, often $2,500; (c) special ex-
perimental, developmental, or research items.

Preference to Small Businesses

Exceptions to standard bidding procedure other
than those mentioned above are made in an attempt
to assign contracts to certain specific classes of
suppliers--those of small size and those operating
in depressed areas. If a business that falls in
one of these categories can meet contractual specifications at an equal price, it may receive preference. These exceptions are limited, however, in
that they do not allow the government to pay a

higher than competitive price, and no allowance is
made for such related community benefits as work
training, development of local entrepreneurship,
reduced welfare transfers.

The Department of Defense attempts to secure
a greater share of government business for small
establishments by urging large contractors to subcontract to smaller ones. Firms receiving contracts of $500,000 or more are required to desig-
nate a Small Business Liaison Officer to seek out
such subcontractual opportunities. This requirement has no real force, for no subcontract need be
let, and a prime contractor's sole reward for his
effort comes in the form of good will.

The Role of the Small
Business Administration

The Small Business Administration (SBA) is the
federal agency charged specifically with providing
assistance in various forms to small businesses
generally, and, more recently, to ghetto businesses
in particular. For SBA purposes, "small" is interpreted generously: firms are considered small if
they are independently owned and operated and are
not dominant in their field of operation. Terms
may vary with specific industrial classifications,
but those firms with fewer than 500 employees regularly qualify.

Section 8a of the SBA Act makes this agency a
promising source of assistance in the securing of
government contracts. This section is as old as
the SBA Act but has never been extensively used.
Recently, however, federal executive officers have
been instrumental in furthering its use, and SBA
officials believe that, with franchising activities,
it provides the most effective vehicle for immediate assistance to ghetto enterprises.[1]

Section 8a of the SBA Act empowers and requires the agency (a) to enter into contracts with
any U.S. Government procurement agencies obligating

SBA to furnish articles, equipment, supplies, and
materials to the government; (b) to subcontract to
small business concerns for the performance of all
or portions of its contracts. SBA may also contract for such management services as may be necessary to enable it to perform such contracts.

In effect, SBA says to a government buyer,
"We'll get this for you at a competitive price,"
and then, through its regional offices, it finds
small businesses to supply the items. SBA then
furnishes a variety of aids to these firms. This
program can help achieve some of the social and
economic objectives of ghetto investment. It recognizes that by dealing with ghetto firms, the government can receive social benefits along with low
prices; it recognizes, too, that the government can
afford to underwrite the costs incurred in activities which support less efficient ghetto firms.

Emphasis on Section 8a programs, coupled with
other methods of SBA assistance, seem to offer the
best vehicle for the sustained growth of ghetto
firms. These other forms of assistance include the
use of surplus land and equipment, available from
the GSA and the Department of Defense, as well
as manpower training and development funds from
the Department of Labor. These assistance programs
must be explored in great detail; the discussion in
this brief chapter is only suggestive. If Harlem
firms are to be successful in securing government
contracts, the assistance available from SBA should
be maximized--subject, of course, to HCC's political constraints.

Analysis of Government Demand

The proper use of the administrative and legal
intricacies of the procurement process is the single
most important element in determining strategies
for selling to the federal government. However, the
question of which goods Harlem businesses should
produce for federal consumption is critical. A
development strategy must concentrate on those

industries which further the community's over-all
development, those goods local businesses are capable of supplying, and those types of goods in the
greatest demand by the government. The presence of
local multiplier effects and the existence of external economies described in Chapters 2 and 3 are
considerations that must be weighed in the development program. These issues are, of course, pervasive and are not limited to a strategy for selling materials to the government. Government demand
should be investigated with the intention not only
of satisfying existing Harlem industries but also
of identifying those areas of demand which can be
most easily captured by new or expanded ghetto
businesses--subject to the requirement that they
be in both current and projected short supply. A
primary objective in studying government demand
and, in particular, identifying goods in short supply is to provide Harlem firms with a bargaining
tool in their negotiations with procurement officials. Full knowledge of the quantity of various
goods bought by government agencies and of their
respective scarcities can allow Harlem representatives to maximize their bargaining position with
federal agencies.

The problem of estimating the government's demand for particular goods can be attacked in two
separate ways. In the first approach, procurement
officials in different agencies can be contacted
and an attempt made to collect quantitative information on the types of goods purchased and the nature of the firms which supply them, the average
size of contract, payment schedules, and contract
terms by agency and by type of commodity. Although
this approach has the obvious advantage of simplic-
ity, it may not work well in practice. The idio-
syncrasies of individual procurement officers and
the decentralized structure of procurement may
frustrate attempts to collect data. It is unlikely
that any single official, even if well-intentioned,
could supply more than scattered bits of information.

The experience of several of our Harlem project consultants--one of them a lawyer--serves to indicate the decentralization of the federal procurement system and the difficulties inherent in an attempt to break into the system without prior contacts or experience:

> We approached the U.S. Department of Commerce on the matter of clothing; Commerce suggested the Defense Services Administration in Philadelphia, since DSA does buy for many agencies on the East Coast. DSA sent us to the Defense Industrial Supply Center, which in turn suggested GSA, who suggested the Regional Commerce Defense Branch. These people referred us to DSA, Commerce Business Daily and the Washington Central Office. Eventually some factual data was obtained at the New York GSA office (Federal Supply Services). They said, however, that one part of the material might be classified and that they would like to withhold it from our interviewers until the Clearance Officer in Washington made a decision on the release. They made available some other material for examination in their offices and, for the sake of completeness, they reported this to the Clearance Officer. Exactly at 5 P.M. the Clearance Officer let them know that the material they had been withholding from us was not classified and that the information that had already been released was classified. The longhand notes that we made in their office could not even be removed from the premises.[2]

If experienced professional investigators can encounter such difficulties, what kind of reception awaits a contingent of ghetto businessmen?

The second, and perhaps more useful, approach is through a statistical analysis of government demand. A methodology for such an analysis was devised but could not be put into practice given the resource limitations of our project. It is based on the construction of a time series using the Commerce Business Daily as the prime data source. This publication serves as a basic reference in preparing a comprehensive listing of the quantity of particular goods and services demanded by federal government agencies. Analysis of time series generated from a large and consecutive sample of current and past issues of the Daily indicates the following characteristics of government demand: (a) classification of demand by 4-digit SIC code; (b) goods and services in current short supply; (c) yearly, quarterly, and monthly demand fluctuations; (d) trends in the demand for specific goods and services; (e) apparent product mixes.[3]

The large volume of data that can be generated by this approach can be immediately reduced. Initial activity selection can be confined to the manufacturing sector, because the services required by federal agencies tend to be highly specialized and location-specific; they are generally provided by firms or universities employing small numbers of highly educated or skilled personnel. Time-series data indicate trends in the levels of purchasing. Only those goods indicating a strong upward demand need be considered. A desirable feature in an activity or product mix is the identification of those goods whose demand fluctuations are negatively related. A positive association between the demand levels of individual commodities may lead to situations where a reduction in the demand for one good brings on a corresponding reduction in the demand for another. A benefit of diversification--protection against demand shifts--is thereby lost. It is a proper strategy, then, for Harlem firms to manufacture and sell, for example, both umbrellas and suntan lotion.

Our survey of opportunities for government contracting has of necessity been brief, since in

the course of our field study we could not fully
enter into, let alone exhaust, the ramifications of
the federal procurement system. In Appendix B we
provide a listing of useful leads for further work
on this problem.

In sum, we have found that there are opportunities for the support of existing enterprises in
the Harlem ghetto by means of opening up access to
new internal, institutional, and governmental markets. Yet the mere existence of such potential
markets does not mean that the scattered small businesses constituting a major part of the area's economic base will, given their resource limitations,
be in a position to exploit such markets by their
own efforts. On the contrary, we have identified
major obstacles, both frictional and systematic,
which impede the entry of Harlem firms into these
markets. Among these is the existence of established sources of supply that place new entrants at
a great disadvantage.

We regard affiliation under the sponsorship of
a community development corporation as the foremost
institutional device for overcoming this disadvantage while at the same time rendering a series of
supportive services to the area's small businesses.
This device assures the community an equitable share
in the benefits that accrue to such efforts. By
means of an affiliation strategy, small local businesses can be integrated into a more powerful network which will generate more income for the area
and improve the level of local services. It will
also establish a basis for new industries through
forward and backward linkages to existing enterprises.

NOTES

1. The Wall Street Journal, July 10, 1969,
p. 1.

2. A Proposed Investment Program for the Economic Development of Central Harlem, Final Report
of the Center for Economic Planning (New York: The
New School for Social Research, 1968) (Grant No.
CG-8730, U.S. Office of Economic Opportunity),
p. 5.16.   (Mimeographed)

3. See ibid., Chapter 5, for a detailed discussion of this statistical model.

CHAPTER 5 RECOMMENDED
DEVELOPMENT
PROJECTS

This chapter surveys the development projects
for which feasibility studies have been prepared as
part of our demonstration economic development program for Harlem. These include: an automotive
diagnostic service center; an auto mechanics training school; a cooperative supermarket; a food-canning facility; a computerized hospital accounting
service; and a community antenna television network.*
Each project is treated as an activity complex in
accordance with the theoretical considerations de-
lineated in Chapter 3. The projects represent a
package of functionally interdependent modules which
may be susceptible of staged construction. They are
potentially capable of generating a wide range of
social benefits for the Harlem community.

In terms of the selection criteria discussed
in Chapter 3, all of these projects rank high, and
all have been recommended for inclusion in Harlem's
development program. Some are in the process of
implementation, although the precise sequence has
not been determined in accordance with the formal
procedure suggested in Chapter 3. The available
quantitative information on resource availabilities
did not justify the definition of secondary project
variants. Decisions regarding the timing of project implementation were governed by such down-to-
earth considerations as the ability of the HCC to

---

*Each project received a detailed treatment in
the final report of the New School consulting team.

interest potential sponsors, the place of the individual project in HCC's over-all strategy, and
other matters of practical judgment.

AN AUTO SERVICE CENTER AND
MECHANICS SCHOOL

The Service Center

Even in a subway city like New York with a
dense network of mass transit facilities, auto use
continues to increase. Moreover, automobiles have
become increasingly complex mechanisms for reasons
of convenience and safety, while facilities to service these increased technical requirements are
lagging behind. The main difficulty seems to be a
shortage of trained manpower. This shortage of
skilled automotive service personnel is attested to
by the New York State Department of Labor, private
and public schools, labor union organizations, gas
stations, garage and dealer organizations, as well
as the general public. The occupational outlook,
according to the U.S. Department of Labor, is for
continually increasing demand for automotive service workers.

Our recommended service center provides comprehensive repair services specifically for residents
of Harlem, upper Manhattan areas contiguous to Harlem, the South Bronx, northwest Queens and, more
generally, for the residents of all of Manhattan
and the New York metropolitan area. The center
would be developed around a modern automotive diagnostic clinic and an auto mechanics training school
based on the training-ladder concept.

The computerized diagnostic clinic offers an
organized and efficient method of testing and analyzing every major safety and performance factor of
a motor vehicle. All tests and inspections are conducted with the most sophisticated electronic and
dynamic equipment. The repair facility provides
guaranteed repair service to correct those defi-
ciencies noted by the diagnostic clinic, as well as

repair services for those who come in directly, without a prior evaluation by the clinic. The clinic and repair center would operate under a unified management. Finally, the diagnostic and repair center would be complemented by a gasoline service station so that the complete plant could offer a full range of automotive services.

Such a center would provide high-quality employment for Harlem residents in the automotive service industry. The inventory of occupations--including diagnostic technicians, master mechanics, servicewriters, shop foremen, parts department managers, and service managers--is structured to offer a career-ladder approach to training (see Figure 8).

An auto mechanics training school would be located on the same site as the automotive diagnostic and repair center and would constitute a major component. The school would provide classroom as well as practical and on-the-job training in every aspect of automotive service so that trainees can progress from low-skilled gasoline station attendants to highly skilled auto mechanics and thence to the management level. The graduates of this program would be able to fill the need for qualified auto mechanics, a skill which is in short supply in the New York metropolitan area and elsewhere in the country, as noted earlier.

The center and school form only a part of what is possible and desirable in the automotive service field. A fully developed multifaceted service center might include a new car dealership with new and used car sales, financing and insurance, an auto driving school, renting and leasing, sale of parts and supplies, body repair and painting, washing and polishing, parking and storage, as well as wrecking and scrapping. These enterprises could be added to the center, resulting in economies of scale based on horizontal integration. The larger economic power represented by a fully developed automotive service center would permit the spawning of departments and/or affiliated businesses. An organizational plan for such an augmented multifaceted

FIGURE 8

Organization and Manpower Needs of the Automotive Center[a]

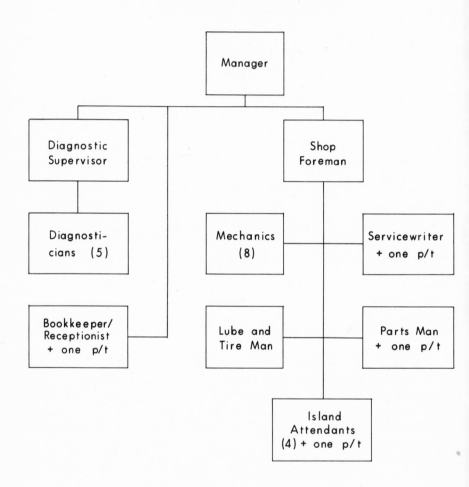

[a]Total employees: 24 plus 4 part-time.

automotive service center is shown in Figure 9.
Some activities are recommended for immediate implementation as representing a realistic first
stage of development. The other modules can be
added later in steps.

There would be a number of cooperative services
tied in with the center. These would include a
credit union, consumer cooperative, and a consumer
advisory service. As a means of encouraging community response, the center might offer the use of
its plant, tools, and technical assistance in a do-
it-yourself program. The pricing of tool rental
and the use of facilities should reflect a break-
even price and the activities would take place during low-volume hours.

The center would be located in that part of
Harlem which has access to major highways and public transportation. A location near the Triborough
Bridge would permit customers to drive in from
Queens and the Bronx, as well as from upper Manhattan via the Harlem River Drive, from lower Manhattan via the East Side Drive, and from the West Side
via 125th Street. For those who wish to leave their
cars for repair while they go to work, subways and
buses are nearby. Since there is a large volume of
automobile traffic in the area, drivers would undoubtedly become familiar with the services offered,
thereby reducing the need for advertising.

The following assumptions were used in the cost
analysis of the automotive service project.

On the diagnostic clinic:

Hours: 7:00 A.M. to 9:00 P.M. plus one shift on
Saturday. Total, 78 hours per week.

Capacity: 3 cars per hour, 42 per day, 1,050
per month.

Assumed capacity utilization in first year: 50
per cent, or roughly 500 cars per month.

FIGURE 9

Organization Plan for Augmented Automotive Center

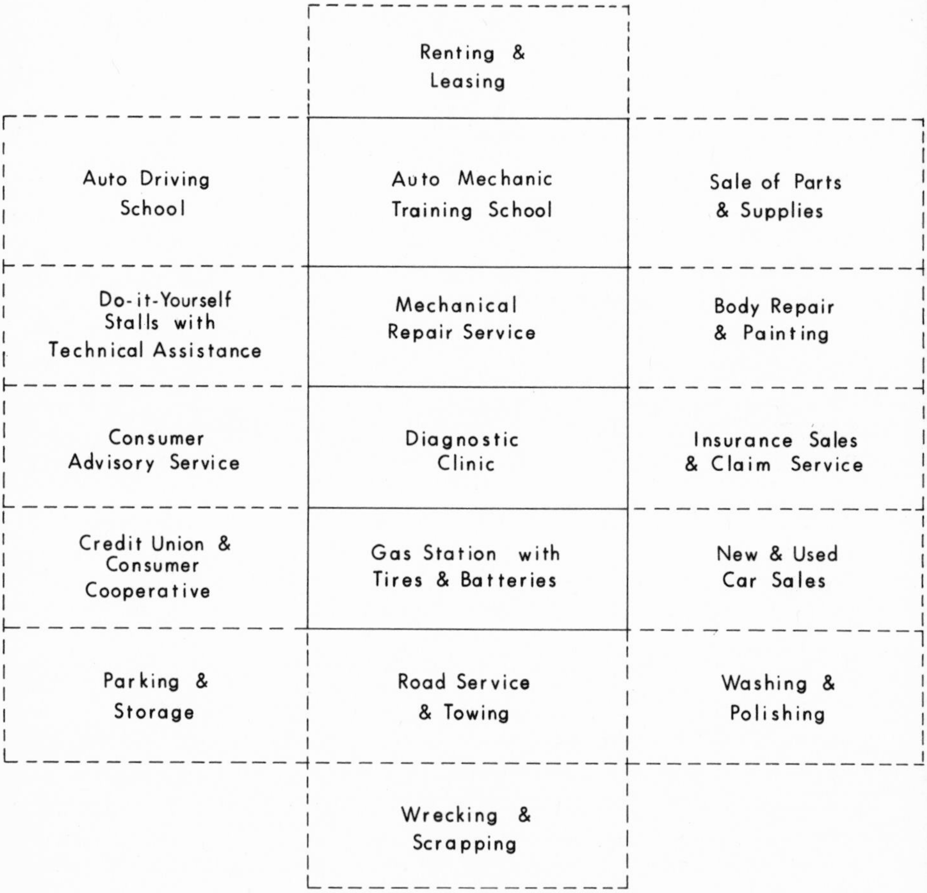

```
              ┌ ─ ─ ─ ─ ─ ─ ─ ─ ─ ─ ─ ─ ┐
              ¦        Renting &         ¦
              ¦        Leasing           ¦
┌ ─ ─ ─ ─ ─ ─ ┼──────────────────────────┼ ─ ─ ─ ─ ─ ─ ┐
¦             │                          │             ¦
¦ Auto Driving│    Auto Mechanic         │  Sale of Parts ¦
¦   School    │    Training School       │   & Supplies  ¦
¦             │                          │             ¦
├ ─ ─ ─ ─ ─ ─ ┼──────────────────────────┼ ─ ─ ─ ─ ─ ─ ┤
¦ Do-it-Yourself                         │             ¦
¦ Stalls with │   Mechanical             │  Body Repair ¦
¦ Technical Assistance  Repair Service   │  & Painting  ¦
├ ─ ─ ─ ─ ─ ─ ┼──────────────────────────┼ ─ ─ ─ ─ ─ ─ ┤
¦  Consumer   │   Diagnostic             │ Insurance Sales ¦
¦ Advisory Service  Clinic               │ & Claim Service ¦
├ ─ ─ ─ ─ ─ ─ ┼──────────────────────────┼ ─ ─ ─ ─ ─ ─ ┤
¦ Credit Union &                         │             ¦
¦  Consumer   │ Gas Station with         │  New & Used  ¦
¦ Cooperative │ Tires & Batteries        │  Car Sales   ¦
├ ─ ─ ─ ─ ─ ─ ┼ ─ ─ ─ ─ ─ ─ ─ ─ ─ ─ ─ ─ ┼ ─ ─ ─ ─ ─ ─ ┤
¦  Parking &  ¦  Road Service            ¦  Washing &   ¦
¦  Storage    ¦  & Towing                ¦  Polishing   ¦
└ ─ ─ ─ ─ ─ ─ ┼ ─ ─ ─ ─ ─ ─ ─ ─ ─ ─ ─ ─ ┼ ─ ─ ─ ─ ─ ─ ┘
              ¦   Wrecking &             ¦
              ¦   Scrapping              ¦
              └ ─ ─ ─ ─ ─ ─ ─ ─ ─ ─ ─ ─ ┘
```

LEGEND

Solid lines: activities recommend for immediate implementation.
Broken lines: activities to be added.

Charge: $12.95 per diagnosis not rebated for repairs.

Two-shift diagnostic bay operation.

On the repair facility:

Conversion ratio (number of diagnosed cars repaired: 43 per cent, or 215 cars per month.

Average diagnosed car repair bill: $80.00.

Direct business customers: 400 per month.

Average direct business car repair bill: $28.00.

Eight service bays, including one for quick service.

One-shift mechanic operation: 8:00 A.M. to 5:30 P.M.

Parts sales average, 120 per cent of labor cost on repair bill.

On the gasoline service station:

Sales at 60,000 gallons monthly; regular at 28,000 gallons, premium at 32,000 gallons.

Gasoline prices: regular $0.349, premium $0.389.

Gross profit per gallon: regular $0.061, premium $0.064. Oil company assumed to offer $0.0175 per gallon reduction in wholesale price based on volume, to return $0.01 per gallon of this to the management and to make available the remainder of $0.075 per gallon for investment in station development (five years of given volume--about $27,000 for station renovation and improvement).

The capital which will probably be required for fixed investment in land, buildings, and equipment and the projected operating capital costs are shown in Table 21.

TABLE 21

Projected Capital Needs for
Automotive Service Center

Fixed investment
(land, buildings, equipment)

Demolition	$ 3,000	
Building construction - center	275,000	
Outside construction - station	15,000	
Diagnostic and repair equipment	45,000	
Total		$338,000

Projected operating
capital costs

Working capital (1 month costs)	$ 50,000	
Inventory	15,000	
Total		$ 65,000
Total fixed and operating capital required		$403,000

Total projected sales of the automotive diagnostic and repair center should amount to roughly
$33,000 per month. This assumes that the price of
a diagnosis will hold at $12.95 per car, and that
some 40 per cent of the diagnosed cars will have
their repairs done at the center. These assumptions
appear reasonable based on one major oil company's
successful experience in raising the price from
$9.95 to $14.95 and typical in-shop repair ratios
of 40-45 per cent. Specific assumptions were also
made regarding the average repair ticket on cars.

These estimates were based on averages observed at
the diagnostic centers run by the Mobil Oil Company.

Operating expenses (principally labor) will
total approximately $28,000, and projected opera-
ting profits before taxes will exceed $4,000. The
estimate for real estate expenses are subject to
some variation, in that a firm price for the property to be used by the center had not been determined. This will depend in large part on the out-
come of the negotiations between HCC and the
property-owners. The figure for depreciation is
an estimate based upon the likely costs of the
diagnostic equipment, the repair bay, tools, and
other items.

Total sales in the gasoline service station
should amount to roughly $25,000 per month. This
assumes sales of 60,000 gallons of gasoline per
month, together with oil, tires, and batteries.
The gasoline volume assumption is critical, but,
according to an independent evaluation, it is a
realistic volume goal. This projection is based
on the sale of gasoline for 4 cents less than the
going rate without the use of trading stamps.

The cost of goods included in these sales
should come to approximately $20,000. Operating
expenses, mainly labor, total nearly $4,900, and
include a figure for lease cost and taxes of $2,600.
Profits before taxes should exceed $4,000, a figure
which, while relatively modest, will nonetheless
enable the station to help cover some portion of
the operation's overhead, such as land and other
expenses.

On this basis, total profitability before
taxes for the center and the station taken together
should approximate $5,000 per month. Assuming a
total investment of $340,000, this comes to a 16
per cent rate of return before tax with a payout
period of 6-2/3 years, or an 11 per cent rate of
return after tax with a payout period of 9 years.
This assumes that the entire $5,000 per month would

be subject to tax. However, it is likely that a
good portion of these earnings would be plowed back
into business expansion. Therefore, the before-
tax rate would be a better indicator of the strength
of the business than the after-tax rate.

It should be recalled that these projections--
and particularly those associated with rates of
profit--refer only to the three modules which constitute the first stage of the center's development.
As the other community-service modules depicted in
Figure 9 are incorporated gradually into the over-
all design, there will inevitably occur a substitu-
tion of external community benefits for commercial
profits. This is precisely what recommends the
project as a desirable candidate for inclusion in
a ghetto development program.

Finally, it may be noted that there exist
still other linked industrial activities which
might eventually be spun off from a reasonably mature center. For example: a modern tire-recapping
facility employing some 15 men could supply an annual volume of recapped auto and truck tires to
local and institutional customers (especially the
truck fleets of various city agencies) sufficient
to return an annual estimated profit of about
$15,000. Moreover, such an activity is potentially
capable of saving Harlem consumers some $42,000 an-
nually in tire expenses.

The Auto Mechanics Training School

The shortage of qualified auto mechanics has
been thoroughly documented by educational, governmental, industrial, and labor sources; public and
private schools have attempted to fill the need,
but without notable success. The Board of Education in New York City has automotive training programs for out-of-school youths and adults, but for
one reason or another, these programs have not met
the need. For example, the city's evening trade
schools are designed for those already employed in
the industry who wish to improve their job skills;

unemployed youth and adults are not eligible. The
Board of Education's manpower development and training program (which cooperates with the N.Y. State
Employment Service and the federal manpower development and training program, or MDTA) could meet the
needs if it offered training in auto mechanics at
locations easily accessible to Harlem residents
with on-the-job training--and if more cordial rela-
tions existed between the Board of Education and
the Harlem community. Unfortunately, this is not
the case.

Private, profit-making trade schools (which
also cooperate with the N.Y. State Employment Service and the MDTA) do offer fairly accessible locations for skill training in auto mechanics. However they are deficient in on-the-job training and
basic education. In addition, and perhaps as important a factor, is the identification problem
that is likely to arise between the black student
and the white, middle-class instructors who make
up a large part of the faculty of such schools.
Industry schools train dealer employees who have
received basic auto mechanic training elsewhere.
Here a student is highly motivated because poor
school performance can result in the loss of his
job. The teacher is also highly motivated because
he can easily be fired for poor performance since
he does not have the tenure protection of a Board
of Education teacher. Also, the curriculum is more
up-to-date because of the need to service late-
model cars. These schools are excellent for those
who have basic automotive training and who can be
hired by a dealer in the first place, but unfortunately in Harlem there is a scarcity of both
prior training and local dealerships.

The training of unemployed and subemployed
Harlem workers for scarce and relatively well-
paying skills which can be easily transferred to
industrial activities apart from automotive service is one of the most important community benefits that can be generated by the Harlem project.
Yet, as noted above, existing training institutions

in New York City are either unwilling to accept
minorities, or are inherently incapable of providing those whom they <u>have</u> enrolled with either adequate or relevant vocational preparation.

In view of the community benefits stemming from
a training program which seeks to upgrade the skills
of marginally employed and unemployed workers and
the lack of commercial profitability generally associated with such a program, it is necessary to by-
pass the profit motive by substituting, in its
stead, a community-oriented organization--HCC.

A Harlem auto mechanics training school located on the premises of the auto diagnostic service center would offer a program of skill training
in auto mechanics combined with basic education in
an on-the-job setting. It would combine the major
features of both the sheltered workshop and on-the-
job types of training. The program is strictly for
skills delivery and is not a work-readiness training program. The course would comprise 750 hours
of instruction spread over approximately 20 weeks
and would cover all of the technical areas recommended by the Bureau of Apprenticeship Training.
The communications and mathematics areas would be
heavily work-related and would have an immediate
application to the student's training. The available physical plant could handle approximately 75
students at any one time. This number would be
divided into classes of no more than 15 trainees
and classes could be held on a recycling basis.

The methods used for the automotive part of
the training would be lecture, discussion and demonstration, controlled laboratory experiences, and
selected live-auto repair. Half of the selected
live-auto repair instruction would be given in the
school shop and half in the HCC repair shop. In
addition to automotive instruction, the curriculum
would contain related science topics, communications skills, and mathematics. The school would
also provide a counselor for guidance and similar
services.

The school would be a private, nonprofit, vocational school under community control. It would
operate in cooperation with the N.Y. State Department of Labor's Division of Employment and the Department of Health, Education and Welfare's Office
of Education under the Manpower Development and
Training Act. The State Education Department would
have to pass on the qualifications of the school,
and the State Employment Service on the eligibility
of its students. HEW could provide training sti-
pends under MDTA. The school would charge no tui-
tion, thus meeting the needs of those who are not
eligible for the programs of the N.Y. City Board of
Education or industry-sponsored programs.

Because it is tied in with the HCC repair shop,
the school could also offer a small apprentice
training program which would, in effect, be a greenhouse operation. The limited size of the repair
shop would be the only constraint on the extent of
the apprentice training program.

The curriculum would include four basic courses
of study: the structure of automobile systems; related science topics (e.g., "mechanics and machines,"
"friction"); remedial mathematics; and basic communication skills. The school's physical plant
might be designed by an advocacy planning team such
as the Architects' Renewal Committee in Harlem
(ARCH). It is expected that some of the equipment
would be donated by industry sources, some purchased
outright, and the rest factored by the vendors.

MDTA and N.Y. State Employment Service participation are attendant on securing approval from
the N.Y. State Education Department in Albany.
Such approval would be contingent on the school's
ability to meet several state criteria: qualifications of the director and associated instructional
staff; adequacy of the curriculum and course con-
tent; standards for the physical plant; and financial competence. None of these requirements are
inherently difficult to meet. Approval usually
takes two to six months.

The director must have five years' trade experience plus a high school diploma or equivalency.
The instructors must have two years' trade experience plus high school. Since the quality of instruction is so critical, the instructors' qualifications should exceed the minimum of two years.
State Employment Service approval of the trainees
should present little difficulty, especially when
the service realizes the motivational aspects of
an HCC school which can also provide on-the-job
training. The physical standards of the school
building can be easily met in a design proposal already submitted by ARCH.

The instructional staff would consist of two
full-time auto mechanics teachers and one half-time
basic education teacher. A half-time secretary is
also required. This secretary could be the same
person who works in the diagnostic and repair center. A part-time counselor is required for guidance and counseling services. The tool crib attendant would be the same parts man who works in the
diagnostic and repair center. The supervisor would
also be the manager of the diagnostic and repair
center.

Prospective trainees would be recommended by
HCC to the State Employment Service for inclusion
in the program. Persons whose incomes are at a
poverty level would be given preference since the
training program is primarily aimed at those who
are either unemployed or subemployed.

If each trainee is paid a wage of about $55
per week plus a $2 transportation allowance, then
total annual costs for the project may be estimated
at almost $94,000, or just over $1,200 per trainee
A complete projected cost profile is shown in Table
22.

TABLE 22

Projected Cost Profile for
Auto Mechanics Training School

Student wages		$24,750
Instructional services		37,936
Instructional salaries only	$22,500	
Instructional supplies, including shipping cost	2,863	
Rental of instructional equipment	50	
Local supervision	5,263	
Guidance and counseling salaries	5,760	
Other allowable items	1,500	
Fixed charges		21,119
Rental of nonpublic space	17,500	
Employer share of employee benefits	3,619	
Other fixed charges	--	
Equipment maintenance and repair		1,000
Repair and servicing of equipment	1,000	
Other maintenance and repairs	--	
Equipment purchase		4,684
Initial purchase of instructional equipment	3,000	
Minor equipment, tools, and reference books	1,184	
Minor remodeling of school plant	--	
Other capital expenditures	500	
Other costs not elsewhere classified		4,469
Utilities (including telephone)	684	
Custodial or janitorial salaries	1,875	
Incidental student charges	750	
Trainee transportation	900	
Other miscellaneous costs	260	
Cost of 5 sections of this course (75 students)		$93,958
Estimated cost per trainee	$1,253	
Estimated cost per trainee hour	$1.68	

COOPERATIVE SUPERMARKETS

According to the 1960 census, the residents of Harlem spent 30 per cent of their disposable income for food. This expenditure amounted to a total of some $177 million. Any relative improvements that can be achieved in the area of food distribution can, therefore, operate on a large consumer base and be highly significant. At the same time, any successful venture in food manufacturing will be able to tap a broad market. Efforts to identify promising investment projects in the food sector accordingly should have a very high priority in a ghetto development strategy.

There is now some evidence that food prices in Harlem may be higher and food quality lower than in the rest of Manhattan. A study by David Caplovitz documents this problem for many lines of purchases in East Harlem.[1] Typical anecdotes give accounts of supermarket chains which take their left-over, wilted vegetables from their stores in middle- or upper-income city neighborhoods and truck them to ghetto branches, where they are often sold at higher prices than those offered at the original store.

An August, 1966, New York Post survey indicated that the price of a dozen eggs in Harlem was 20 cents higher than the city-wide average, and the price of butter was 20 cents higher per pound. The same meat sold in Harlem for $1.69 per pound sold elsewhere for only $1.15. The Bureau of Labor Statistics concluded late in 1966, with respect to Harlem, that for equivalent rents, poor families get poorer housing than families with higher incomes and that they also pay more for credit. The problem, in other words, is not restricted to food retailing.[2]

Besides higher prices and poorer quality (or perhaps as a factor contributing to these conditions), Harlem's residents are faced with an insufficient number of food stores. The data shown in Table 23 document this shortage.

TABLE 23

Employment in Food Retailing
New York City (1962) and Harlem (Winter, 1967/68)

	Employees per 1,000 Population	Food Retailing Employees as % of Employees in All Retailing
New York City	14	25
Central Harlem	5	14

Source: U.S. Census of Business 1963 and
Harlem Business Inventory.

        Clearly, the amount of food retailing service
available in Harlem was almost three times lower
than for New York City as a whole. Some of this
difference may be discounted by noting that since
the level of disposable income in Harlem is less,
absolute per capita food purchases would be expected to be lower. This might reduce the number
of employees needed in food retailing. With many
little "Mom and Pop" stores tending to stay open
longer than the average food retail store, the difference in terms of manhours per 1,000 population
is probably less than the observed difference in
terms of employment. Nevertheless, the difference
is just too great to permit a fully satisfactory
explanation by recourse to these observations.
This is confirmed by the second column of Table 23,
which measures employment in food retailing as a
percentage of employment in all retailing. The effects of differentials in disposable income should,
in this case, cut exactly the opposite way since,
according to Engel's law, at lower income levels,
higher percentages of disposable income are spent
on food. Yet the figure for Harlem is almost twice
as low as for the city as a whole.

Not only does Harlem appear to need additional
retail food distribution; it also appears to want
additional food stores. This has been documented
in a recent sociological and economic survey conducted in an area adjacent to Central Harlem. In
this survey, residents of the East Harlem Triangle,
a largely black area, were questioned as to which,
in their opinion, were the most deficient or most
needed retail and service functions in their area.
The question was posed in several different ways in
order to avoid the danger of putting words into the
mouths of the respondents. Yet the results were always the same--people overwhelmingly felt a need
for additional and better food stores within easy
walking distance.[3]

We have therefore identified two strategies
through which HCC could enter the retail food distribution field. The first of these concerns the
development of cooperative supermarkets. This form
of organization is controlled by its membership and
can therefore dedicate itself not only to profit-
making, but also to significant improvements in the
quality of service and a reduction in price levels.
Co-ops can be established in new locations, thereby
adding to the available food retailing network, or
they can be organized to take over existing supermarkets, in which case their benefits come from service and price improvements. In addition, local
control over a co-op system can yield indirect benefits such as management and labor-skill training.

An alternate strategy is the affiliation of independent grocers and small supermarkets by an affiliating institution. The aim here is primarily to
upgrade existing retail food stores, but this can
be expanded to include the establishment of additional food stores, affiliating them from the out-
set. The affiliation strategy has been discussed
in Chapter 4.

We decided to recommend the cooperative strategy for initial implementation. A co-op supermarket
requires capitalization in the $250,000-$300,000

range, whereas an affiliating organization may require capitalization at a figure running into several millions of dollars.

Co-op and affiliated-independent modes are not
necessarily mutually exclusive alternatives. A
ghetto development organization could well sponsor
a network of co-op food stores that are either new
stores or are established by buying out existing
private supermarkets. At the same time, it would
proceed to affiliate the smaller independent food
retailers in the area. By increasing the efficiency
of small stores, it may be possible to increase
their profitability, while at the same time enforc-
ing higher quality and lower prices under threat of
exclusion from the affiliation network. This, of
course, serves to raise disposable incomes of Harlem residents--most of whom belong to low-income
groups.

A co-op strategy can:

1. <u>Confer a substantial equity base</u>. Co-ops
are initiated by selling equity shares to the public. In this way, signing up several thousand families can create a substantial equity base which
makes possible the solicitation of bank loans and
other financing. A co-op supermarket venture in
Harlem, the Harlem River Consumers Cooperative,
Inc., has managed to sell several thousand shares
and has opened a store in the area.

2. <u>Encourage community participation</u>. The
door-to-door effort in selling equity shares can
bring the sponsoring organization to the attention
of the community. This benefit is attained even
if some families do not sign up. We believe that
a ghetto development institution should work out a
strategy for establishing a network of systematic
face-to-face contacts in the community, and the
door-to-door selling of co-op shares creates both
an occasion for doing so and an immediate payoff
that justifies the effort.

The one-man one-vote feature of co-op control
is an excellent device for giving community members
a sense of participation in decisions affecting
their lives, and can serve as the entering wedge in
a process of systematically increasing the public
consciousness of the large passive majority in the
community.

3. Demonstrate the legitimacy of the local
organization. The co-op, owned by its members, is
an instrument of direct democracy in the local community. Given the fact that a favorite tactic of
those suspicious of ghetto self-improvement efforts
is to question the legitimacy of a local group push-
ing for significant changes, co-op ventures with a
broad popular base help to refute such criticism.

4. Confer direct economic benefits. Co-ops
can be used to improve quality and reduce prices.
They either add to the food retailing network or
bring large private supermarkets under community
control. They have management and labor training
functions. They create an economic surplus that
can be either distributed as a membership rebate
or, alternatively, can be plowed back into community development.

5. Obtain support from existing trade asso-
ciations. One of the important potential economies
for retail consumer co-ops in New York City is the
existence of at least one major wholesale food
co-op network. It is owned by member retail food
co-ops, each of whom appoints one member to a board
of directors. The wholesale co-op has a warehouse
which supplies the retail stores and a house brand
under which it makes available some 200 items of
merchandise. It also assists member retail co-ops
with management and labor training and provides
capital assistance.

6. Permit backward integration. A single
retail co-op store does not furnish much of a basis
for backward integration into food manufacturing.
The required minimum economical scale of production

for most items sold in supermarkets is well above
the sales made by even a large single store. The
existence of the wholesale co-op, however, creates
an entirely new perspective for backward integration. A member store can exert some influence, as
the sponsor of a given food manufacturing operation,
to have this product accepted for marketing under
the house brand not only on its own shelves but
also on the shelves of all associated retail co-op
stores. If several retail co-ops are established
by a single community development institution, increased representation on the board of the wholesale co-ops will improve chances for the acceptance
of sponsored manufacturing operations as suppliers
for co-op house brands.

A service module which could easily be integrated with food co-ops in ghetto areas--not for
the sake of commercial profitability but in order
to supply a desperately needed community service--
is an ethical pharmacy. Independent pharmacies can
rarely afford to counsel their clients on the use
of generic rather than brand-name drugs, since to
do so would tend to reduce their profits. Neither
can they afford to offer all-night service, as the
volume of business transacted during these hours
will not cover the expense of a registered pharmacist who, under state law, must be present when
drugs are being dispensed.

Adding a prescription section to a co-op supermarket could be done with a minimal sacrifice in
competing floor space use. The cosmetics, drugs,
toiletry, and household goods sections could be
slightly expanded to support drugstore operations.
In all, the marginal costs of adding pharmacy operations are considerably less than the costs of
establishing a separate drugstore. The principal
problem is that of designing the physical plant so
that the pharmacist has access to the drugstore
items and is provided with a measure of personal
security. A separate street entrance with a customer area sealed off from the rest of the store, except for a service counter protected by bullet-proof

glass, probably could satisfy these requirements. The costs of such an arrangement will be offset by the community service rendered.

For the first HCC cooperative supermarket, a site at upper Eighth Avenue seemed to offer the best location available at the time of the study. This facility, which HCC was urged to purchase, is the largest supermarket in Harlem with 15,000 square feet of selling space and 15,000 square feet for the storage of stock. Located within several blocks of 125th Street, it is in the heart of the community. There are more than 7,000 families for whom this site is the nearest market, and they will, according to estimates provided by the Community Council of Greater New York, spend $8,686,000 a year on food. Assuming that only 25 per cent of this trade is given to the proposed cooperative supermarket, the total annual sales volume would be some $2,170,000. With co-op management concerned with service and not profit maximization, it should be possible to draw customers from well beyond this primary market area.

Projected capital and operating budgets are as shown in Tables 24 and 25.

TABLE 24

Proposed Capital Budget for Co-op Supermarket

Needed		
Working capital	$ 30,000	
Inventories	75,000	
Fixtures and equipment	175,000	
Prepaid items	10,000	
Total		$290,000
Sources		
Trade creditors (suppliers)	50,000	
Financing of equipment		
(2/3 of cost)	117,000	
Membership shares (at $10 each)	50,000	
Loans, bonds, etc. (capital		
to be raised)	73,000	
Total		290,000

TABLE 25

Proposed Yearly Operating Budget for Co-op Supermarket

Sales

Grocery	$1,300,000	65	%
Meat	500,000	25	%
Produce	200,000	10	%
Total sales	$2,000,000	100	%

Gross margin

Grocery	$ 214,500	16.5	%
Meat	125,000	25.0	%
Produce	54,000	27.0	%
Total gross margins	$ 393,500	19.67	%

Operating expenses

Payroll & payroll expense	$ 200,000	10.0	%
Occupancy expenses (rent & utilities)	60,000	3.0	%
Repairs & maintenance	2,000	.1	%
Wrapping supplies	20,000	1.0	%
Advertising	20,000	1.0	%
Cleaning, rubbish removal, etc.	2,000	.1	%
Office expenses	40,000	2.0	%
Total operating expenses	$ 344,000	17.2	%
Net savings (earnings)	$ 49,500	2.47	%

A FOOD-CANNING FACILITY

The development of a network of cooperative and/or affiliated retail stores and supermarkets can lead to the acquisition of an increasing volume of local shelf space. The more shelf space controlled, the greater the feasibility of backward integration into the manufacturing of products (not necessarily or exclusively foods) to stock those shelves.

In considering candidate projects of this type it is crucial that the local or regional distribution network be able to produce a sales volume that represents a substantial portion (if not all) of the capacity of the manufacturing plant. Of course, it may not be necessary to rely on this protective device; contracts with government or institutional buyers may be an acceptable complement. The problem with this arrangement, however, is that both the ghetto manufacturer and his community sponsor may find themselves at the mercy of these outside organizations. Such power could conceivably be turned against the community and used as a lever to force acquiescence on apparently unrelated issues. The chance of this would be minimized if the outlet to the market were secured by adequate control of the distribution system. This is one of the key reasons why those manufacturing projects that are integrated to a distribution system serving community demands are preferable to projects which feed into uncontrollable outside activities, such as military procurement.*

Given the above extremes of controlled shelf space versus unstable "export" type subcontracts, one can readily perceive an intermediate possibility, namely some degree of control over a distribution system outside the ghetto. Once several co-op

---

*This is not an argument against accepting such subcontracts per se. Rather, we believe it to be a matter of common business sense to restrict sales to these markets to some fraction--perhaps 20-25 per cent--of the total.

food stores have been successfully set up in ghetto
areas, it is reasonable to consider setting up
others in mixed or middle-class areas as well, provided that financing can be made available. Simi-
larly, given a well-working affiliation system
within the ghetto, outside affiliates may be permitted to join on some limited basis. These devices stabilize "exports" of manufactured goods outside the ghetto. This has a parallel in international business practice; the foreign manufacturers
who have been most successful in penetrating the
U.S. market are the ones who established, or had
access to, distribution networks reaching the ultimate customer, for example, Volkswagen automobiles with their unique network of exclusive sales
and service representatives, or Japanese industrial-
ists with their access to hundreds of independent
Japanese retail stores.

Finally, to the extent that ghetto residents
can be persuaded to purchase local products, the
typically high advertising costs of established competitive products may provide a buffer for local
activities conducted at less than fully satisfactory scales or under other less-than-ideal conditions.

A technical consultant to the U.S. Agency for
International Development (AID) has suggested that
"an urban population of between 100,000 and 200,000
should be enough to support the output of a canning
plant producing 400,000 cans per year."[4] The more
than 200 food and grocery retailers located inside
Central Harlem--together with others operating in
the neighboring areas of East Harlem, Bedford-
Stuyvesant, Brownsville, and the Central Ward of
Newark--provide a substantial market for the output of a black canning factory.

One idea presents itself which, if practical,
can obviate the necessity for having to compete
with established companies in the supply markets.
There are at present many black farm cooperatives
located in the South and in various Northern areas.

These groups would benefit from the development of
what could be, for them, a regular customer. Subsequently, other such canneries might be established around the country to service these suppliers. The network of linkages suggested here could,
it would seem, be publicized quite dramatically in
searching for equity capital. Location of a canning
facility in New York City which purchases the produce of a Mississippi farm cooperative is not at
all implausible. As noted in an AID technical report, the value of most vegetables and fruits is
rather low, relative to the price of the can. This
tells the regional economic planner that unit transportation freight charges for the uncanned food-
stuffs are likely to be relatively low and that
the facility ought probably to be located close to
the source of the cans and, above all, close to the
ultimate market--the grocers' shelves. We have already discussed the availability of shelf space.
As to the local availability of can manufacturers,
the classified New York City Telephone Directory
lists over 60 firms operating in the metropolitan
area.

Having indicated that local location of a canning facility is probably desirable, we must now
investigate its spatial requirements. A canning
facility may require as much as 2-5 acres of land
for its operation. Typically, this is allocated
to a one-floor plant (see Figure 10), a warehouse
for finished goods, storage space, outdoor parking,
and land for future expansion. For a center city
location, the parking area can be eliminated. Depending on produce origin and output destination,
rail lines might be partially substitutable for
trucks, thus reducing the necessary land area still
further. Finally, imaginative technological experiments might yield new multistory, land-saving
design alternatives.[5]

Nevertheless, the fact remains that a canning
facility is likely to require a substantial amount
of land, with access to rail and/or trucking routes.
Should a physical development program (such as

FIGURE 10

Suggested Layout, Food Canning Plant

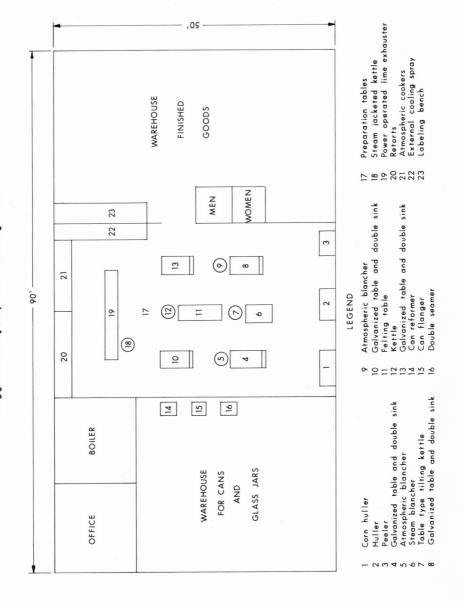

LEGEND

1 Corn huller
2 Huller
3 Peeler
4 Galvanized table and double sink
5 Atmospheric blancher
6 Steam blancher
7 Table type tilting kettle
8 Galvanized table and double sink
9 Atmospheric blancher
10 Galvanized table and double sink
11 Felting table
12 Kettle
13 Galvanized table and double sink
14 Can reformer
15 Can flanger
16 Double seamer
17 Preparation tables
18 Steam jacketed kettle
19 Power operated lime exhauster
20 Retorts
21 Atmospheric cookers
22 External cooling spray
23 Labeling bench

153

Model Cities) create the necessary space within or adjacent to Central Harlem, then location in the immediate area becomes feasible. If not, it might become necessary to look elsewhere--the Brooklyn Navy Yard Industrial Park, for example.

These general considerations suggest the desirability of further research into an HCC-sponsored canning facility. According to a Tronchemics Research Inc. consulting report to the U.N. Center for Industrial Development (Document 64-03105), and based on New York area statistics for 1963, for 20 fruits and vegetables locally canned, the average number of cans per case was 24, and the mean wholesale price per case was $8.00. A fully operative 800,000 cans per year capacity facility might, therefore, earn as much as $264,000 a year. Capital investment would be between $56,000 and $89,000. AID Industry Fact Sheets permit the estimation of annual operating costs for a firm of this size; these are about $252,000, distributed as shown in Table 26.

We estimate that an 800,000 cans per year capacity plant could return a $12,000 annual profit and create perhaps 50 jobs--of which a quarter would be skilled, semi-skilled, or clerical (thus providing the opportunity for an internal training ladder, since the plant could offer on-the-job training to as many as 36 unskilled workers per program)--at an average capital-labor ratio of from $1,100 to $1,800. These are extremely favorable (i.e., labor-intensive) capital-to-job ratios.

UN and AID documents suggest at least four alternative scales of operation, summarized in Table 27. The capital requirements enumerated in the table will cover the costs of equipment and installation, building construction, water supply, and so forth. The plant scale which we recommended is shown as Plant B in Table 27; it constitutes a two-shift variant of Plant A. The manpower requirements associated with this design are listed in Table 28, together with the technical processes to be performed.

TABLE 26

Estimated Annual Operating Cost for Canning Plant
(800,000 cans/year capacity; 2 shifts @ 400,000)[a]

Direct materials		
Vegetables	$ 25,000	
Cans, cartons, labels	25,000	
		$ 50,000
Labor		
5 skilled workers @ $3.00/hr	$ 30,000	
7 semi-skilled workers @ $2.00/hr	28,000	
36 unskilled workers @ $1.50/hr	108,000	
1 manager	12,000	
1 clerical @ $2.50/hr	15,000	
		$193,000
Overhead		
Supplies	$ 1,000	
Power, fuel, water	1,500	
		$ 2,500
Administrative and sales costs		
Interest, insurance, legal, audit	$ 3,000	
Sales commissions, freight out, travel	5,000	
		$ 8,000
Depreciation @ 6% (maximum)		$ 9,000
		$262,000

[a]For capital cost of canning plant of this
capacity, see Table 29, Plant B.

Source: Estimation from U.S. Agency for International Development, Industry Fact Sheets.

TABLE 27

Estimated Capital Costs and Alternative Capacity Scales for Canning Plant[a]

	Capacity #2 Cans/Hr.	Capital Equipment	Total Capital Cost	Manpower Req'd.	Capital/ Labor Ratios	Estimated Max. Storage and Plant Area
Plant A	100-200	$ 17,050	$ 56,300- 88,850	28	$ 2,011- 3,173	5,550 sq. ft.
Plant B	100-200 (2 shifts)	$ 17,050	$ 56,300- 88,850	50	$ 1,126- 1,777	5,550 sq. ft.
Plant C	1,000	$ 59,400	$176,500- 291,300	42	$ 4,202- 6,936	19,700 sq. ft.
Plant D	10,000	$223,500	$601,600- 852,900	66	$ 9,116- 13,000	41,100 sq. ft.

[a]Capital costs for other scales may be estimated by the following formula:

$$I_2 = I_1 \left(\frac{C_2}{C_1}\right)^x$$

where C_1 = capacity of a plant whose capital cost is known

C_2 = intended capacity of the desired plant

I_1 = capital cost of known plant

I_2 = unknown capital cost of desired plant

x = 0.75 for capacities between 100 and 1,000 cans/hr.

x = 0.50 for capacities greater than 1,000 cans/hr.

TABLE 28

Labor Needs for Canning Plant

Process Step	Machine	Manpower Needs per Shift
Inspection, grading, receiving, etc.	(a)	4
Peeling	FMC-Dixie lye peeler	2
Washing	(a)	2
Blanching & cooling	FMC-Dixie steam jacketed kettle	3
Filling & brine making	(a)	3
Exhausting	FMC-Dixie line exhauster	1
Sealing	FMC-Dixie electric sealer	1
Retorting	FMC-Dixie No. 3 retorts	2
Labeling	(a)	2
Casing & storing	(a)	2
Can reforming	(b)	3
Total essential manpower for recommended equipment		25
Other: Foreman-mechanic		1
Clerical office worker		1
Manager		1
Total essential manpower		28

[a] Minor equipment and hand tools (tables, knives, etc.).

[b] Includes FMC flange reformer, die flanger, roll former, and closing machine.

AN ELECTRONIC DATA-PROCESSING CENTER
FOR PUBLIC HOSPITALS

A project HCC can establish which will offer
career-ladder training leading all the way to the
sophisticated and highly priced skills of computer
programming and systems analysis is an electronic
data-processing service center. This project would
also provide its sponsor, HCC, with a high-powered
tool for undertaking primary data-gathering surveys,
programming tasks, and management assistance functions.

However, a commercial computer center would,
by itself, not be a particularly attractive proposition, since the general run of business in this
line is characterized by intense competition that
leaves, at best, only slim margins of benefit, and
poses the risk of a losing operation unless extremely efficiently run from the start--an unlikely even-
tuality for any fresh undertaking.

The idea could be placed on a completely different footing if the computer center were established to deliver a unique or specialty service
which would permit the negotiation of a firm contract with a client and would assure definite benefits from the start. The computerization of certain hospital management functions for the New York
City hospital system would offer such a unique service.

It is well-known that public hospitals are
poorly managed. With this in mind, U.S. Research
and Development Corporation and Mathematica, Inc.
expressed interest in researching hospital management and computerization techniques.

These firms met with us to discuss possible
approaches to the hospital computerization and management problem. One approach was to develop a
computer service package for an HCC-affiliated
electronic data-processing center in Harlem, and
to offer it on a contract basis to the city. This
system would then be used as an entry into the

much more difficult hospital management area. The
other strategy was to pose a more ambitious management approach.

After the initial sessions, however, the group
did not hold together to decide between these strategies. Mathematica decided to submit a proposal to
the city on its own, and U.S. Research and Development Corporation's interest in an early joint effort
lapsed. Their initial proposals do, nevertheless,
merit further review. Thus, the purpose of this
section is to evaluate differing approaches to a
health-services-oriented electronic data-processing
system.

One approach would concentrate on the conditions under which an electronic data center could
serve a group of Harlem hospitals (approximately
4,000 beds) on a break-even basis. The other proposal assumed that the city, instead of purchasing
the service, would manage its own computer operation, based on a computer installation of its own,
or on computer hours rented from commercial or university computer centers. It would service 14 municipal hospitals with a total of 13,500 beds.

The services to be offered under the first
study would cover the following functions: bill-
ing, accounts receivable, accounts payable, payroll,
personnel, inventory and purchasing, insurance pro-
ration (including Medicare), equipment maintenance
scheduling, and pharmacy system. There were two
available computer systems that could handle the
majority of desired applications: The IBM Shared
Hospital Accounting System and the Honeywell Hospital Computer Sharing System. The IBM system works
with a punched card terminal input, while the Honeywell system uses typewriters, paper tape, and
Frieden add-punches. In both cases, terminals in
the hospitals feed through leased telephone lines
into the proposed HCC computer center.

The second proposal offered the following services: patient admission, patient discharge, reser-
vations, report requests, and updating of basic

TABLE 29

Alternative Computer Systems for Hospital Management

(1) Author, System, Functions	(2) Notes	(3) Terminals	(4) Capacity	(5) Hospitals Served	(6) Total Beds
1. Reed IBM 360/30 house- keeping functions	manual back-up existing programs	keypunch	10 hosp. 1,500 beds	Harlem Sydenham Fr. Delafield	1,230
2. Reed IBM 360/30 house- keeping functions	manual back-up existing programs	keypunch	15 hosp. 4,000 beds	Harlem Sydenham Fr. Delafield Metropolitan Harlem Eye & Ear	3,880
3. Reed Honeywell 200/1800 house- keeping functions	machine back-up existing programs	typewriter, paper tape, Frieden add-punch	8 hosp. 3,700 beds reserve capac in ctrl com- puter with more eq't	Harlem Sydenham Fr. Delafield Metropolitan	3,880
4. Mathe- matica IBM 360/50 patients' status & records	internal new programs req'd.	typewriter	initially 12-14 hrs slack per day	All 14 municipal hospitals	13,500

(7)	(8)	(9)	(10)	(11)	(12)	(13)	(14)
						$/bed-month	
						both	housekeeping
Cost Item	No.	@	$/yr	$/mo	as shown	functions	only
hardware				11,800			
data set				300			
telephone lines				25			
hosp. terminals	3	359		1,100			
			159	13,225			
staff			142				
rent, etc.			49				
			350	29,200	23.7	-	23.7
hardware				16,800			
data set				300			
telephone lines				25			
hosp. terminals	5	400		2,000			
			229	19,125			
staff			142				
rent, etc.			49				
			420	35,000	9.1	-	9.1
hardware				19,500			
terminals &)	5	275		1,380			
communications)			251	20,880			
staff			142				
rent, etc.			49				
			442	36,800	9.5	-	9.5
hardware			452				
oper. staff			105				
util., space			24				
supplies, tel.,							
furn.			24				
			605				
communications:			89				
terminals	40	100	(48)				
data sets	80	25	(24)				
10-mile leased							
phone lines	40	35	(17)				
system staff			49				
			743	61,900	4.6	5.8	5.3

(continued)

TABLE 29 (continued)

(1) Author, System, Functions	(2) Notes	(3) Terminals	(4) Capacity	(5) Hospitals Served	(6) Total Beds
5. Mathe- matica IBM 360/50 patients' status & records	commercial service org. new programs req'd	typewriter		All 14 municipal hospitals	13,500
6. Mathe- matica IBM 360/50 patients' status & records	university computing center new programs req'd	typewriter		All 14 municipal hospitals	13,500
7. Vietorisz IBM 360/50 both kinds of functions	university computing center existing and new programs	typewriter & keypunch		Harlem Hosp.	750
8. Vietorisz IBM 360/50 both kinds of functions	university computing center existing and new programs	typewriter & keypunch		Harlem Sydenham Fr. Delafield	1,230

162

(7)	(8)	(9)	(10)	(11)	(12)	(13)	(14)
						$/bed-month	
Cost Item	No.	@	$/yr	$/mo	as shown	both functions	housekeeping only
computer rental,							
hrs	700	500/hr	350				
dedicated							
peripheral							
storage			72				
			422				
communications			89				
system staff			49				
			560	46,600	3.5	6.9	4.4
computer rental,							
hrs	700	250/hr	175				
dedicated							
peripheral							
eq't			101				
			276				
communications			89				
system staff			49				
			414	34,500	2.6	4.9	3.5
computer rental,							
hrs	80	250/hr	20				
dedicated							
peripheral							
eq't			20				
terminals	3	100/mo	4				
terminals	3	400/mo	16				
data sets	6	25/mo	2				
10-mi leased							
phone lines	3	35/mo	1				
			63				
system staff			49				
			112	9,350	12.5	12.5	10.9
computer rental,							
hrs	128	250/hr	32				
dedicated							
peripheral							
eq't			25				
terminals	5	100/mo	6				
terminals	5	400/mo	24				
data sets	10	25/mo	3				
10-mi leased							
phone lines	5	35/mo	2				
			92				
system staff			49				
			141	11,800	9.6	9.6	8.1

system statistics. The expansion of the system
could add the following functions: monitoring of
patient records, retrieval of medical records,
scheduling outpatient clinics, and extension of the
system to include, in addition to municipal hospitals, the voluntary hospitals in the city. While
the existing IBM and Honeywell systems cover ordinary housekeeping and administrative functions in
hospitals that are very similar to analogous functions in commercial enterprises, this proposal is
directed at the computerization of the distinctive
hospital functions related to patients' status and
records. Table 29 presents a summary of hospital
computer system alternatives. After a careful analysis of the merits of both systems, we recommended
that HCC consider offering to the city a service
which would consist of the standard housekeeping
functions, based on the existing IBM system, but
covering all 14 municipal hospitals. In Table 29,
the entries of systems 4 to 6 in column 14 give the
unit costs of such systems. Given the $10 per bed-
month estimate for acceptable price, this would generate acceptable profits. This system could be
made operational within a short time; it is limited
only by time lags for equipment delivery and set up.

An alternative recommendation is shown under
systems 7 and 8. These are small demonstration systems which can apply either to Harlem Hospital
alone (system 7) or to the three municipal hospitals (Harlem, Sydenham, Francis Delafield) in the
Harlem area (system 8).

While these systems are not meant as commercial propositions, they do come close to meeting
commercial standards.

It is recommended that system 8 be formally
proposed as a demonstration project covering the
three Harlem area municipal hospitals. This proposal should be submitted to the U.S. Department of
Health, Education and Welfare (HEW) by HCC and the
Health Services Administration of the City of New
York. If the city will finance part of the required

$141,000, HEW can be requested to finance the proj-
ect as the central component in a major computerized
public health service in Harlem.

A proposal to HEW and the installation of a
demonstration system in Harlem area hospitals would
be the best way for an HCC-sponsored computer service operation to develop a working relationship
with the Health Services Administration of the City
of New York. This demonstration project would
achieve at least two objectives: It would allow
the establishment of a functioning HCC-sponsored
computer service group, and it would open a door to
subsequent service contracts with the city. A demonstration project would also make it much easier
for the Health Services Administration to take the
initial step in the direction of introducing the
new computerized techniques into its hospitals.

The initial operations of the HCC-sponsored
computer service group could conveniently be based
on rented computer time, preferably at a university
computer center. From this start, it would then be
comparatively easy for the group to make the transi-
tion to the operation of its own computer installation.

A COMMUNITY ANTENNA TELEVISION SYSTEM

Many studies have shown that ghetto residents
not only own television sets, but use them as their
major source of entertainment. This is especially
true among young people.[6]

A major thrust in expanding television facilities is through the use of cable transmission which
requires no Federal Communications Commission (FCC)
approval, takes advantage of the unused portion of
the VHF spectrum, and exhibits low costs and maintenance.[7]

The use of cable for television transmission
has been in existence for almost 20 years. Some

2,000 communities in the United States receive
their television programs via cable transmission
through community antenna systems (CATV). Furthermore, several hundred of these CATV systems do
their own broadcasting over unused channels.

Under a slight modification of CATV it is possible to establish a Harlem television station operating in one or more buildings or even in an entire
neighborhood. The station would not require licens-
ing and would reach those families in the building
or neighborhood wired for the purpose. The station
could operate on any unused channel as often as desired. It would be planned, operated, and pro-
grammed by the community which it would serve.

The opportunities for such a facility are almost limitless. Among other things, it could:

1. Provide a wide variety of cultural and
educational programs which would be produced by and
directed to ghetto residents.

2. Serve as a community stimulator and infor-
mational center for many types of activities.

3. Train hundreds of minority group individuals in the field of television technology, broadcasting, programming, editing, and so forth.

Precise costs are difficult to estimate because they depend upon the kind of equipment desired, which in turn depends on such questions as
color versus black-and-white, live broadcasting
versus videotape or film chains, the use of one or
multiple channels, problems of local interference,
the number of buildings to be interconnected, and
so on.

Assuming minimum complexity, a black-and-white
television station, including videotape could be
established for less than $50,000. If the facility
were mounted on a truck, an additional $10,000
would be required. If program production is

separated from program distribution via truck videotape units, each such unit would add about $25,000
to the cost. These costs do not include staffing
or promotion, both of which are of prime importance.
It might be possible for Harlem television to use
existing commercial cable facilities to quickly and
inexpensively enlarge the area it desires to serve.

The Teleprompter Corporation is franchised for
cable television in the northern half of Manhattan.
However, to date, relatively little cable has been
laid. The cost of laying cable runs into the millions, and can be commercially justified only if
programming is to be distributed into high-income
residential areas, where it is sold on a subscrip-
tion basis.

In upper Manhattan, cable has been laid through
Central Harlem in order to establish a connection
with the more affluent Washington Heights section
and neighboring areas. It is very possible that
the Teleprompter Corporation would be willing to
cooperate with a Harlem television project by per-
mitting taps from their main cable as it runs through
Harlem. This would have the effect of reducing costs
since the amount of cable to be laid would be minimal, i.e., some feeder cable into master antenna concentration. Since no existing CATV system reaches
more than 20,000 homes, advertising revenue, based
upon reach, would be less than $50 per minute.
There are no examples of successful CATV ventures
based exclusively on advertising revenues.

All in all, there is no doubt that a demonstration project is far preferable to the commitment of
major funds to lay cable in ghetto areas, since
little or no experience is available regarding exactly what television can accomplish in the ghetto.

In the initial stages, the proposed CATV
project cannot be self-supporting as a commercial
venture because few residents could afford to become paid subscribers. If this mode of financing
were adopted, precisely those families in greatest

need of community service would be cut off from the
benefits. Commercial financing through advertising
revenues is not a viable proposition--consequently,
it is necessary to rely on public or foundation
funding.

This does not mean, however, that the entire
operation is permanently linked to subsidies. If
introduced into the 100-200 largest urban ghettos
in the United States, which comprise a total audience of perhaps 5 to 10 million potential viewers
(depending on how the strategies aimed at establishing outreach in the course of the initial demonstration project in Harlem actually work out) the same
system provides the basis, on a nation-wide scale,
for a self-supporting operation. In this context,
CATV in Harlem, while of prime interest in itself,
also becomes a demonstration project for a subsequent nation-wide effort. A nation-wide effort,
logically, should be organized under the sponsorship of a nation-wide organization with local af-
filiates--for example, the Congress of Racial
Equality.

Many ghetto-based groups are currently expressing interest in CATV. Several applications have
already been received for CATV in ghettos (including Bedford-Stuyvesant).

In order to preserve the impact and unity of a
nation-wide project, it is essential to coordinate
it carefully with other aspects of an over-all anti-
poverty strategy, particularly the ghetto development aspects as well as recruitment and job training.

The expectation that the project could be self-
supporting on a nation-wide scale rests on the premise of creating outreach to a large audience. For
example, with an audience of 5 million, the value
of one minute of prime time rises to $12,500 at
current commercial rates. There is, however, a
reasonable expectation that the unit rate ($2,500
per million viewers) could well be raised, since a
special audience is being reached. From a purely

commercial point of view, this audience represents
a potentially huge untapped market. In order to
penetrate this large potential market, many national
advertisers may consider buying CATV time.

In addition, a good deal of institutional and
public-relations advertising is almost sure to be
directed at these ghetto audiences. Indeed, this
can already be seen on network television. Given a
break-through in the area of private and institutional advertising, it is within the realm of possibility that a television system for Harlem and other
ghetto areas, reaching several hundred thousand
homes, might be largely or fully self-sustaining.

A number of technological developments now in
the experimental stage may provide the advantages
of cable television without the use of either cable
or video trucks. Two of these developments are the
Theta Corporation's rooftop "soup dish" antenna
now in small-scale use under FCC license; and the
Chrome Alloy Corporation's quasi-laser link (a reported improvement over the "soup dish" antenna).
The quasi-laser system is expected to be operational
in Brooklyn in 1970. Should these technological developments prove successful, "cable" television, on
a large scale, could become available at a considerably reduced cost, thereby making it all the more
probable that a nation-wide ghetto television system could become a financially strong, self-
supporting venture.

The potential benefits of CATV in ghetto communities are enormous. Such projects would be highly attractive even if they had to be entirely subsidized. Preliminary investigation already indicates that on a nation-wide basis, there is a reasonable chance for an operation that could break
even, on the basis of currently available technology. Although this goal might not be altogether
possible to accomplish, the more modest goal of
having a nearly self-supporting nation-wide operation appears to be entirely possible. Technological improvements that are now in the pilot stage

promise to yield considerable cost reductions that
would greatly increase the chances of self-supporting
or even profitable operation.

We recommended that HEW be approached to ex-
plore potential aspects of television programming
having a bearing on the Head Start program and on
both student and adult education. Funding possibilities supporting the educational aspects should
also be explored with the New York City and New
York State governments and with private funding organizations active in the field of education, such
as the Ford Foundation.

Commercial or foundation funding might be secured for program experimentation concerning both
the ghetto audience and the extension of the same
technical idea of master-antenna interconnections
served by video playback units to nonghetto areas.
The whole question of programming impact is now
very difficult to investigate experimentally, since
commercial television is far too expensive for meaningful program experimentation. There is no well-
founded knowledge, for example, about what kinds of
programs will effectively reach the black audience,
the Spanish audience, or various other audience segments. Support for program experimentation should
be sought from large institutional advertisers as
well as from other commercial firms having major
television advertising budgets. A carefully worked
out proposal in this area might conceivably turn
the Harlem CATV venture from a subsidized demonstration project into a highly profitable undertaking
for the HCC, with additional resources to be plowed
back into local community development.

PROJECTS RECOMMENDED FOR FURTHER STUDY

In addition to our prospectuses and detailed
studies, we made several investigations at the pre-
feasibility level. These projects interested us
for different reasons; each is based on some specific characteristic of Harlem's economy. This

section, then, is a discussion of several of those projects that we recommended for further investigation.

Metalworking

There are steadily growing intermediate and final demands for the products of the metalworking sector--particularly in urban areas.[8] The broad variety of metalworking products and the technological characteristics of the sector are favorable to a core city location. These characteristics include a medium range capital-labor ratio, a large number of only moderately skilled operations that can be readily learned by previously marginal workers, and generally low to moderate space requirements. These industries also provide excellent opportunities for on-the-job development of high-level industrial skills that can be readily transferred from job to job and from industry to industry.*

Evidence indicates that there are opportunities for ghetto-based metalworking enterprises to compete successfully in urban markets. An extensive study of the Philadelphia economy has shown not only that there are strong local intermediate demands for metalworking products but also that significant local supply gaps (excess local demand relative to the existing metalworking base in the city) exist.[9]

The multipurpose nature of metalworking equipment makes investment in such activities extremely flexible. A machine shop can produce a large product mix, but the prevalence of scale economies leads most small firms to specialize in the output of only a restricted assortment of items.

---

*We are defining the metalworking sector to include the following classes of the Standard Industrial Classification: 332, iron and steel foundries; 336, nonferrous foundries; 339, miscellaneous primary metal products; 34, fabricated metal products; 35, machinery, except electrical; 36, electrical equipment and supplies; 37, transportation equipment; 38, instruments and related products; and several industries from 25, furniture and fixtures.

Recent innovations in planning methodologies
for the metalworking sector, including several that
we and our colleagues have developed, now make it
possible to design activity complexes that mesh with
the industrial and commercial program recommended
for Harlem.[10]

As is the case in the construction sector, development of metalworking industries provides the
community with a pool of workers skilled in those
operations which must form the basis for any comprehensive program for rebuilding the physical capital stock in the ghetto.

Industrial Parks

Substantial economies can be gained through
the locational clustering of industries or firms.
This principle is by now so well understood by the
business community that the development of industrial parks has become a dominant planning strategy
since World War II. Most industrial parks are concentrated in metropolitan areas; few, however, are
located in the central city itself.

The general class of industrial parks found in
New York City consists of two types: (a) the industrial park proper (a centralized location of a large
number of firms) and (b) the vest-pocket industrial
park (the decentralized location of small clusters
of firms in various neighborhoods throughout the
city). Industrial parks are in the design process
for the Brooklyn Navy Yard, College Point, Hunt's
Point, and Staten Island areas. It is logical to
expect that occupancy preference will be granted to
firms whose blue-collar jobs could be filled largely by local minority group workers. With respect
to the Brooklyn Navy Yard Industrial Park, this is
an explicit requirement established by the City
Planning Commission.

A number of small areas in the south Bronx and
in Queens have been proposed for the location of
vest-pocket industrial parks. These would be

developed on vacant land, on land now occupied by
abandoned or deteriorating structures, and under or
over existing facilities such as elevated express-
ways or railroad freight yards. The City Planning
Commission might consider the possibility of re-
zoning selected areas in Harlem and the south Bronx
to permit a mix of residential and light vest-pocket
industrial development. The proposed south Bronx
parks could be scattered throughout the almost 600
acres at the southern tip of the borough. It is
possible to create perhaps as many as 5,000 new
jobs in this area alone.* These parks could be devoted to locally owned and locally managed greenhouse industries. The payoff from such vest-pocket
park developments could be significant in terms of
skill training and immediate employment gains.

Government Office Buildings in Harlem

The construction of government office buildings in Central Harlem--a policy announced in 1967
by Governor Nelson Rockefeller and Mayor John
Lindsay--could confer several immediate benefits
to the local economy. Harlem firms and workers
could be employed in the demolition of the structures occupying the sites. Harlem's labor force
could be employed in the construction of the building, thereby providing immediate training in this
industry, provided that the local construction
unions can be prevailed upon to admit black workers.
The maintenance contract for building services
could be let to Harlem-based firms, or to a group
such as HCC, thereby creating business opportunities for existing firms as well as providing the
impetus for the establishment of new black-owned
firms in this growing industry.

The design of the buildings themselves could
act to stimulate the local economy. For example,
we feel the buildings should be designed without

---

*This area coincides with that designated by
the New York City Human Resources Administration's
Manpower and Career Development Agency as the impact area for the South Bronx Concentrated Employment Program.

cafeteria facilities so that their occupants would
be encouraged to patronize local restaurants--
which are virtually all black-owned. If, however,
such facilities are incorporated into the design,
then HCC could perhaps obtain a cafeteria franchise.
It might even be possible to mesh this operation
with the various food-industry projects discussed
above.

The presence of large numbers of additional
workers in the area would undoubtedly improve the
sales of the existing area businesses that provide
consumer-oriented goods and services. Local establishments should, in fact, be upgraded prior to the
construction of such a large employment complex.

In June, 1969, Governor Rockefeller announced
that a state office building project begun several
months earlier was being suspended temporarily.
Local residents apparently objected to the fact
that they were not going to participate in the
building's ownership, and, more importantly, felt
that they and their children would benefit more
from the construction of a playground and school on
the site. This does not, however, mean that our
proposed strategy is not workable or desirable.
Political leaders may continue to pose large-scale
construction as a development strategy; Harlem's
leaders should be prepared to maximize the community's participation in such projects.

Stationery Supplies

The affiliation strategy discussed earlier is
readily applicable to many of Harlem's small industries. For example, if HCC were to affiliate the
existing stationery wholesaling and office supply
firms in Harlem, it might reap economies of scale
as well as the control of a part of the distribution network. Thus, an HCC-sponsored organization
could negotiate for favorable trade prices, insurance, and sales contracts from institutional purchasers of office supplies and equipment. Such an
organization should be able to secure repair fran-
chises from the major office machine manufacturers.

Control over the distribution network may even make it possible for the organization to integrate backward into the manufacture of such office items as small machines and business forms. The business service and supply industry is growing rapidly in the New York City area; it should be exploited because of the relative ease with which it can be entered.

Phonograph Recording Company

Harlem, as the political and cultural center of black America, should be able to sustain at least one major recording company. A Harlem-based recording firm specializing in "soul" music and spoken-word recordings of black theater group performances could surely enjoy the protection of a differentiated product, in the same manner as the Detroit-based Motown Records. It is conceivable that the export of this music from Harlem to the national market could provide a substantial business base ranging from local broadcasting to the publication of sheet music.

This completes our discussion of recommended Harlem development projects. We now turn to the question of how these projects fit in with the general development trends in the New York metropolitan area.

NOTES

1. David Caplovitz, The Poor Pay More: Consumer Practices of Low Income Families (New York: The Free Press, 1963).

2. An additional source is Herbert Hill, "Demographic Change and Racial Ghettos: The Crisis of American Cities," Journal of Urban Law, Winter, 1966. An alternative hypothesis proposes that the inefficiencies of small-scale retailing may be as much the cause of poor service and high prices as deliberately exploitative behavior. For a comprehensive econometric examination of these issues,

see Roger Alcaly, "Food Prices in New York City,"
in The Economy of Harlem, Final Report of the Development Planning Workshop (New York: Columbia University, 1968) (Grant No. CG-8730, U.S. Office of
Economic Opportunity), I. (Mimeographed)

3. Social Dynamics Corporation, East Harlem
Triangle Feasibility Study (Oct./Nov., 1967), pp.
53-57. (Mimeographed)

4. U.S. Department of State, Agency for International Development, Industry Fact Sheets, 1965.

5. The general urban crisis, i.e., the physical, social, and fiscal deterioration of core cities,
is necessarily going to require experiments with new
technologies in production, transportation, and construction. See Athelstan Spilhaus, "Technology,
Living Cities, and Human Environment," American
Scientist, LVII, 1 (1969), pp. 24-36. One industrial example of an imaginative technological solution to the urban space shortage is the design by a
Chicago firm of a prototypical "high-rise industrial building," with capability for vertical
materials-handling, truck access to every floor via
graded roadways which circle the building, and
subterranean parking and loading areas: John H.
Alschuler and Irving M. Footlik, "Industry Can Cut
Costs with Multi-Story Buildings," Mid-Chicago Economic Development Study (Chicago: Mayor's Committee for Economic and Cultural Development, 1966), I.

6. Social Dynamics Corporation, op. cit.

7. Harold J. Barnett and Edward Greenberg,
"The Best Way to Get More Varied TV Programs,"
Trans-action, May, 1968, pp. 39-45.

8. Regional Science Research Institute, Economic Development Study for the Philadelphia Model
Cities Community: Proposal (March, 1969), pp. 13-
23. Thomas Vietorisz and Bennett Harrison partici-
pated in the drafting of this Proposal.

9.   Regional Science Research Institute, Philadelphia Region Input-Output Study; Working Papers (1967-68).

10.   Thomas Vietorisz and Richard Lissak, The Role of the Metalworking Sector in the Development of Harlem, Consulting Report to the Harlem Commonwealth Council (September, 1968).   This study develops several basic analytical units, including "product clusters," "process clusters," and "resource elements."   See also Thomas Vietorisz and Richard Lissak, "The Planning of Production and Exports for the Metalworking Industries," United Nations Document No. ID/WG.10/1 (Vienna: United Nations Industrial Development Organization, February, 1967); Thomas Vietorisz, "Programming of Production and Exports for Metalworking: Models and Procedures," United Nations Document No. ID/WG.10/2 (Vienna: United Nations Industrial Development Organization, February, 1969); and Thomas Vietorisz, The Engineering Industries, a monograph of the Athens International Symposium on Industrial Development (Vienna: United Nations Industrial Development Organization), in press.

6

INTERFACING HARLEM
DEVELOPMENT WITH THE
GROWTH OF THE
NEW YORK CITY ECONOMY

Chapters 4 and 5 described the most important commercial activities selected as candidates for a Harlem economic development program. These are listed in Table 30.

Important questions arise regarding the extent to which these investments mesh with the growth patterns of the broader economic system of which Harlem is a part. Which are the industries whose growth rates, especially in terms of their employment size, have been the greatest in the city, the metropolitan region, and the United States? Which industries have been leaving the city, and why do they leave? The activities selected as development projects following the criteria developed earlier must be matched against the broad development trends within New York City, the New York SMSA, and the U.S. economy. Specifically, do the commercial activities we recommended for Harlem's economy belong, or are they linked, to industries which have been relatively successful in the city-wide economy? Have they at least this measure of survival potential?

LEADING AND LAGGING INDUSTRIES IN
THE CITY ECONOMY

The U.S. Bureau of Labor Statistics has examined the sectoral employment growth which has taken place in New York City since 1950 (Figure 11). At the level of aggregation of industry sectors shown in Figure 11, services and government

employment demonstrate the fastest growth; together
they added almost 50,000 jobs to the central city
by 1967.

TABLE 30

Leading Activities Proposed for Harlem's
Economic Development
(by Standard Industrial Classification)

Manufacturing
    2033   Food canning
     322   Glassware

Communications
    4833   Community antenna television

Wholesale
     504   Groceries, frozen foods, dairy
                      products
    5077   Air-conditioning and refrigeration
                      equipment and supplies
    5096   Stationery supplies

Retail
    5221   Plumbing, heating, and air-
                      conditioning equipment
    5411   Cooperative supermarkets
    5541   Gasoline stations

Services
    7341   Window cleaning
    7392   Computerized hospital accounting
                      services
    7534   Tire recapping
    7623   Refrigerator and air-conditioning
                      repairs
    7949   Computerized automotive diagnostic
                      center
    8242   Auto mechanics training school

FIGURE II

Employment Trends in New York City, 1950-67

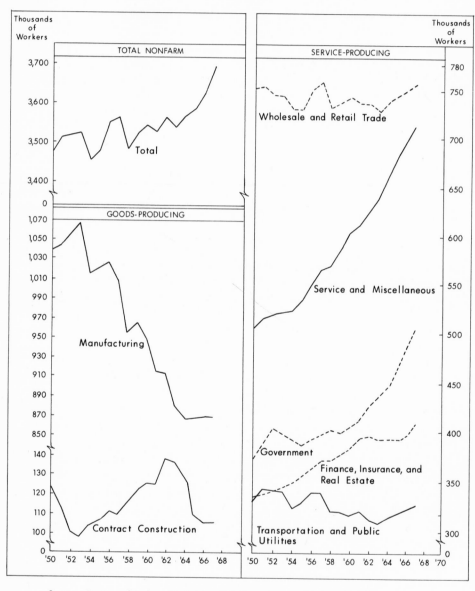

Source: Bureau of Labor Statistics, U.S. Department of Labor, Middle
Atlantic Region, <u>Changing Patterns of Employment, Income
and Living Standards in New York City</u>, April, 1968.

On the other hand, manufacturing employment has declined; since 1947 the city has lost over 200,000 manufacturing jobs. Compared with national employment growth since 1947, all of New York City's sectors have lagged. The area with the greatest loss was manufacturing, which is illustrated in Figure 12. The sectors in which New York City's performance was most encouraging were services and government (Figure 13).

These sectoral overviews, while indicative of general trends, are not adequate for a detailed analysis. Greater precision is required to identify, at least in an approximate fashion, the specific industry groups to which recommended Harlem development projects belong. Table 31 shows those industry groups that have contributed the largest number of job gains or losses from 1958 to 1967. In absolute terms, the activities of local governments were the most important source of new central-city jobs. In the private sector, business service activities were dominant, with almost half of the 54,000 gain in service jobs occurring during the three-year period 1964-67. Business service activities consist of building maintenance, advertising, credit agencies, management services, laboratories, private employment agencies, and the like.

One of our recommended projects is a food-processing and canning facility. Choice of this activity is not consistent with the city-wide trends observed here. Between 1958 and 1967, employment in this industry group declined by some 22,000 jobs, demonstrating the largest percentage loss of any group. The reasons for including this activity among our recommendations have been discussed in earlier chapters.

In order to proceed to a comprehensive and disaggregated level of analysis it was necessary to construct our own time series. Table 32 tabulates the nonretail industry groups in which are included the specific projects recommended for

Harlem.* Exhibiting positive growth rates were
wholesale paper products and hardware, plumbing,
and heating; business services; auto repair, service,
garages, tires; miscellaneous repair; and education.
The city suffered job losses in food and kindred
products; stone, glass, clay, and concrete products;
and wholesale groceries. Employment levels in the
communications industry were relatively unchanged
over this period.

      Thus a significant number of our candidate
activities belong to industries whose postwar employment growth in New York City has been relatively
satisfactory.

FIGURE 12

Employment in Manufacturing Industries
United States and New York City
Annual Averages, 1947-67

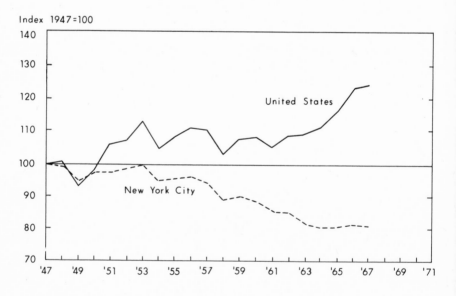

Source: Bureau of Labor Statistics, U.S. Department of Labor,
        Middle Atlantic Region.

_____

      *Data for retail activities by a 2-digit SIC
code are not readily available from published sources.

FIGURE 13

Employment in Nonagricultural Industries, United States and New York City, 1950-67

WHOLESALE AND RETAIL TRADE

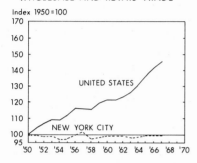

FINANCE, INSURANCE, AND REAL ESTATE

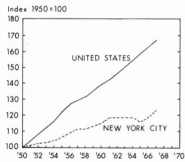

CONTRACT CONSTRUCTION

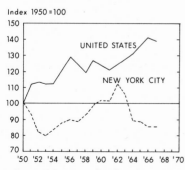

TRANSPORTATION AND PUBLIC UTILITIES

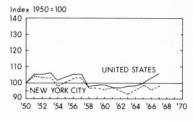

SERVICE AND MISCELLANEOUS

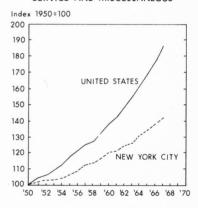

GOVERNMENT

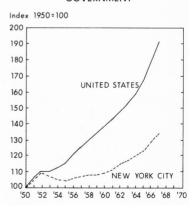

Source: Bureau of Labor Statistics, U.S. Department of Labor.

183

TABLE 31

Change in Number of Jobs in Leading Sectors,
New York City, 1958-67

Industry Sector	Number of Jobs 1967	Employment Change	
		1958-67	1964-67
Sectors of job growth			
Local government	362,000	97,000	53,000
Business services	179,000	54,000	25,000
Medical and health services	126,000	40,000	18,000
Securities brokers and exchanges	69,000	28,000	14,000
Education (nongovernment)	70,000	27,000	7,000
Air transportation	49,000	21,000	11,000
Banks	103,000	20,000	9,000
Nonprofit membership organizations	91,000	16,000	8,000
Miscellaneous services	51,000	12,000	6,000
State government[a]	34,000	11,000	10,000
Sectors of job decline			
Apparel manufacturing	233,000	-44,000	- 8,000
Food processing	62,000	-22,000	- 9,000
Railroad transportation[a]	17,000	-14,000	- 9,000
Water transportation	60,000	-12,000	- 3,000
Fabricated metals	37,000	-10,000	- 3,000
Contract construction	105,000	- 9,000	-25,000
Real estate	96,000	- 9,000	- 4,000
Federal government	111,000	- 7,000	- 5,000
Insurance carriers and agents	119,000	- 7,000	- 3,000
Chemical manufacturing	42,000	- 5,000	- 2,000

*Reflects shift of Long Island Rail Road to public ownership.

Source: U.S. Department of Labor Bureau of Labor Statistics, Middle Atlantic Region, Changing Patterns of Employment, Income, and Living Standards in New York City (April, 1968).

TABLE 32

Employment in New York City, 1958-66, Nonretail Enterprises Recommended for Harlem

Standard Industrial Classification	Employment (thousands)			
	1958	1962	1965	1966
20 Food and kindred products	84.4	76.3	66.0	63.4
32 Stone, glass, clay, and concrete products	11.0	11.0	9.8	9.5
48 Communications	75.0	72.1	74.7	76.2
504 Wholesale groceries[a]	35.4	32.4	31.8	31.4
507 Wholesale hardware, plumbing and heating[a]	8.4	8.0	9.4	9.0
5096 Wholesale paper products, office supplies[b]	12.0	14.0	15.0	16.6
73 Business services	125.2	140.0	162.0	167.5
75 Auto repair, service, garages, tires	14.5	16.0	17.6	18.0
76 Miscellaneous repair	8.9	9.9	10.8	11.1
82 Education	42.9	59.8	66.0	67.6

[a]1958 data from Census of Business, IV, Wholesale Trade Area Statistics, Chapter 32.

[b]1958 data from Census of Business; 1963 data from Census of Business for that year. From these two observations, the 1962 point was interpolated and the 1965 and 1966 points extrapolated.

Source: U.S. Department of Commerce, Office of Business Economics, The National Income and Product Accounts of the U.S. 1929-65, Table 6.3.

THE OUTMIGRATION OF FIRMS AND THE
IMPORTANCE OF THE CORE CITY

Only recently have urban economists begun to
study the migration of industrial firms from central
cities to their suburban rings.[1] It now appears,
however, that this trend has been under way for at
least twenty years. Table 33 tabulates recent
changes in New York City's employment, as well as
employment change in the surrounding ring of the
New York SMSA. The industries listed in the table
are those that have contributed the most to the central city's job loss. In every case employment
levels in the metropolitan ring increased as central
city employment fell. This was especially pronounced
for apparel, which for many years has been a major
New York City industry. Between 1958 and 1966 the
central city lost almost 36,000 apparel jobs, while
the ring gained 4,000 new ones.

Approaching this trend from another perspective,
Table 34 shows the distribution of new private nonresidential building permits issued in the central
city core and ring of the New York SMSA. Over the
period 1954-65, 75 per cent of all new industrial
buildings were constructed in suburban areas.
Herbert Bienstock, Director of the Bureau of Labor
Statistics' Middle Atlantic Regional Office, has
called this industrial outmigration an important
source of friction in the urban labor market. Bienstock goes on to say that "the long-term tendency is
for major sources of employment to be located at a
considerable distance from the residence of those
workers with a very high incidence of unemployment
and poverty."[2]

Indirect evidence does not prove that job losses
in the core, or job gains in the suburbs, represent
the physical relocation of specific firms. Changing
patterns of new business incorporations and business
failures could, at least in part, explain these observations. Abraham Burstein, formerly with the
New York City Department of Commerce and Industrial

TABLE 33

Change in Employment in Key Industries in New York,[a] Core City and Ring, 1958-66 (in thousands)

Standard Industrial Classification	1958		1966		Net Change	
	Core	Ring	Core	Ring	Core	Ring
20 Food	84.4	12.5	63.4	13.3	-21.0	+0.8
23 Apparel	276.9	13.6	241.4	17.6	-35.5	+4.0
27 Printing and publishing	125.9	12.7	125.1	17.6	- 0.8	+4.9
34 Fabricated metal products	46.4	10.1	40.5	14.5	- 5.9	+4.4

[a]Standard Metropolitan Statistical Area.

Sources: U.S. Department of Labor, Bureau of Labor Statistics, Employment and Earnings Statistics for States and Areas, 1939-66, pp. 508-22; N.Y. State Department of Labor, Employment Review (August, 1967), pp. 17-22.

TABLE 34

Per Cent of New Private Nonresidential Building Inside and Outside Central Cities[a]
United States and New York Area, 1960-65 and 1954-65[b]

Type of New Nonresidential Building	Per Cent of Valuation of Permits Authorized for New Nonresidential Building			
	United States		New York Area	
	Inside Central City	Outside Central City	Inside Central City	Outside Central City
	1960-65			
All types[c]	53	47	62	38
Business	53	47	61	39
Industrial	38	62	39	61
Stores and other mercantile buildings	48	52	36	64
Office buildings	73	27	79	21
Gasoline and service stations	49	51	49	51
Community	55	45	69	31
Educational	55	45	71	29
Hospital and institutional	65	35	75	25
Religious	45	55	45	55
Amusement	53	47	81	19

	1954-65[d]			
All types[c]	51	49	56	44
Business	54	46	56	44
Industrial	37	63	25	75
Stores and other mercan- tile buildings	47	53	29	71
Office buildings	73	27	82	18
Gasoline and service stations	47	53	35	65
Community	55	45	62	38
Educational	50	50	66	34
Hospital and institu- tional	64	36	68	32
Religious	46	54	39	61
Amusement	52	48	67	33

[a] Central cities of Standard Metropolitan Statistical Areas.

[b] Data for groups of years are used to avoid erroneous impressions from erratic year-to-year movements in building construction.

[c] Includes types not shown separately and excludes major additions and alterations for which type of building is not known.

[d] Excludes data for 1959, for which comparable information is not available.

Source: Unpublished data of the Bureau of the Census, tabulated at the request of the Bureau of Labor Statistics. Based on a sample of over 3,000 permit-issuing places.

Development, attempted to identify the reasons and
magnitudes of the outmigration problem. He interviewed 153 plant managers in manufacturing activities. As a group, they were responsible for taking
some 12,000 jobs out of New York's central city.
These did not represent migration to low-wage areas
in the South, or to the new growth areas such as
suburban Washington, D.C. Nine out of ten plants
leaving the city in 1965 relocated in nearby New
York and New Jersey counties.

Eighty-five of the managers (accounting for
8,300 employees) gave specific reasons for relocating
outside of the city's core (Table 35). The most important one concerned spatial requirements. This
may reflect changing industrial technologies--in
particular the efficiences derived from substituting
techniques which require an extended horizontal
space for those techniques using vertical, or multi-
storied, space.

To identify the types of manufacturing activities leaving the city, Burstein constructed a distribution of the 153 firms by SIC code (Table 36).
The food industry accounted for the largest employment loss.

This analysis is carried one step further in
Table 37, which identifies changes in employment
patterns between the core city, the metropolitan
area, and the country as a whole. Between 1958 and
1966, the core's share of total metropolitan employment declined in every sector of the economy. The
largest absolute decreases took place not in manufacturing activities but in wholesaling; the core's
share of metropolitan wholesaling employment declined by 8 percentage points. During this time a
parallel shift took place in the metropolis' share
of total U.S. employment; this share, with but a
single exception, decreased or remained stationary.
Taken together, the parallel shifts in the core-
city-to-metropolis and metropolis-to-U.S. employment
ratios over the eight-year period illustrate that
(at least in the case of New York) the much discussed job crisis of the core cities is part of a

TABLE 35

Reasons Advanced by 85 Manufacturers for Relocation
Out of New York City in 1965

Category of Reason Advanced	Number
Space	
Additional space	35
Cost of space	31
Horizontal space	18
Condemnation	10
Zoning regulations	4
Access-loading-park	8
Space combinations	–
Taxes	
Gross receipts	22
Commercial occupancy	20
Sales taxes	9
Real estate	2
Sewer and water charges	1
Labor	
Skill shortage	4
High cost of labor	5
Consolidations	18
Miscellaneous	
City business climate	4
Harassment	4
Personal convenience	7
Cost of doing business	4
Air pollution	2
Financing	2
Freight costs	2

Source: A. Burstein (unpublished report of
the New York City Department of Commerce and Industrial Development).

TABLE 36

Manufacturing Plants Relocated from New York City
in 1965 by Industry, Number of Plants, and
Number of Jobs

Standard Industrial Classification	No. of Plants	No. of Jobs
20 Food & kindred products	8	1,678
35 Nonelectrical machinery	16	1,261
27 Printing and publishing	11	1,259
28 Chemicals & allied products	13	1,210
38 Professional & scientific instruments	9	1,149
26 Paper & allied products	13	1,030
34 Fabricated metal products	16	961
36 Electrical machinery	24	925
23 Apparel & related products	11	878
39 Miscellaneous manufacturing	12	762
22 Textile & mill products	8	465
31 Leather & leather products	1	200
30 Rubber & miscellaneous plastic products	2	178
25 Furniture & fixtures	1	90
37 Transportation equipment	2	55
32 Stone, clay, and glass products	1	51
24 Lumber and wood products	2	35
33 Primary metal industries	2	16
21 Tobacco manufactures	1	3
Totals	153	12,206

Source: A. Burstein (unpublished report of
the New York City Department of Commerce and Industrial Development).

TABLE 37

Shifts in Sectoral Employment Distribution,
New York City, New York Area,[a] and
United States, 1958 and 1966

| | 1958 | | 1966 | |
| | NYC as % of NYSMSA | NYSMSA as % of US | NYC as % of NYSMSA | NYSMSA as % of US |
Sector				
Contract construc- tion	69	6	64	5
Manufacturing	84	7	78	6
Infrastructure	90	9	87	9
Wholesale trade	95	11	87	13
Retail trade	78	7	71	6
Finance, real es- tate, insurance	94	16	91	14
Services	84	10	81	9
Government	78	6	75	6

[a]Standard Metropolitan Statistical Area.

Sources: U.S. Department of Commerce, Office
of Business Economics, The National Income and
Product Accounts of the United States, 1929-65;
U.S. Department of Labor, Employment and Earnings
(December 1967), p. 43; U.S. Department of Labor,
Bureau of Labor Statistics, Employment and Earnings
Statistics for States and Areas, 1939-66; and N.Y.
State Department of Labor, Employment Review, August
1967, pp. 17-22.

broader phenomenon. Accompanying the progressive urbanization of U.S. society, there is a gradual dispersal of economic activities within the urban areas that spills over the edges of the standard metropolitan statistical areas as defined by the Census Bureau. This dispersal is directly related to increases in population density and to metropolitan expansion induced by the urbanization process. Residential land use competes with industrial, commercial, and other nonresidential land uses, and pushes commerce outward from the core by bidding up land rents.[3] At the same time, population increases in suburban and nearby exurban areas attract market-oriented activities to locations at increasing distances from the core. Inmigration of population and outmigration of jobs are therefore the statistical manifestations of these underlying trends.

The observations in Table 37 are plotted in Figure 14. Among linear, quadratic, and log-linear regression specifications, we chose the log-linear form as giving the best fit to the data:

$$\log Y_i = \alpha_{0i} + \alpha_{1i} \log X_i + \epsilon_i ;$$

$$i = 1, 2, \ldots 8 \text{ sectors}$$

where Y_i equals New York City's percentage share of total New York SMSA employment, and X_i equals the New York SMSA's percentage share of national employment, both in sector i.

The results are, with standard errors in parentheses:

$$1958: \quad \log Y = 1.68 + 0.26 \log X;$$
$$(0.07) \quad (0.07)$$

$$R^2 = .70$$

$$1966: \quad \log Y = 1.65 + 0.28 \log X;$$
$$(0.05) \quad (0.05)$$

$$R^2 = .81$$

Pooled sample: $\log Y = \quad 1.66 \quad + \quad 0.28 \quad \log X$;
$$\qquad\qquad\qquad\quad (0.04) \qquad (0.04)$$

$$R^2 = .75$$

The differences between the 1958 and 1966 regression coefficients are clearly not statistically significant; the pooled regression is therefore representative of the relationship.

Since we had no more reason to suppose that Y depends on X than the converse, we reran these regressions with the variables interchanged. The results in terms of statistical significance are no different from those given above (standard errors in parentheses).

1958: $\log X = -4.12 \quad + \quad 2.63 \quad \log Y$; $R^2 = .60$
$$\qquad\qquad (1.36) \qquad (0.71)$$

1966: $\log X = -4.69 \quad + \quad 2.95 \quad \log Y$; $R^2 = .82$
$$\qquad\qquad (1.09) \qquad (0.58)$$

Pooled: $\log X = -4.21 \quad + \quad 2.80 \quad \log Y$; $R^2 = .75$
$$\qquad\qquad (2.69) \qquad (0.42)$$

FIGURE 14

Employment Shares of the City in the Metropolis,
and the Metropolis in the Country,
by Major Sectors, 1958 and 1966

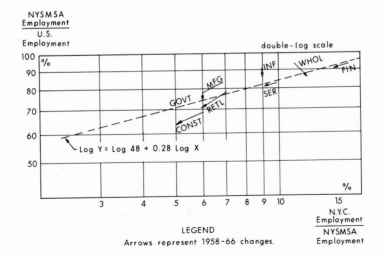

LEGEND
Arrows represent 1958-66 changes.

We find a highly significant positive relationship between the city's share of metropolitan employment (Y) in a sector and the metropolis' share
of national employment (X) in the same sector. The
elasticity of Y with respect to X is low; its value
in the pooled regression is .28, given by the log-
linear coefficient of Y on X (the inverse elasticity
[d log X/ d log Y] is 2.80). Thus, a 1 per cent
increase in the "relative importance" of the SMSA to
the national economy is associated with a .28 per
cent increase in the "relative importance" of the
core city to the metropolitan economy. (Alternatively
a 1 per cent increase in the "relative importance"
of the city to the metropolitan economy is associated
with a 2.80 per cent increase in the "relative importance" of the SMSA to the national economy.)

We interpret these results to mean that the
metropolitan area sectors which have most of their
employment located in the central city are the same
sectors for which the metropolitan area is most important nationally. The metropolis, in other words,
derives its distinction vis-à-vis the nation from
those of its sectors whose employment is most heavily concentrated inside the city, not in its suburbs.[4] Our elasticity measure indicates, however,
that large differences in the national importance
of metropolitan sectors translate into considerably
smaller differences in their core-city concentration,
and vice versa.[*]

We have repeated these calculations with a
more detailed sectoral classification.[**] The data
are given in Table 38 and plotted in Figure 15.

---

[*]The absolute level of core-city concentration,
as distinct from differences in this level, depends
on where the boundary of the core is drawn. If
Manhattan alone were defined as the core of the
New York SMSA, concentration levels for all sectors
would decrease.

[**]For the underlying data, see Appendix C.

The arrows in the plot, designating 1958-66 shifts, show a downward and leftward trend, signifying an outward migration of economic activity.

The statistical regression based on these data yields even lower differences in core-city concentration than the ones found for the major-sector regression (a coefficient of 0.10 in place of 0.28). We have omitted transportation equipment (SIC 37; see lowest arrow in Figure 15), which shows the influence of aircraft manufacturing on Long Island. Our justification is that the regression is designed to reflect the spatial pattern of many moderate-sized units for which marginal adjustments can be reasonably postulated, and not the special circumstances associated with the location of giant individual units.

The regression equations, with standard errors in parentheses, are:

$$1958: \quad \log Y = 1.86 + 0.08 \log X \;;$$
$$(0.02) \quad (0.03)$$

$$R^2 = .21$$

$$1966: \quad \log Y = 1.81 + 0.11 \log X \;;$$
$$(0.03) \quad (0.03)$$

$$R^2 = .22$$

$$\text{Combined sample:} \quad \log Y = 1.83 + 0.10 \log X \;;$$
$$(0.02) \quad (0.02)$$

$$R^2 = .25$$

The cluster of arrows in the upper right-hand corner of Figure 15 indicates those activities, represented in our survey, for which the New York metropolitan area is most specialized relative to the nation, and which are also most concentrated in the core city. These are apparel, printing and publishing, wholesale drugs, wholesale groceries, wholesale stationery and office supplies, wholesale

TABLE 38

Shifts in Industrial Employment Distribution, New York City, New York Area,[a] and United States, 1958 and 1966

Standard Industrial Classification	1958		1966	
	NYC as % of NYSMSA	NYSMSA as % of US	NYC as % of NYSMSA	NYSMSA as % of US
Manufacturing				
20 Food & kindred products	87	6	83	4
21 Tobacco products	97	3	100	3
22 Textiles	94	4	92	4
23 Apparel	95	25	93	19
24 Lumber & wood	81	1	83	1
25 Furniture	88	6	81	5
26 Paper & allied products	88	6	82	5
27 Printing & publishing	91	16	88	14
28 Chemicals	82	7	75	6
29 Petroleum	97	4	96	4
30 Rubber & plastics products	85	4	74	3
31 Leather products	98	9	96	9
32 Stone, glass, clay, & concrete products	78	3	73	2
33 Primary metals	72	2	68	2
34 Fabricated metal products	82	5	74	4
35 Machinery (except electrical)	78	3	59	3
36 Electrical machinery, equipment, supplies	71	6	61	5
37 Transportation equipment	27	4	18	3
38 Instruments: scientific, optical	48	1	53	1

Infrastructure				
20/47	Transportation	97	9	92	9
48	Communications	97	9	83	10
49	Utilities	75	6	76	5
Wholesale trade				
501	Motor vehicles & automotive equip-ment	83	8	65	6
502	Drugs, chemicals	94	30	99	21
504	Groceries	88	23	86	17
507	Hardware, plumbing & heating goods	82	8	81	9
5096	Paper products & office supplies	94	20	89	18
5097	Furniture	95	28	87	27
Services				
73	Miscellaneous business	93	21	86	16
75	Auto repair, service & garages	78	8	75	7
76	Miscellaneous repair	72	10	77	9
80	Medical & health	80	7	76	7
82	Education	65	10	77	10
Government				
91	Federal	91	3	86	2
92/93	State & local	91	5	73	6

[a]Standard Metropolitan Statistical Area.

Source: Appendix C.

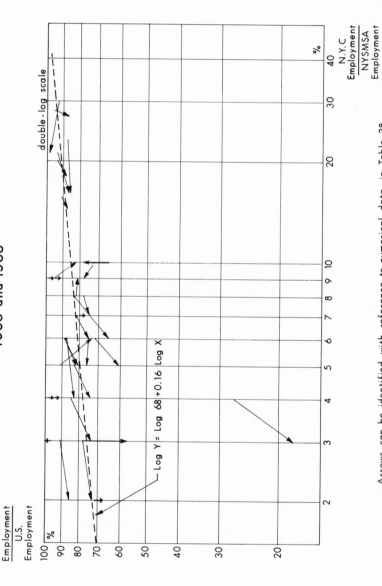

FIGURE 15

Employment Shares of the City in the Metropolis,
and the Metropolis in the Country,
by Industry Groups,
1958 and 1966

Arrows can be identified with reference to numerical data in Table 38.

200

furniture, and business services. To these should
be added finance, real estate, and insurance, which
occupy a similar position in the diagram of major
sectors (see Figure 14). Relative to the metropolitan area and the nation, these are New York City's
most important industries--since they remain heavily
concentrated in the center city rather than in the
suburbs in spite of the general outward migration
of jobs. Failure to maintain a hospitable economic
environment in the city--a policy, or lack of it,
that allows the core to deteriorate further--can
jeopardize the very activities that give the New
York metropolitan area its national distinction.

Can we interpret the importance of a given activity, derived from its position within the upper
right-hand cluster in Figure 15, to signify a comparative advantage? This question is particularly
relevant to New York's apparel industry. This industry grew at an annual rate of 2.4 per cent nationally from 1958 to 1966, yet declined at a rate
of 1.45 per cent in the New York metropolitan area
and by 1.76 per cent per year in the core city over
the same period. Its national level in terms of
wages was among the lowest-paying that we investigated, yet its city wage level was well above the
national average.* Can a locally declining low-wage
industry with an unfavorable locational cost differential demonstrate any comparative advantage? We
think it can.

New York is the fashion and wholesaling center
for the industry, and continues to organize a much
higher proportion of total U.S. apparel manufacturing than its employment figures suggest--New York
firms let a large volume of subcontracts to facto-
ries in the South. These elements of advantage
have, in the past, largely offset an unfavorable
wage gap, which now seems to be closing. Compared

----

*
See Appendix C.

with the U.S. average, this gap declined from 10 per cent in 1958 to 6 per cent in 1966.

The measure of national specialization and central-city concentration emerging from this analysis implies that a core-city industry will indeed have a comparative advantage--at least as long as the industry is not in the process of a rapid collapse. The reason for not including the apparel industry in our recommendations to the HCC is its prevailing low wage level, not pessimism concerning its future importance within the city.

In our recommendations we stressed the potential of community-sponsored affiliating institutions in supporting existing food and other retail and service activities. As affiliating institutions will be organized around the wholesaling function, our recommendation meshes with the comparative advantage of this function in the city and the New York metropolitan area. We also recommended an affiliation-like approach for rationalizing the scatter of small printing shops now operating in Harlem; this activity, again, is in a group with the greatest comparative advantage. Automotive diagnostic and repair services and cooperative food retailing (two of our major feasibility studies) are in the middle range of the distribution, as are the other retail and service activities mentioned in the introductory section of this chapter.[*]

Throughout this investigation of the region's economy, we noted high rates of growth in local government employment. In a city such as New York, how much of the job problem can private enterprise

-----

[*] Food retailing is not among the detailed sectors listed in Table 38; therefore we used the retail sector as a whole from Table 37 as a proxy for this activity. Other detailed classes not individually represented were dealt with in a like manner.

TABLE 39

Fastest-Growing Industries in United States, New York Area,[a] and New York City,
1958-66

Rank	United States	New York Area[a]	New York City
1	Misc. business services	Govt. (state & local)	Govt. (state & local)
2	Educational services	Educational services	Paper & paper products
3	Medical & health services	Paper & paper products	Medical & health service
4	Rubber & plastics products	Medical & health services	Misc. business services
5	Paper & paper products	Misc. business services	Educational services
6	Motor vehicle & automotive equipment	Rubber & plastic products	Misc. repair service
7	Electrical equipment & supplies	Misc. repair services	Auto repair, services, garage
8	Machinery (except electrical)	Auto repair, services, garage	Rubber & plastics products
9	Auto repair, services, garage	Communications	Textile mill products
10	Govt. (state & local)	Machinery (except electrical)	Hardware: plumbing & heating equipment

[a]Standard Metropolitan Statistical Area.

Source: Appendix C.

realistically solve? Or, conversely, how important
is the public sector's employment potential?[5] Table 31 indicates that between 1958 and 1967, local
government activities accounted for the largest number of additional jobs in the city, over half of the
nearly 100,000 job gain in that sector occurring in
the last three years of the period.

Table 39 lists the ten fastest-growing industry
groups in New York City, the New York SMSA, and the
United States from 1958 to 1966. They are ranked in
descending order based on their percentage rates of
employment growth over the period.

On a national basis, state and local government
activity ranks tenth. In the city and the metropolis,
however, government employment ranks first. The
implication then is clear: in addition to its own
business development and capital improvement programs,
the HCC--as a community development corporation--will
make significant contributions to the employment of
Harlem residents by using its prestige and political
influence to place black workers in public service
employment.

In sum, the activities we have stressed in our
recommendations concerning development projects in
Harlem--both projects involving support to existing
enterprises and projects involving new ventures--
mesh well with the observed development trends of
major sectors and more specific industrial branches
in the city and the region.

NOTES

1. John F. Kain, "Housing Segregation, Negro
Employment, and Metropolitan Decentralization,"
Quarterly Journal of Economics, May, 1968, pp. 175-
98; John F. Kain, "The Distribution of Jobs and In-
dustry," in The Metropolitan Enigma, James Q. Wilson,
ed. (Cambridge: Harvard University Press, 1968);
John R. Meyer, John F. Kain, and Martin Wohl, The
Urban Transportation Problem (Cambridge: Harvard

University Press, 1965), Chapter 3; Dorothy K. New-
man, "The Decentralization of Jobs," Monthly Labor
Review, May, 1967, pp. 7-13; Joseph D. Mooney,
"Housing Segregation, Negro Employment and Metropolitan Decentralization: An Alternative Perspective,"
Quarterly Journal of Economics, May, 1969, pp. 299-
311.

2. U.S. Department of Labor, Changing Patterns
of Employment, Income, and Living Standards in New
York City, Bureau of Labor Statistics Middle Atlantic
Region Report Number 10 (June, 1968), p. 22.

3. On the joint determination of industrial
and residential location, see W. Alonso, Location
and Land Use (Cambridge: Harvard University Press,
1964).

4. After observing a similar positive correla-
tion for 117 New York City manufacturing industries
(using the 1954 census), Raymond Vernon concluded
that "most of the industries whose national employment was heavily concentrated in the [metropo-
lis] . . . also had an unusually heavy concentration
in New York City . . . it was in the City that one
found an unusual portion of the activity which gave
the [metropolis] its distinctive place in the nation": Metropolis 1985 (New York: Anchor Books,
1963), p. 136.

5. The issue of public employment programming
for the urban poor has been investigated at some
length; see Bennett Harrison, "Public Service Jobs
for Urban Ghetto Residents," Good Government, LXXXVI
(Fall, 1969).

CHAPTER **7** CONCLUSION: THE
PROSPECTS FOR
GHETTO DEVELOPMENT

In this book, we believe we have shown that
strategically planned development of the urban
ghetto--in the immediate instance, of Harlem--is
possible, technologically and financially. The resources, both material and human, exist for accom-
plishing this objective.

The slum communities, individually and considered as a loosely knit network, contain a sufficient number of consumers with enough purchasing
power to make ghetto industries producing and dis-
tributing for local consumption a viable proposition. Moreover, the city has a host of public and
private institutions which might be made to purchase goods and services from ghetto industries as
a matter of public policy, thereby opening up a
market for export production. The ghetto itself
has a narrow but substantial commercial base upon
which to build, particularly if existing establishments which are uneconomically small can be organized into various cooperative forms, recommended
earlier, and if the strategy of backward integration is employed imaginatively.

The creative application of new technologies
in building construction, industrial processing,
and transportation can make core city industrial
locations feasible again. Moreover, new technologies in training--to the extent that they integrate
prevocational (motivational) and on-the-job training within the context of career ladders (as embodied in the "greenhouse industry" concept) and
against the background of improved community-oriented

public schools--will ensure these ghetto industries
an adequate supply of capable local labor.

Finally, there are a number of new mechanisms
available for channeling outside financial resources into ghetto development. Many conduits for
performing this function already exist, having been
developed gradually during the Kennedy-Johnson
years.[1] That these conduits, never full, virtually
dried up during the closing years of the 1960's is
perhaps less important than the fact that imaginative executives in several government agencies have
found it possible to restructure selected functions
of public and private organizations in order to accommodate the financial needs of ghetto enterprises.

Granted that ghetto development can be achieved,
the decisive question is: Will it be achieved?
This is a political, not an economic question.

From the over-all economic point of view, enterprises that help in developing the ghetto are
enormously attractive, because both the money costs
and the social costs of the ghettos are intolerably
high. These islands of underdevelopment in the
world's richest society lead to an appalling waste
in the form of forgone productivity, quite apart
from the invisible cost of plain human suffering.
For Harlem alone, lost production can be estimated
(from per capita incomes) as a billion and a quarter dollars annually. Over and above this short-
fall, there are vast cash expenditures involved in
running the fire departments, police stations,
courts, prisons, hospitals, mental asylums, reha-
bilitation centers, welfare departments, and other
social institutions required for keeping the lid
on the ghetto.

Yet in an economy organized by commercial
motivations, it is not the over-all economic benefit that decides if an activity will be undertaken,
but its commercial profitability. This is why the
problem is primarily political. Money-making ventures in the ghetto are invariably exploitative:

slum-lordism, numbers, vice, drugs, consumer credit
frauds. Few and far between are the constructive
activities that generate large enough profits--10
to 15 per cent after taxes--to attract investment
by the core institution of the American economy,
the large corporation. Things being as they are,
the ghetto is the last place to establish a business having the option of alternative locations.
Rents are high; labor skills, morale, turnover, and
absenteeism unfavorable; crime and casualty losses
frightening; insurance sky-high or unavailable;
public services miserably lagging behind those in
more prosperous areas. The ideal business for
ghetto development, one that is highly constructive
and hugely profitable, is rare indeed. The idea of
ghetto development based on large numbers of self-
contained, profit-making businesses that would generate their own capital for expansion is a fantasy.

When we assert that ghetto development is economically feasible, we have no illusions about the
commercial prospects of isolated ghetto enterprises.
Our strategy relies on tightly planned coordination
and mutual support between individual activities,
to bring them up to the level of profitability that
assures survival in an economy geared to commercial
success. Survival implies no more than the modest
bookkeeping profits needed for paying off bank
loans. This level of commercial performance, we
have shown, is feasible. But it will not motivate
the massive investments needed to develop the
ghettos.

Investments for ghetto development must be
motivated by over-all economic worth, not by commercial success; that is to say, in a private-
enterprise economy, they must be generated by the
political process. If the needed political motivation cannot be or is not provided, ghetto development and the private-enterprise economy are incom-
patible.

Will government and the corporate establishment make development aid available to community

leaders on the latter's own terms? More important,
will ghetto leaders have the courage, the tenacity,
and the backing from their communities to exact
from the establishment those terms that are necessary for a planned, strategic approach to ghetto
development? For the immediate future, our predic-
tion is "No," on both counts.

In dealing with urban poverty, government and
private industry have declared a definite preference for a conventional job-oriented business approach, to the nearly total exclusion of the development approach. Nascent development mechanisms
such as the SBA's Project OWN are being virtually
dismantled; "token" agencies such as the Office of
Minority Enterprise established in the Department
of Commerce under President Nixon are not taken
seriously, even by the administration which created
them; and many of the urban coalitions across the
country have become inert.[2] The private sector in
general is showing signs of a loss of interest in
developing the economic base of the ghetto, particularly as it is perceived that outside investments
in slum industry are unlikely to generate large
profits.[3] Meanwhile, the strategy of conventional
job training for conventional jobs is receiving the
greatest emphasis. The private sector, being the
chief beneficiary of these public investments in
urban labor, will continue to support this priority.
Local training and placement agencies, particularly
the state employment services, will of course lend
their support, since they are generally the implementing institutions. Indeed, President Nixon's
official request for a national program of public
welfare assistance tied to jobs proposes to operate within these conventional parameters; the employment services and the urban corporations will
decide who works where and in what kind of job.
Meanwhile, direct assistance to ghetto leaders to
aid them in becoming employers has been reduced to
a trickle of highly expensive SBA loans.

The pure "jobs" strategy won't work; it is
not working. The orthodox organizations do not

know how to reach into the ghetto systematically to
find the persons in need of vocational assistance.
Training methods and personnel are seldom geared to
providing the sustained concern and encouragement
which recruits from the ghetto so badly need. The
jobs themselves are often of low quality and--what
is more important--of doubtful permanency. Already,
member companies of the National Alliance of Businessmen have begun to shut down several of their
much publicized inner-city recruiting centers and
to release the most recently hired of the hard-core
unemployed.[4] Finally, the practice of racial discrimination in American industry and in state and
local government is so pervasive that the possibilities for promotion above entry levels, let alone
the availability of fully articulated career ladders, must seem remote indeed to the newly recruited
ghetto worker.[5] Moreover, there is no indication
that the legal instruments for attacking discrim-
ination--whether they be the Equal Employment Opportunity Commission for jobs, the 1966 Civil
Rights Act for schools and accommodations, or the
1968 Civil Rights Act for housing--are at least
going to be used vigorously in the next several
years, if not sharpened. Probably the only hope
for a jobs strategy lies in an effective policy of
bringing the urban poor into the local public service through modifications in the merit system.[6]
But this, too, will require major changes in the
attitudes of the establishment. And, in any case,
even the most well-conceived jobs program can never
be sufficient. The ghetto worker's labor cannot
indefinitely be exported to an industrial job on
the beltway or to a clerical post at city hall if
that worker must return each night to the same
pathological environment; we made this point in
Chapter 2, in discussing the writings of Oscar
Lewis. A jobs program is not a substitute for a
development program. At the very least, they are
complements.

The current debate over national priorities
recently elicited an admission from the administration that, war or no war, there is likely to be

little budgetary slack within existing priorities
for public investment in <u>any</u> form of urban development in the United States over the next several
years at least.[7]

We do not, therefore, perceive either government or private industry as being prepared to provide more than token aid, on any terms, to ghetto
leaders seeking development assistance; and certainly they will not provide aid on the terms most
consistent with the planned, strategic approach to
community development recommended in this book.   In
any case, the latter issue is moot for the moment.
The present generation of militant ghetto political
leaders--or rather, those within this leadership
who still maintain a dialogue with the white government and business establishment--have chosen not to
insist on such terms.   It is to this not altogether
unexpected retreat that we now turn our attention.

Taken individually, none of the components of
the development strategy recommended herein is
either radical or new.   Consumers' and producers'
cooperatives have been established in white communities for over a hundred years.   A great many
small towns in America have their own nonprofit development corporations, which assemble land, organize local entrepreneurs, and--sometimes--attempt
to take community preferences into account when laying out industrial parks.   The use of captive shelf
space as a lever for backward integration to producing units is a technique prominently employed
by the large food chains.   The "infant industry"
strategy is well-known and quite commonly advo-
cated in international economic development, e.g.,
by AID.   Finally (as noted in Chapters 2 and 4),
white food-merchants with small shops have in recent years taken up the affiliated-independents approach to industrial organization to such an extent
that their networks have surpassed the market
shares of the large chains.   We have not made any
attempt to disguise or deny the fundamentally
eclectic character of the elements in our economic
development strategy.

What is new in our approach is the articulation of these techniques into a program, and the suggestion that blacks might use this mix of techniques to organize their communities. Used in combination--which is all that is meant by a planned, strategic approach--these not unconventional techniques constitute a formidable economic planning instrument. Since economic power confers considerable political power as well, it is perhaps not surprising that the white government and business establishment is reluctant to assist ghetto leaders in implementing such a development plan. Within the context of the plan--within, that is, the coordinated mix of techniques--ghetto businesses are considerably more than vehicles for generating profits for a black bourgeoisie. In this context, ghetto businesses become development instruments in their own right; that is, devices which the community can manipulate toward many objectives, both economic and political. The public and private officials who are reluctant to assist in the implementation of such a plan understand this perfectly.

Yet many militant ghetto leaders apparently do not. They have chosen to pursue an orthodox, atomistic business development strategy, to identify and build unrelated ghetto enterprises whose only common attribute is the expectation that they will yield maximum profits. This will, these leaders believe, provide them with access to the board rooms of American industry and with sufficient countervailing power to hold city hall to a standoff in their (thoroughly legitimate) quest for local control of community political institutions.

In our opinion, these expectations will not and cannot be realized by the ghetto leaders unless and until they recognize that the communities which they seek to represent must be mobilized and given the opportunity to participate in the development process--as workers, as organizers, as co-op members, as voters, and as critics of each new proposal. It is the collective political strength of the community--not the asset portfolios of a small

number of its "barons"--which will confer on the
new leadership the power and legitimacy to enable
them to confront effectively the mayor's office,
the governor's mansion, the White House, or the
Chase Manhattan Bank.

In short, our experience in Harlem and our
familiarity with ghetto development projects across
the country has led us to the conclusion that the
present generation of militant leaders, insofar as
they are oriented toward action on the economic
front, are for the most part not yet prepared to
lead an effort toward genuine community development.
Their present mood does not favor the unorthodox
use of the orthodox planning techniques without
which community development cannot be achieved.
And ultimately, even if a group of highly profitable yet nonexploitative businesses could be established within the geographic confines of the
ghetto--which we consider totally implausible--it
is the development of the community qua community
and not isolated black businesses per se which will
confer political power upon the community's leaders.

Probably, the new ghetto leadership will not
turn to the planned strategic community development
approach unless their more traditional approach to
"economic" (read "business") development fails.
We believe that it will fail; indeed, that it is
already failing. Meanwhile, people within the
ghetto are going to bring more and more pressure to
bear on their leaders, the more intolerable becomes
their perceived situation. This is likely to be
especially true for the young men in the ghetto.
Pressure for change, as economists and psychologists
long ago observed, is a function of the relative
and not the absolute position of an individual or
group within society, and it feeds upon preceding
changes. In these terms, there is every reason to
expect an increase of tensions within the ghetto.
This projection is supported by the Census Bureau's
finding (reported in Chapter 2) on the recent increase in residential segregation in American
cities, and by our own statistical result (reported

in Chapter 1) which shows that, at least for full-
time employed, married Harlem men, additional edu-
cation--up to college and possibly beyond--does not
translate into perceptibly higher wages.

As such pressures build, those militant ghetto
leaders who are now committed to a conventional
business approach--or the next generation of leaders following them--may be increasingly willing to
experiment with unconventional economic and organizational strategies. We perceive their present reluctance to attempt planned ghetto development as,
more than anything, a matter of motivation and
political style. America has been built by the decentralized efforts of individuals and small groups;
there is simply no successful political tradition
to draw on for organizing broad, sustained social
action that follows a comprehensive economic and
political design. In one word, there is no mainstream tradition for planning; on the contrary,
every inbred political reflex of the average individual over thirty is "conditioned" to fend off
planning, seen as conveying the threat of social
coercion. Given this tradition, no American minority group that views itself as fighting for its
freedom will lightly commit itself to planned community development.

Yet concerted group action in the economic and
social sphere is becoming more inevitable every day,
not only in relation to the problem of the urban
ghetto, but also in relation to almost every aspect
of modern living. Advancing population densities,
the growing sophistication of technology, the rapid
deterioration of the environment through all manner
of pollution, the shrinkage of the globe through
high-speed transport--all of these are carrying us
toward a fundamentally changed world. In this
world the entire material basis of meaningful human
social existence will depend on highly articulated,
carefully designed technical and organizational
systems, rather than on the commercially motivated
maneuvering of large numbers of small social units,
be they enterprises, households, or traditional

political pressure groups. Political styles and
structures will either ride this advancing wave or
be crushed by it. We are advocating planned community development within the ghettos in the conviction that such planning is also urgently needed
in regard to practically every aspect of middle-
class metropolitan living right now, and will in
all certainty become a condition of sheer physical
survival within our lifetimes. The only conceivable
guarantee of an open society under the material conditions facing us is the organization of the needed
planning process by socially meaningful communities
of limited size, as in urban neighborhoods, and the
broadest possible participation of individuals in
all aspects of planning, all the way down to the
grass-roots level. The approach we recommend is
thus designed to become part of the future, not
merely to serve as a palliative for the mistakes
of the past.

In the case of the ghetto, the need is so
great and the alternatives so bleak that the logic
of a comprehensive planning approach, we feel, has
a reasonable chance of being given an early try by
militant ghetto leadership. The political issue of
providing the massive investment needs of ghetto development will then be clearly joined. Ghetto leaders may seek outside alliances to press the white
government and corporate establishment for development funds; or they may turn inward in an attempt
to generate reinvestible surplus out of the resources of the ghetto itself. The first strategy
places the main burden of change in attitudes and
motivations--both in the formation of political
alliances and in the renunciation of stubbornly
held vested interests--on white society outside the
ghetto. The second strategy, on the contrary,
makes enormous demands on the internal political
cohesion of the ghetto, for this strategy cannot be
successful unless it generates a consensus on the
extent and distribution of self-imposed savings,
voluntarily surrendered for ghetto development.

In spite of these obstacles, we are confident
that a sustained effort at comprehensive ghetto

development will have a reasonable chance of success because, once initiated, it has an inherent
ability to gather momentum rapidly. Concerted community action on the economic front translates itself into increased political power which, in turn,
improves the probable success of further economic
action. Alternately, initial political pressure
oriented toward community-wide economic goals, even
if moderately successful, will achieve a secondary
political payoff that gives the wheel yet another
turn. Beyond a point, the process may well prove
strong enough to fend off powerful vested interests,
both outside and inside the ghetto.

Notwithstanding the cumulative and self-
reinforcing nature of this political and economic
evolutionary process, we believe that it cannot run
its full course as long as society outside the
ghetto continues to be organized on predominantly
commercial principles. And it would be illusory to
expect that, by itself, the process of planned
ghetto development might be capable of generating
fundamental changes in the core institutions of
American society. Yet, if carried forward insis-
tently, it can become one of several centers of
accelerating change that prepare the way for the
society of the future.

To reiterate our opening argument: The idea
of comprehensive planned ghetto development is
technologically and financially feasible. Its
time, we trust, will not be long in coming.

NOTES

1. Some of these were discussed in Chapter 2.
For a fuller description of the legal structure of
these and other working mechanisms, written by one
of their principal architects, see Eugene P. Foley,
The Achieving Ghetto (Washington, D.C.: The National Press, 1969).

2. On the demise of SBA's effectiveness, see
Robert Samuelson, "SBA Funds Limited, Direct Loans
Curbed," Washington Post, March 29, 1969; Rowland
Evans and Robert Novak, "Catholic Cleric Suddenly
Surfaces as SBA Administrator's Key Advisor," Wash-
ington Post, April 9, 1969; Rowland Evans and Robert
Novak, "SBA Purge," Washington Post, May 4, 1969;
and "Black Capitalism: Still a Promise," Newsweek,
August 4, 1969. The original plans for the Com-
merce Department's Office of Minority Enterprise
are described at length in Monroe W. Karmin,
"Nixon's Plan to Assist Minority Entrepreneurs
Makes Faltering Start," The Wall Street Journal,
July 10, 1969. The total failure of this agency
is described in the Newsweek article cited above.
Finally, for a discussion of at least one local
urban coalition "on the verge of collapse," see
Robert L. Asher, "Urban Coalition Is Tottering in
Confusion," Washington Post, August 23, 1969.

3. A recent study at the Center for Manpower
Policy Studies of George Washington University concluded, after analyzing industries that have already established subsidiaries in core city areas,
that "the experience generally has not been favorable and the business environment of ghetto areas
does not seem to be profitable." The most highly
publicized of the branch plants has been Aerojet-
General's tent-manufacturing facility established
in Watts in 1966. By May of 1969, and despite
Labor and Defense Department subsidies and contracts totaling well over $2 million, the project
had lost "several hundred thousand dollars" and employment had been cut back from 500 to 300 ghetto
workers: John Herbers, "Economic Development of
Blighted Inner-City Areas Is Running into Snags,"
The New York Times, May 4, 1969. Few experts believe that tax credits will be sufficient to permit
corporations to earn the high profits they require
as a matter of course; see Frank C. Porter, "Manpower Experts Cool to Tax Credits," Washington Post,
January 8, 1969; William Cris Lewis, "Tax Concessions and Industrial Location: A Review," Reviews
in Urban Economics (Fall, 1968); and the final

218   THE ECONOMIC DEVELOPMENT OF HARLEM

reports of the National Commission on Urban Problems
(former Senator Paul H. Douglas, Chairman), released
December 14, 1968.

4.   In January, 1969, Leo Beebe (formerly
Executive Vice Chairman of the National Alliance of
Businessmen) announced that by January 1 about
120,000 people had been placed in jobs under Labor
Department Manpower Assistance Act Section 3 subsidies during the National Alliance's first year, and
that 85,000 were still at work: Murray Kempton,
"The Private Sector," The New York Post, January 8,
1969. By the end of the first quarter of 1969, the
Alliance's momentum had slowed down considerably;
only about 5,000 new workers had been hired. Altogether, these 125,000 workers were distributed among
some 12,500 companies, for an average of only ten
new hires per company. Moreover, between 15,000 and
20,000 companies had been contacted: Business Week,
March 8, 1969, p. 62. Ghetto workers are traditionally the last hired but the first fired in private
labor markets. Thus, by the middle of March, 1969,
the Ford Motor Company was announcing the closing
of two special hiring centers in central Detroit
and the layoff of several hundred newly hired workers from the ghetto: Business Week, March 22, 1969,
p. 41.

5.   See, for example: U.S. Civil Rights Commission, For All the People, by All the People
(1969); U.S. Equal Employment Opportunity Commission, Job Patterns for Minorities and Women in
Private Industry, 1966, Equal Employment Opportunity Report No. 1 (3 volumes; 1969); and Joseph
Featherstone, "Career Ladders for Bottom Dogs,"
The New Republic, September 13, 1969.

6.   The National Civil Service League--with
contracts and grants from the U.S. Departments of
Housing and Urban Development and Labor and the
Office of Economic Opportunity--has undertaken the
task of stimulating public employment of the disadvantaged under modified merit principles at state

and local levels; see Bennett Harrison, "Public Service Jobs for Urban Ghetto Residents," Good Government, LXXXVI, Fall, 1969.

7. Referring to the budget projections of Herbert Stein of the Council of Economic Advisors, Presidential Assistant Daniel P. Moynihan described the so-called peace dividend as "somewhat evanescent, like the morning clouds around San Clemente" (the summer White House): "Nixon Is Skipping the Peace Dividend," Business Week, August 30, 1969.

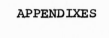

APPENDIXES

APPENDIX A STATISTICAL
PROFILE OF THE
HARLEM ECONOMY

APPENDIX TABLE 1:   INCOME AND
EMPLOYMENT PROFILE

In 1966, the U.S. Department of Labor conducted a survey of 37,330 individuals aged 14 and
over living in ten urban ghettos including Central
Harlem.

The 1966 Urban Employment Survey (UES) cov-
ered the following areas (sample sizes are in
parentheses): Roxbury, Boston (3,945); Central
Harlem, New York City (3,581); East Harlem, New
York City (4,217); Bedford-Stuyvesant, New York
City (4,220); North Philadelphia (3,969); North
Side, St. Louis (4,068); slums of San Antonio
(3,770); Mission-Fillmore, San Francisco (2,617);
Salt River Bed, Phoenix (3,314); and slums of New
Orleans (3,629).

For each individual record in the UES, there
are four income variables: gross income of the
person's family during the past year, his or her
own wages for the preceding week, whether or not
the family had received any form of public assistance during the past year (a 0-1 variable), and
whether or not the family had received income from
any source other than wages or welfare during the
past year (also a 0-1 variable). Since the UES
was conducted during the month of November, 1966,
"past year" refers to November, 1965-November,
1966; "past week" refers to one of the five weeks
from about October 24 to November 29, 1966.

It is possible to aggregate the interview
data so as to produce family as well as individual
data files. Whether we tabulate the income distributions in terms of family units or in terms of
their component individuals depends, of course, on

225

the purposes at hand. Much can be learned from
either approach.

Our first interest is in the relationship between the incomes and labor force status of Harlem
workers. Since so many nonwhite families have
multiple wage-earners,* this relationship is best
studied in terms of <u>family</u> units. Thus, columns
1-5 and column 8 of Appendix Table 1, Part I, contain tabulations of family income, distributed by
the labor force status of those members of the family aged 14 or more.

Next, we are concerned with the contrast between the income profiles of Harlem families headed
by males on the one hand and females on the other.
Again, therefore, the appropriate unit of analysis
is the <u>family</u>. The tabulations are shown in columns 6-8 of Appendix Table 1, Part I.

So far, we have related quantitative data on
gross incomes and wages and qualitative information
on welfare and "other income" to labor force status
and sex of the household head. Now, we turn to the
relationship between income and occupation. Since
the latter is an inherently individualistic attribute, the unit of analysis will be the <u>individual</u>,
whether or not related. Cross-tabulations of "individual" income with occupation are shown in Appendix Table 1, Part II. It would, of course, be desirable to have information on each person's own
contribution to annual family income, such as that
collected periodically by the Bureau of the Census

---

*In the Harlem sample, of 1,377 families with
at least one labor force participant, 465 (or 34
per cent) had 2 or more wage-earners. Nationally,
in 1966, 55 per cent of all Negro families in the
labor force had multiple wage-earners, compared
with 49 per cent of the white families: U.S. Department of Labor, Bureau of Labor Statistics,
<u>Social and Economic Conditions of Negroes in the
United States</u>, Report No. 332 (October, 1967), p. 19.

in the Current Population Surveys. In the present
instance, however, we are forced to rely upon the
variable "family income" once again. Therefore,
measures of central tendency are computed for wages
but not for income.

Under "Reported Gross Annual Family Income,"
an upper limit of $11,999 was assumed for the open
class. Of all nonwhite families living in the central cities of SMSA's in 1967, about 90 per cent received incomes of less than $12,000;* for the ghetto
(i.e., the most disadvantaged subset), the proportion is almost certainly even higher than that.

Under "Reported Weekly Family Wages," an upper
limit of $11,999 per year, or $220 per week, was
assumed, on the following argument: In 1967, about
10 per cent of all nonwhite families earned more
than $11,999 in gross income, while about 11 per
cent of all central city metropolitan nonwhite families earned more than this amount. About 7 per
cent of all nonwhites earned more than $11,999 in
wages alone.** Assuming proportionality between
the gross income and wage distributions for nonwhites, then only about (.10/.11 = .07/x =) 8 per
cent of all central city nonwhite families earned
more than $11,999 in wages. For the ghetto (i.e.,
the most disadvantaged subset), an upper annual income limit of $11,999 therefore contains at least
92 per cent of the observations, and probably more.
The sum $11,999 divided by 50 weeks is approximate-
ly equal to $220 per week.

Under "Reported Weekly Family Wages," an upper
limit of $200 per week was assumed: In 1967, only

---

*See Bureau of the Census, Current Population
Reports, Series P-60, No. 59, "Income in 1967 of
Families in the United States" (Washington, D.C.,
1969), Table 9.

**Ibid., Tables 20, 9, and 1.

2 per cent of all nonwhite individuals earned more
than $9,999 gross income, while about 4 per cent
of all central city metropolitan nonwhite individuals earned more than $9,999 in wages alone.* Assum-
ing proportionality, then only about (.02/.04 =
.02/x =) 4 per cent of all central city nonwhite
individuals earned more than $9,999 in annual wages.
In the ghetto, an upper annual wage limit of $9,999
probably includes about 100 per cent of the observations. The sum $9,999 divided by 50 weeks is
approximately equal to $200 per week.

---

*Ibid., No. 60, "Income in 1967 of Persons in
the United States" (Washington, D.C., 1969), Tables
3, 1, and 16.

APPENDIX TABLE 1

Income and Employment Profile of the Harlem Labor Force, November, 1966

I. Families, by Labor Force Status of Members and by Sex of Head[a]

Income Status		Families with One or More in the Labor Force				With None in the Labor Force	Families with Male Head	Families with Female Head	Total
		Total	With None Employed	With One Employed	With More Than One Employed				
Total Reporting		1,377	63	849	465	495	989	883	1,872
$0 -1,499	no.	97	19	64	14	269	79	287	366
	pct.	7.0	30.2	7.5	3.0	54.3	8.0	32.5	19.6
$1,500-1,999	no.	53	8	36	9	63	45	71	116
	pct.	3.8	12.7	4.2	1.9	12.7	4.6	8.0	6.2
$2,000-2,499	no.	76	10	59	7	67	56	87	143
	pct.	5.5	15.9	6.9	1.5	13.5	5.7	9.9	7.6
$2,500-2,999	no.	87	3	68	16	30	47	70	117
	pct.	6.3	4.8	8.0	3.4	6.1	4.8	7.9	6.2
$3,000-3,499	no.	146	8	117	21	28	70	104	174
	pct.	10.6	12.7	13.8	4.5	5.7	7.1	11.8	9.3
$3,500-3,999	no.	136	4	102	30	14	89	61	150
	pct.	9.9	6.3	12.0	6.5	2.8	9.0	6.9	8.0
$4,000-4,999	no.	212	4	157	51	16	157	71	228
	pct.	15.4	6.3	18.5	11.0	3.2	15.9	8.0	12.2
$5,000-	no.	570	7	246	317	8	446	132	578
	pct.	41.4	11.1	29.0	68.2	1.6	45.1	14.9	30.9
	mean[b]	5,344 (2,808)	2,817 (2,309)	4,701 (2,619)	6,862 (2,488)	1,674 (1,362)	5,513 (2,873)	3,099 (2,564)	4,374 (2,985)
	median[c]	4,438 (3,445-5,610)	2,199 (1,570-2,790)	3,892 (3,195-4,645)	6,324 (5,000-6,590)	1,325 (0-1,875)	4,687 (3,520-5,811)	2,477 (490-3,390)	3,566 (2,410-4,700)

(Labels reading vertically in left margin: (1), REPORTED GROSS ANNUAL FAMILY INCOME)

(continued)

APPENDIX TABLE 1 (continued)

Income Status		Families with One or More in the Labor Force				With None in the Labor Force	Families with Male Head	Families with Female Head	Total
		Total	With None Employed	With One Employed	With More Than One Employed				
Total Reporting		1,339		866	473		850	489	1,339
$0 - 29	no.	98		88	10		57	41	98
	pct.	7.3		10.2	2.1		6.7	8.4	7.3
(2) REPORTED $30 - 59	no.	151		143	8		57	94	151
	pct.	11.3		16.5	1.7		6.7	19.2	11.3
WEEKLY $60 - 89	no.	378		342	31		194	179	373
	pct.	27.9		39.5	6.6		22.8	36.6	27.9
FAMILY $90 -119	no.	362		293	69		269	93	362
	pct.	27.0		33.8	14.6		31.6	19.0	27.0
WAGES $120-149	no.	140		0	140		101	39	140
	pct.	10.5		0.0	29.6		11.9	8.0	10.5
$150-	no.	215		0	215		172	43	215
	pct.	16.1		0.0	45.5		20.2	8.8	16.1
	mean[d]	101 (54)		74 (29)	150 (47)		110 (52)	85 (46)	101 (54)
	median[c]	93 (74-114)		77 (64-92)	145 (134-164)		103 (85-120)	78 (64-94)	93 (74-114)

(3)								
FAMILIES RECEIVING PUBLIC ASSISTANCE								
all forms[e] no.	151	37	83	31	202	120	233	353
pct.	10.9	58.7	9.8	6.7	40.9	12.1	26.4	18.9
unemployment insurance	68	17	37	14	10	54	24	78
aid to dependent children	86	21	48	17	184	67	203	270
other welfare	9	0	7	2	12	7	14	21
(4)								
FAMILIES RECEIVING[f] OTHER INCOME no.	167	16	118	33	193	156	204	360
pct.	12.1	25.4	13.9	7.1	39.0	15.8	23.1	19.2

(Part II of Appendix Table 1, "Individuals, Whether or Not Related, by Occupation," continues on following page.)

II. Individuals, Whether or Not Related, by Occupation[g]

Income Status			Total	Full Time[h]	Part Time[h]	Profes- sional	Craftsman
	Total Reporting		2,036	1,567	297	161	97
(1)	$0 -1,499	no.	139	64	39	3	5
		pct.	6.8	4.1	13.1	1.9	5.2
REPORTED	$1,500-1,999	no.	64	30	21	0	0
		pct.	3.1	1.9	7.1	0.0	0.0
GROSS							
	$2,000-2,499	no.	90	52	22	0	0
ANNUAL		pct.	4.4	3.3	7.4	0.0	0.0
INCOME	$2,500-2,999	no.	108	79	22	2	1
		pct.	5.3	5.0	7.4	1.2	1.0
OF THE							
	$3,000-3,499	no.	181	135	24	5	1
INDIVIDUAL'S		pct.	8.9	8.6	8.1	3.1	1.0
FAMILY	$3,500-3,999	no.	181	135	29	6	3
		pct.	8.9	8.6	9.8	3.7	3.1
	$4,000-4,999	no.	278	222	42	15	14
		pct.	13.7	14.2	14.1	9.3	14.4
	$5,000-	no.	995	850	98	130	73
		pct.	48.9	54.2	33.0	80.7	75.3
(2)	Total Reporting		1,899	1,590	309	164	101
	$0 - 19	no.	146	72	74	13	6
REPORTED		pct.	7.7	4.5	23.9	7.9	5.9
WEEKLY	$20 - 39	no.	129	10	119	2	2
		pct.	6.8	0.6	38.5	1.2	2.0
INDIVIDUAL							
	$40 - 59	no.	266	214	52	5	3
WAGES		pct.	14.0	13.5	16.8	3.0	3.0

| | IN THE LABOR FORCE | | | | | | | |
| | CURRENTLY EMPLOYED | | | | | Now | Not in the | |
Clerical-Sales	Operative	Laborer	Domestic	Other[i]	Unemployed	Labor Force	Total
341	311	273	154	527	172	1,453	3,489
15	11	13	21	35	36	417	556
4.4	3.5	4.8	13.6	6.6	20.9	28.7	15.9
5	7	4	11	24	13	117	181
1.5	2.3	1.5	7.1	4.6	7.6	8.1	5.2
7	9	8	21	29	16	148	238
2.1	2.9	2.9	13.6	5.5	9.3	10.2	6.8
12	12	20	18	36	7	90	198
3.5	3.9	7.3	11.7	6.8	4.1	6.2	5.7
27	36	28	18	44	22	108	289
7.9	11.6	10.3	11.7	8.3	12.8	7.4	8.3
26	27	35	14	53	17	93	274
7.6	8.7	12.8	9.1	10.1	9.9	6.4	7.9
44	54	38	15	84	14	145	423
12.9	17.4	13.9	9.7	15.9	8.1	10.0	12.1
205	155	127	36	222	47	335	1,330
60.1	49.8	46.5	23.4	42.1	27.3	23.1	38.1
350	316	278	158	532			1,899
16	15	22	20	54			146
4.6	4.7	7.9	12.7	10.2			7.7
23	10	16	40	36			129
6.6	3.2	5.8	25.3	6.8			6.8
22	38	60	60	78			266
6.3	12.0	21.6	38.0	14.7			14.0

(continued)

Income Status			Total	Full Time[h]	Part Time[h]	Profes-sional	Craftsman
REPORTED	$60 - 79	no.	562	525	37	11	10
		pct.	29.6	33.0	12.0	6.7	9.9
WEEKLY	$80 - 98	no.	785	758	27	128	80
		pct.	41.3	47.7	8.7	78.0	79.2
INDIVIDUAL	$99 -	no.	11	11	0	5	0
WAGES		pct.	0.6	0.7	0.0	3.0	0.0
(continued)		mean[d]	68	74	39	81	80
			(25)	(21)	(24)	(26)	(21)
		median[c]	74	79	38	87	87
			(64-87)	(68-90)	(27-43)	(83-93)	(83-90)
(3)	all forms[j]	no.	205	105	35	3	4
		pct.	10.1	6.7	11.8	1.9	4.1
WORKERS IN	unemployment	no.	101	53	15	1	2
FAMILIES	insurance	pct.	49.3	50.5	42.9	33.3	50.0
RECEIVING	aid to depen-	no.	108	53	20	2	2
	dent children	pct.	52.7	50.5	57.1	66.7	50.0
PUBLIC	other welfare	no.	12	9	2	0	0
ASSISTANCE		pct.	5.9	8.6	5.7	0.0	0.0
(4) WORKERS IN FAMILIES RECEIVING OTHER INCOME[f]		no.	208	109	69	13	3
		pct.	10.2	7.0	23.2	8.1	3.1

234

| | CURRENTLY EMPLOYED | | | | Now | Not in the | |
Clerical-Sales	Operative	Laborer	Domestic	Other[i]	Unemployed	Labor Force	Total
IN THE LABOR FORCE							
118	101	94	37	191			562
33.7	32.0	33.8	23.4	35.0			29.6
170	150	85	1	171			785
48.6	47.5	30.6	0.6	32.1			41.3
1	2	1	0	2			11
0.3	0.6	0.4	0.0	0.4			0.6
73	73	65	45	65			68
(22)	(22)	(24)	(20)	(26)			(25)
79	78	68	46	70			74
(69-90)	(68-90)	(57-79)	(35-56)	(60-80)			(64-87)
27	26	26	11	43	65	411	616
7.9	8.4	9.5	7.1	8.2	37.8	28.3	17.7
16	18	9	6	16	33	62	163
59.3	69.2	34.6	54.5	37.2	50.8	15.1	26.5
14	8	18	5	24	35	344	452
51.9	30.8	69.2	45.5	55.8	53.8	83.7	73.4
1	1	3	2	4	1	21	33
3.7	3.8	11.5	18.2	9.3	1.5	5.1	5.4
29	16	23	37	57	30	421	629
8.5	5.1	8.4	24.0	10.8	17.4	29.0	18.0

(continued)

NOTES TO APPENDIX TABLE 1

[a] The number of families interviewed in Central Harlem was 1,918.

[b] Computed from the grouped data. Figures in parentheses are standard errors. For the open class, an upper limit of $11,999 was assumed.

[c] Computed from the grouped data. Figures in parentheses represent a 95 per cent confidence interval, based on a 9 per cent relative error of estimate computed by the Department of Labor.

[d] Computed from the grouped data. Figures in parentheses are standard errors. For the open family wage class, an upper limit of $11,999/year or $220/week was assumed. For the open class in the individual wage distribution, an upper limit of $200/week was assumed.

[e] Since families may receive more than one form of assistance, the numbers in each column do not necessarily add to the figure at the head of the column.

[f] Income from all sources other than wages and public assistance, e.g., entrepreneurial and perhaps illegal income.

[g] The number of individuals in Central Harlem on whom data files were constructed was 3,581.

[h] Full-time: 35 hours/week or more regularly;
    part-time: less than 35 hours/week, regularly.

[i] Includes farm workers, new workers not yet assigned, and "all other."

[j] The figure under "all forms" represents the percentage of the total sample receiving some form of public assistance. The other figures represent percentages of the subsample which actually receives aid. These need not add to 100.0, since workers' families may receive more than one type of public assistance.

Source: U.S. Department of Labor, 1966 Urban Employment Survey (unpublished data files).

236

APPENDIX TABLE 2:   DEMOGRAPHIC PROFILE

The source for Appendix Table 2 is also the 1966 UES.

First, we tabulate the age distributions of the Harlem sample, by race, and compute medians for each column of Appendix Table .2. Blacks comprise 85 per cent of the sample; 96 per cent of the sample is nonwhite.

Family size is then tabulated, again by race. Over-all, about 22 per cent of the sample includes single-person families, some (or possibly all) of whom may be truly "unrelated individuals."

Finally, we examine several aspects of the educational status of the Harlem population. The first of these is the frequency distribution of the variable "highest grade attended and completed." Medians are computed for each class. Secondly, we tabulate the reasons offered by respondents for not finishing high school. In the case of multiple responses, only the one which the individual considered to be the most important is tallied.

APPENDIX TABLE 3:   EMPLOYMENT IN
HARLEM BUSINESSES

During the winter of 1967/68, the New School for Social Research project team undertook a comprehensive telephone survey of business establishments in Central Harlem. From the Sanborn Company's land-use maps and the telephone company's reverse directory (with listings arranged by address rather than by name), we were able to compile a universe of all nonresidential addresses in Central Harlem having telephones; the number was about 4,500. Of these, slightly less than 3,000 were engaged in commercial activity.

Each of the 3,000 establishments was telephoned
a maximum of three times. In this way, 2,690 valid
records were obtained. A pretest of the telephone
interview schedule on 200 establishments indicated
the general willingness of respondents to provide
us with the desired information. The data--includ-
ing comments and opinions expressed more or less at
random by many of the Harlem entrepreneurs--were
edited and subsequently revised through the use of
Dun and Bradstreet credit reports and a small sample
survey of Harlem druggists, truckers, and printers
conducted for us by the New York City Planning Commission.

Appendix Table 3 tabulates reported employment
in Harlem businesses, distributed by 4-digit Standard Industrial Classification (SIC) code. The
table shows the distribution of establishments by
number of employees and estimates total employment
in each industry.

APPENDIX TABLE 4:   AGE AND OWNERSHIP

In Appendix Table 4 we tabulate two variables:
whether the business property is owned or rented by
its present tenants, and the number of years in
which the business has been at its present location.
An age distribution by SIC code is presented.

APPENDIX TABLE 5:   RACE OF OWNERS

"Race of owners" is one of the most contro-
versial variables with which we dealt. Of the
2,690 owners or managers interviewed, 1,078, or 40
per cent, reported on the owner's race; 629, or
about 60 per cent of these, reported black ownership.

Demographic Profile of the Harlem Population, November, 1966

Demographic Category		Major Racial Group[a]				
		Black	White	Spanish-Speaking	Other	Total
TOTAL SAMPLE		3,038	153	374	16	3,581
	Males	1,312	60	176	7	1,554
	Females	1,726	83	198	9	2,027
DISTRIBUTION BY AGE						
Number Reporting		2,894	153	374	16	3,437
14-15	No.	102	1	17	3	123
	Pct.	3.5	.7	4.5	18.8	3.6
16-19	No.	240	9	39	3	281
	Pct.	8.3	5.9	10.4	18.8	8.5
20-24	No.	214	17	49	0	280
	Pct.	7.4	11.1	13.1	.0	8.1
25-44	No.	1,098	45	161	3	1,307
	Pct.	37.9	29.4	43.0	18.8	38.0
45-54	No.	538	22	57	1	618
	Pct.	18.6	14.4	15.2	6.3	18.0
55-64	No.	367	28	35	2	432
	Pct.	12.7	18.3	9.4	12.5	12.6
65+	No.	335	31	16	4	386
	Pct.	11.6	20.3	4.3	25.0	11.2
Median age		41.2	46.8	35.2	38.4	40.7

(continued)

APPENDIX TABLE 2 (continued)

Demographic Category		Major Racial Group[a]				
		Black	White	Spanish-Speaking	Other	Total
FAMILY SIZE						
Number Reporting		2,898	153	374	16	3,441
1	No.	668	42	29	6	745
	Pct.	23.1	27.5	7.8	37.5	21.7
2	No.	861	46	47	3	857
	Pct.	29.7	30.1	12.6	18.8	27.8
3	No.	489	24	109	0	622
	Pct.	16.9	15.7	29.1	.0	18.1
4	No.	408	18	62	2	480
	Pct.	14.1	11.8	16.6	12.5	14.2
5-7	No.	414	23	108	5	550
	Pct.	14.3	15.0	28.9	31.3	16.0
8+	No.	58	0	19	0	77
	Pct.	2.0	.0	5.1	.0	2.2
Median size		2.9	2.7	4.0	2.7	3.0

EDUCATION

Highest grade completed:

		2,850	149	363	16	3,378
Number Reporting						
0-6	No.	335	26	93	2	456
	Pct.	11.8	17.4	25.6	12.5	13.5
7-8	No.	392	32	65	2	491
	Pct.	13.8	21.5	17.9	12.5	14.5
9	No.	232	7	32	1	272
	Pct.	8.1	4.7	8.8	6.3	8.1
10-11	No.	607	13	80	4	704
	Pct.	21.3	8.7	22.0	25.0	20.8
12	No.	1,051	52	80	5	1,188
	Pct.	36.9	34.9	22.0	31.3	35.2
13+	No.	233	19	13	2	267
	Pct.	8.2	12.8	3.6	12.5	7.9
Median grade		11.5	11.4	9.7	11.5	11.5

(continued)

APPENDIX TABLE 2 (continued)

Demographic Category		Black	White	Spanish-Speaking	Other	Total
				Major Racial Group[a]		
EDUCATION (continued)						
Reasons for not finishing high school:						
Number Reporting		1,434	78	239	3	1,754
A. health	No.	92	2	18	0	112
	Pct.	6.4	2.6	7.5	.0	6.4
B. support self	No.	502	27	70	1	600
	Pct.	35.0	34.6	29.3	33.3	34.2
C. support family	No.	420	26	64	1	511
	Pct.	29.3	33.3	26.8	33.3	28.1
D. preferred work	No.	118	3	17	0	138
	Pct.	8.2	3.8	7.1	.0	7.9
E. expelled	No.	17	1	5	0	23
	Pct.	1.2	1.3	2.1	.0	1.3
F. not important to future	No.	167	3	28	0	188
	Pct.	11.6	3.8	11.7	.0	11.3
G. other	No.	118	16	37	1	172
	Pct.	8.2	20.5	15.5	33.3	8.8

[a]"Spanish-Speaking": "white Puerto Rican," "black Puerto Rican," and "Mexican" in Labor Department terminology.

"Black": "other black" in Labor Department terminology.
"White": "other white" in Labor Department terminology.
"Other": "Indian," "Chinese," and "other" in Labor Department terminology.

Source: U.S. Department of Labor, 1966 Urban Employment Survey (unpublished

242

APPENDIX TABLE 3

Employment in Harlem Businesses, Winter 1967/68

	Standard Industrial Classification	Total Establishments	Number Reporting	Reported Employment	Employment[a] Distribution by Number of Employees				Total Estimated Employment[b]
					1-3	4-9	10-19	20 or more	
134	Poultry, exc. broiler chickens	1	0	0					0
1511	General building contractors	37	9	66	4	2	1	2	259
1711	Plumbing, heating, air conditioning	16	5	85	1	2		2	272
1721	Painting, paper hanging, decorating	3	0	0					0
1731	Electrical work	16	5	36	2	2		1	112
1742	Plastering and lathing	1	0	0					0
1743	Terrazzo, tile, marble, mosaic work	1	1	1	1				1
1751	Carpentering	5	2	5	1	1			10
1761	Roofing & sheet metal work	4	4	22	1	2	1		22
1791	Structural steel erection	2	2	6	1	1			6
1796	Installing building equip. nec	1	0	0					0
1799	Special trade contractors, nec	2	1	8		1			16
2011	Meat packing plants	2	2	9	1	1			9
2024	Ice cream & frozen desserts	2	1	325				1	650
2051	Bread, cake, & related products	1	1	12			1		12
2086	Bottled & canned soft drinks	2	2	11	1	1			11
2259	Knitting mills, nec	1	0	0					0
2331	Women's blouses & waists	5	4	94			1	3	115
2335	Women's & misses' dresses	5	3	95				3	155
2337	Women's suits & coats	6	3	51			2	1	102
2339	Women's & misses' outerwear	2	2	35			1	1	35
2351	Millinery	1	0	0					0
2355	Hats, caps, & millinery	2	0	0					0
2369	Children's outerwear, nec	1	1	12			1		12
2381	Fabric dress & work gloves	1	1	65				1	65
2512	Upholstered household furn.	4	4	67	2		1	1	67
2515	Mattresses & bedsprings	1	0	0					0
2541	Wood partitions & fixtures	1	1	150				1	150

(continued)

APPENDIX TABLE 3 (continued)

Standard Industrial Classification	Total Establishments	Number Reporting	Reported Employment	Employment[a] Distribution by Number of Employees				Total Estimated Employment[b]
				1-3	4-9	10-19	20 or more	
2711 Newspapers	3	0	0					0
2731 Book publishing	1	0	0					0
2741 Misc. publishing	2	0	0					0
2751 Com. printing, exc. litho.	18	14	57	9	2	3		72
2752 Com. printing, lithographic	3	2	4	2				6
2834 Pharmaceutical preparations	1	1	8		1			8
2842 Polishes & sanitation goods	2	2	4	2				4
2844 Toilet preparations	1	1	4		1			4
2899 Chemical preparations, nec	1	0	0					0
3142 House slippers	1	1	80				1	80
3161 Luggage	1	0	0					0
3231 Products of purchased glass	1	1	2	1				2
3292 Asbestos products	1	1	3	1				3
3433 Heating equip. exc. electric	1	0	0					0
3441 Fabricated structural steel	5	3	19		3			30
3443 Fabricated plate work	1	0	0					0
3449 Misc. metal work	1	1	6		1			6
3561 Pumps and compressors	1	1	7		1			7
3574 Calculating & accounting mach.	1	0	0					0
3585 Refrigeration machinery	1	0	0					0
3599 Misc. machinery, exc. electrical	3	2	5	1	1			6
3652 Phonograph records	1	0	0					0
3679 Electronic components, nec	1	1	4		1			4
3711 Motor vehicles	1	0	0					0
3941 Games and toys	1	1	200				1	200
3942 Dolls	3	2	110				2	165
3962 Artificial flowers	2	1	15			1		30
3993 Signs & advertising displays	1	1	9		1			9
3994 Morticians' goods	1	1	10			1		10
3999 Manufactures, nec	4	2	44				2	88
4119 Local passenger transp, nec	3	0	0					0
4121 Taxicabs	3	0	0					0

SIC	Description							
4172	Bus service facilities	1	0	0				0
4211	Trucking, local & long distance	2	0	0				0
4212	Local trucking, w/o storage	11	7	14	6	1		22
4214	Local trucking & storage	10	4	23	1	3		50
4217	Trucking, exc. local	1	0	0				0
4224	Household goods warehousing	2	2	7	1	1		7
4225	Gen. warehousing & storage	3	1	6	1	1		18
4226	Special warehousing & storage	1	1	1				1
4412	International shipping	1	0	0				0
4712	Freight forwarding	1	0	0				0
4721	Arrangement of transportation	10	2	2	2			10
4821	Telegraph communication	1	0	0				0
5022	Drugs, proprietaries, sundries	1	0	0				0
5033	Piece goods	1	1	1	1			1
5048	Fresh fruits & vegetables	1	0	0				0
5064	Electrical appliances, TV & radio	1	1	1	1			1
5065	Electronic parts & equipment	1	0	0				0
5074	Plumbing & heating equipment	3	3	56			2	56
5081	Com. mach. & equipment	1	1	20			1	20
5082	Constr. & mining machinery	2	1	5	1	1		10
5086	Professional equip. & supplies	2	1	4	1	1		8
5091	Metals & minerals, exc. petroleum	3	0	0				0
5092	Petroleum & petroleum products	1	1	1	1			1
5096	Paper & its products	1	0	0				0
5097	Furniture & home furnishings	1	0	0				0
5098	Lumber & construction materials	8	3	78	1		2	208
5099	Wholesalers, nec	1	1	1	1			1
5113	Trade	2	1	1	1			32
5211	Lumber & other building mtl.	2	2	32	1		2	1,053
5231	Paint, glass, wallpaper stores	9	3	353	1		1	3
5241	Electrical supply stores	3	1	1	10	2		50
5251	Hardware stores	25	12	28	1			9
5311	Department stores	3	1	3	1			0
5321	Mail order houses	1	0	0				102
5331	Variety stores	34	16	63	12	3	1	1
5392	Misc. general mdse. stores	1	1	1	1			84
5399	Misc. general mdse. stores	12	3	23	1	1	1	603
5411	Grocery stores	201	95	339	72	19	3	603

(continued)

APPENDIX TABLE 3 (continued)

Standard Industrial Classification	Total Establishments	Number Reporting	Reported Employment	Employment[a] Distribution by Number of Employees				Total Estimated Employment[b]
				1-3	4-9	10-19	20 or more	
5421 Meat & fish markets	63	32	57	29	3			63
5422 Meat & fish markets	1	1	6		1			6
5431 Fruit stores & vegetable mkts.	5	1	1	1				5
5441 Candy, nut, & confectionary stores	38	13	43	12			1	114
5451 Dairy products stores	3	2	4	2				6
5462 Retail bakeries, baking & selling	11	3	10	1	2			33
5463 Retail bakeries, selling only	2	0	0					0
5499 Misc. food stores	1	0	0					0
5531 Tire, battery, & accessory dealers	5	2	7	1	1			15
5541 Gasoline service stations	29	20	119	10	7	2	1	145
5611 Men's clothing & furnishings	38	10	121	8	1		1	456
5621 Women's ready-to-wear stores	33	9	19	8	1			66
5631 Women's specialty stores	27	12	13	12				27
5641 Children's & infant's wear stores	5	3	11	1	2			15
5651 Family clothing stores	2	1	4		1			8
5661 Shoe stores	29	9	33	6	2	1		87
5671 Custom tailors	16	7	23	5	1	1		48
5681 Furriers & fur shops	3	1	2	1				6
5691 Misc. apparel & accessories	4	1	1	1				4
5699 Misc. apparel & accessories	4	1	2	1				8
5712 Furniture stores	58	30	260	14	9	4	3	464
5713 Floor covering stores	3	0	0					0
5714 Drapery & upholstery stores	1	0	0					0
5715 China, glassware, metalware stores	1	1	1	1				1
5719 Misc. home furnishings stores	3	2	3	2				3
5721 Household appliance stores	2	0	0					0
5722 Household appliance stores	5	2	7	1	1			15
5731 Radio, TV, & music stores	5	3	9	1	2			15
5732 Radio & TV stores	8	0	0					0

SIC	Description								Total
5733	Music stores	22	8	17	7	1			44
5812	Eating places	303	83	470	36	34	10	3	1,615
5813	Drinking places	29	6	34	12	6			145
5912	Drug & proprietary stores	51	30	131	12	17	1		204
5921	Liquor stores	90	44	149	27	15	2		278
5933	Secondhand stores	14	3	18	1	1	1		84
5942	Book stores	8	1	1	1				8
5943	Stationery stores	94	31	60	28	1	2		94
5952	Sporting goods stores	2	1	2	1				4
5953	Bicycle shops	2	2	4	2				4
5971	Jewelry stores	29	11	74	10			1	174
5982	Fuel & ice dealers, nec	3	1	8		1			24
5992	Florists	22	12	20	11	1			22
5993	Cigar stores & stands	7	5	10	5				14
5994	News dealers & newsstands	1	1	1	1				1
5995	Hobby, toy, & game shops	1	1	1	1				1
5996	Camera & photo supply stores	1	1	2	1				2
5997	Gift, novelty, & souvenir shops	7	4	7	4				7
5999	Misc. retail stores, nec	26	8	19	6	2			52
6053	Check cashing & currency exch.	10	3	5	3				10
6151	Business credit institutions	1	0	0					0
6161	Loan correspondents & brokers	1	0	0					0
6411	Insurance agents, brokers & serv.	30	2	3	2				30
6513	Apartment building operators	1	1	23				1	23
6531	Agents, brokers, & managers	87	17	47	14	2	1		174
6611	Combined real estate, insurance	9	4	19	2	1	1		36
6711	Holding companies	1	0	0					0
7211	Power laundries, fam. & com.	2	0	0					0
7212	Laundries, exc. power	22	11	18	10	1			22
7213	Linen supply	2	1	7		1			14
7215	Coin-op laundries & cleaning	17	8	11	8				17
7216	Dry cleaning plants, exc. rug	106	50	144	34	14	2		212
7218	Industrial launderers	1	1	1	1				1
7221	Photographic studios	11	3	3	3				11
7231	Beauty shops	287	53	127	43	9	1		574
7241	Barber shops	123	54	131	44	9	1		246
7251	Shoe repair & hat cleaning	23	8	11	7	1			23
7261	Funeral service & crematories	47	15	47	13	1	1		141
7271	Garment press, alter, repair	11	5	115	3	1	1	1	253

(continued)

247

APPENDIX TABLE 3 (continued)

Standard Industrial Classification	Total Establishments	Number Reporting	Reported Employment	Employment[a] Distribution by Number of Employees				Total Estimated Employment[b]
				1-3	4-9	10-19	20 or more	
7299 Misc. personal services	8	4	10	3	1			16
7311 Advertising agencies	2	0	0					0
7321 Credit reporting & collection	2	0	0					0
7339 Steno & duplicating, nec	2	1	1	1				2
7341 Window cleaning	1	1	72				1	72
7342 Disinfecting & exterminating	2	2	12		2			12
7349 Misc. services to buildings	5	2	22		1	1		65
7351 News syndicates	1	0	0					0
7361 Private employment agencies	17	5	6	5				17
7392 Business consulting services	2	0	0					0
7393 Detective & protective services	14	1	6		1			84
7398 Temp. help supply service	1	0	0					0
7399 Business services, nec	7	3	7	2	1			14
7512 Pass. car rental & leasing	1	0	0					0
7516 Automobile rentals	1	1	4		1			4
7523 Parking lots	3	3	5	3				5
7525 Parking structures	10	7	22	5	2			30
7531 Top & body repair shops	3	1	1	1				3
7538 General auto repair shops	11	3	6	2	1			22
7539 Auto repair shops, nec	1	1	1	1				1
7549 Automobile services, nec	5	1	3	1				15
7622 Radio & television repair	34	12	15	12				34
7629 Electrical repair shops	4	0	0					0
7631 Watch, clock, jewelry repair	2	0	0					0
7641 Reupholstery & furn. repair	9	4	5	4				9
7694 Armature rewinding shops	1	0	0					0
7699 Repair services, nec	11	6	17	5	1			22
7821 Motion picture production serv.	1	0	0					0

SIC	Industry								
7911	Dance halls, studios, & schools	9	1	2	1		1		18
7929	Entertainers & entertainment	2	1	1	1		1		2
7932	Billiard & pool establish-ments	1	0	0					0
7933	Bowling alleys	1	0	0					0
7949	Amusement & recreation, nec	7	0	0					0
8072	Dental laboratories	10	5	21	3	1	1		40
8211	Elementary & secondary schools	2	0	0					0
8242	Vocational schools	1	1	2	1				2
8299	Schools & educational services	8	2	13	1		1		48
8531	Botanical & zoological gardens	1	0	0					0
8611	Business associations	1	0	0					0
8621	Professional organizations	1	1	12		1			12
8811	Private households	1	1	1	1				1
8911	Engineering & arch. services	1	0	0					0
8931	Accounting, auditing, bookkeeping	13	1	1	1				13
	Totals	2,690	983	5,573	659	223	56	45	11,785

nec = not elsewhere classified.

[a] Measured in full-time equivalents, defined as one full-time employee or two part-time employees.

[b] As a first approximation, firms not reporting employment are assigned the average number of employees in those firms in the industry which did report employment. To produce conservative estimates, the calculations employ integer arithmetic operations.

Source: Center for Economic Planning, The New School for Social Research, Harlem Business Inventory.

APPENDIX TABLE 4

Age of Harlem Businesses and Ownership of Property, Winter 1967/68

| | | | | Ownership of Business Property | | | |
| | | Total Establish- | Number Report- | Rent Premises | | Own Premises | |
Standard Industrial Classification		ments	ing	No.	Pct.	No.	Pct.
134	Poultry, exc. broiler chickens	1	0				
1511	General building contractors	37	10	8	80.0	2	20.0
1711	Plumbing, heating, air conditioning	16	5	4	80.0	1	20.0
1721	Painting, paper hanging, decorating	3	0				
1731	Electrical work	16	6	5	83.3	1	16.7
1742	Plastering & lathing	1	0				
1743	Terrazzo, tile, marble, mosaic work	1	1	1	100.0		
1751	Carpentering	5	1	1	100.0		
1761	Roofing & sheet metal work	4	4	3	75.0	1	25.0
1791	Structural steel erection	2	2	2	100.0		
1796	Instal. building equip., nec	1	0				
1799	Spec. trade contractors, nec	2	1	1	100.0		
2011	Meat packing plants	2	2	2	100.0		
2024	Ice cream & frozen desserts	2	1			1	100.0
2051	Bread, cake, & related products	1	1	1	100.0		
2086	Bottled & canned soft drinks	2	1	1	100.0		
2259	Knitting mills, nec	1	1	1	100.0		
2331	Women's blouses & waists	5	4	4	100.0		
2335	Women's & misses' dresses	5	3	3	100.0		
2337	Women's suits & coats	6	3	3	100.0		
2339	Women's & misses' outerwear	2	2	2	100.0		
2351	Millinery	1	0				
2355	Hats, caps & millinery	2	0				
2369	Children's outerwear, nec	1	1	1	100.0		
2381	Fabric dress & work gloves	1	1	1	100.0		
2512	Upholstered household furn.	4	4	3	75.0	1	25.0
2515	Mattresses & bedsprings	1	0				
2541	Wood partitions & fixtures	1	1	1	100.0		
2711	Newspapers	3	0				
2731	Book publishing	1	0				
2741	Misc. publishing	2	0				
2751	Com. printing, exc. litho.	18	14	12	85.7	2	14.3
2752	Com. printing, lithographic	3	2	2	100.0		
2834	Pharmaceutical preparations	1	1			1	100.0
2842	Polishes & sanitation goods	2	2	2	100.0		
2844	Toilet preparations	1	1	1	100.0		
2899	Chemical preparations, nec	1	0				
3142	House slippers	1	1	1	100.0		
3161	Luggage	1	0				
3231	Products of purchased glass	1	1	1	100.0		
3292	Asbestos products	1	1	1	100.0		

Years in Present Location

| Number Reporting | Mean Years | Age Distribution of Establishments | | | |
		1-2	3-9	10-29	30 or more
0					
10	12.9	1	4	4	1
5	12.4	1	1	2	1
0					
6	16.7	1	2	2	1
0					
1	5.0		1		
1	19.0			1	
4	21.0			3	1
2	55.0			1	1
0					
1	17.0			1	
2	6.5		1	1	
1	40.0				1
1	28.0			1	
1	2.0	1			
1	17.0			1	
4	11.5		2	2	
3	10.0	1	1	1	
3	4.3	1	2		
2	4.0	1	1		
0					
0					
1	1.0	1			
1	18.0			1	
4	12.2		2	2	
0					
1	12.0			1	
0					
0					
0					
13	22.2	2	1	5	5
1	22.0			1	
1	33.0				1
2	34.5			1	1
1	6.0		1		
0					
1	34.0				1
0					
1	40.0				1
1	14.0			1	

(continued)

Standard Industrial Classification	Total Establish- ments	Number Report- ing	Ownership of Business Property			
			Rent Premises		Own Premises	
			No.	Pct.	No.	Pct.
3433 Heating equip. exc. electric	1	0				
3441 Fabricated structural steel	5	2	1	50.0	1	50.0
3443 Fabricated plate work	1	0				
3449 Misc. metal work	1	1			1	100.0
3561 Pumps and compressors	1	1	1	100.0		
3574 Calculating & accounting mach.	1	0				
3585 Refrigeration machinery	1	0				
3599 Misc. machinery, exc. electrical	3	2	2	100.0		
3652 Phonograph records	1	0				
3679 Electronic components, nec	1	1	1	100.0		
3711 Motor vehicles	1	0				
3941 Games and toys	1	1	1	100.0		
3942 Dolls	3	1	1	100.0		
3962 Artificial flowers	2	1			1	100.0
3993 Signs & advertising displays	1	1	1	100.0		
3994 Morticians' goods	1	1	1	100.0		
3999 Manufactures, nec	4	2	2	100.0		
4119 Local passenger transp., nec	3	0				
4121 Taxicabs	3	0				
4172 Bus service facilities	1	0				
4211 Trucking, local & long distance	2	0				
4212 Local trucking, w/o storage	11	8	8	100.0		
4214 Local trucking & storage	10	6	6	100.0		
4217 Trucking, exc. local	1	0				
4224 Household goods warehousing	2	2			2	100.0
4225 Gen. warehousing & storage	3	1	1	100.0		
4226 Special warehousing & storage	1	1	1	100.0		
4412 International shipping	1	0				
4712 Freight forwarding	1	0				
4721 Arrangement of transportation	10	3	3	100.0		
4821 Telegraph communication	1	0				
5022 Drugs, proprietaries, sundries	1	0				
5033 Piece goods	1	1	1	100.0		
5048 Fresh fruits & vegetables	1	0				
5064 Electrical appliances, TV & rad.	1	1	1	100.0		
5065 Electronic parts & equipment	1	0				
5074 Plumbing & heating equipment	3	3	2	66.7	1	33.3
5081 Com. mach. & equipment	1	1	1	100.0		
5082 Constr. & mining machinery	2	1	1	100.0		
5086 Professional equip. & supplies	2	1	1	100.0		
5091 Metals & minerals, exc. petroleum	3	0				
5092 Petroleum & petroleum products	1	1	1	100.0		
5096 Paper & its products	1	0				
5097 Furniture & home furnishings	1	0				
5098 Lumber & construction mtls.	1	0				
5099 Wholesalers, nec	8	3	2	66.7	1	33.3

	Years in Present Location				
		Age Distribution of Establishments			
Number Reporting	Mean Years	1-2	3-9	10-29	30 or more
0					
3	32.3			1	2
0					
1	40.0				1
1	4.0		1		
0					
0					
2	30.0	1			1
0					
0					
0					
1	13.0			1	
3	14.7			3	
1	1.0	1			
1	32.0				1
1	59.0				1
2	16.5			2	
0					
0					
0					
0					
8	12.5	2	1	5	
6	13.5	1	2	2	1
0					
2	3.5	1	1		
1	60.0				1
1	1.0	1			
0					
0					
3	14.3		1	2	
0					
0					
1	15.0			1	
0					
1	12.0			1	
0					
3	41.7			1	2
1	20.0			1	
2	68.5				2
0					
0					
1	5.0		1		
0					
0					
0					
3	18.0		1	1	

(continued)

253

Standard Industrial Classification	Total Establish- ments	Ownership of Business Property				
		Number Report- ing	Rent Premises		Own Premises	
			No.	Pct.	No.	Pct.
5113 Trade	1	1			1	100.0
5211 Lumber & other building mtls.	2	2	1	50.0	1	50.0
5231 Paint, glass, wallpaper stores	9	3	2	66.7	1	33.3
5241 Electrical supply stores	3	1	1	100.0		
5251 Hardware stores	25	12	10	83.3	2	16.7
5311 Department stores	3	1	1	100.0		
5321 Mail order houses	1	0				
5331 Variety stores	34	15	15	100.0		
5392 Misc. gen. mdse. stores	1	1	1	100.0		
5399 Misc. gen. mdse. stores	12	4	3	75.0	1	25.0
5411 Grocery stores	201	84	77	91.7	7	8.3
5421 Meat & fish markets	63	34	31	91.2	3	8.8
5422 Meat & fish markets	1	1	1	100.0		
5431 Fruit stores & vegetable mkts.	5	1	1	100.0		
5441 Candy, nut & confectionary stores	38	13	12	92.3	1	7.7
5451 Dairy products stores	3	2	2	100.0		
5462 Retail bakeries, baking & selling	11	4	4	100.0		
5463 Retail bakeries, selling only	2	0				
5499 Misc. food stores	1	0				
5531 Tire, battery, & accessory dealers	5	2	2	100.0		
5541 Gasoline service stations	29	19	17	89.5	2	10.5
5611 Men's clothing & furnishings	38	9	9	100.0		
5621 Women's ready-to-wear stores	33	11	10	90.9	1	9.1
5631 Women's specialty stores	27	13	13	100.0		
5641 Children's & infant's wear stores	5	3	1	33.3	2	66.7
5651 Family clothing stores	2	1	1	100.0		
5661 Shoe stores	29	11	10	90.9	1	9.1
5671 Custom tailors	16	7	7	100.0		
5681 Furriers & fur shops	3	1	1	100.0		
5691 Misc. apparel & accessories	4	1	1	100.0		
5699 Misc. apparel & accessories	4	1	1	100.0		
5712 Furniture stores	58	28	18	64.3	10	35.7
5713 Floor covering stores	3	1	1	100.0		
5714 Drapery & upholstery stores	1	0				
5715 China, glassware, metalware stores	1	0				
5719 Misc. home furnishings stores	3	3	2	66.7	1	33.3
5721 Household appliance stores	2	0				
5722 Household appliance stores	5	3	2	66.7	1	33.3
5731 Radio, TV, & music stores	5	2	2	100.0		
5732 Radio & TV stores	8	2	2	100.0		
5733 Music stores	22	7	7	100.0		
5812 Eating places	303	80	75	93.7	5	6.2
5813 Drinking places	29	8	8	100.0		
5912 Drug & proprietary stores	51	31	27	87.1	4	12.9
5921 Liquor stores	90	44	39	88.6	5	11.4

Years in Present Location

Number Reporting	Mean Years	Age Distribution of Establishments			
		1-2	3-9	10-29	30 or more
1	54.0				1
2	11.0			2	
4	12.5		1	3	
1	30.0				1
12	24.8	1	2	3	6
1	20.0			1	
0					
14	9.3		9	5	
1	23.0			1	
4	17.2		1	2	1
84	13.6	7	34	32	11
34	19.8	5	4	15	10
1	21.0			1	
1	8.0		1		
11	12.1	1	7	2	1
2	11.0			2	
4	14.5		3		1
0					
0					
2	7.0	1		1	
17	7.5	3	10	3	1
10	23.1	1	1	4	4
11	17.6	2		8	1
10	17.2		2	7	1
3	28.0			2	1
1	4.0		1		
10	25.5	1	1	4	4
7	10.4	2	1	4	
1	1.0	1			
1	10.0			1	
1	29.0			1	
30	19.0	2	9	12	7
0					
0					
0					
3	21.0			3	
0					
3	18.3		1	1	1
3	19.0		1	1	1
0					
6	6.3		4	2	
78	12.1	18	26	22	12
6	16.5		2	3	1
29	22.1	2	7	11	9
44	18.8	4	9	17	14

(continued)

Standard Industrial Classification	Total Establish- ments	Number Report- ing	Ownership of Business Property			
			Rent Premises		Own Premises	
			No.	Pct.	No.	Pct.
5933 Secondhand stores	14	3	2	66.7	1	33.3
5942 Book stores	8	4	3	75.0	1	25.0
5943 Stationery stores	94	27	27	100.0		
5952 Sporting goods stores	2	1	1	100.0		
5953 Bicycle shops	2	2	1	50.0	1	50.0
5971 Jewelry stores	29	13	13	100.0		
5982 Fuel & ice dealers, nec	3	1	1	100.0		
5992 Florists	22	11	10	90.9	1	9.1
5993 Cigar stores & stands	7	6	6	100.0		
5994 News dealers & newsstands	1	1	1	100.0		
5995 Hobby, toy, & game shops	1	1	1	100.0		
5996 Camera & photo supply stores	1	1	1	100.0		
5997 Gift, novelty, & souvenir shops	7	4	4	100.0		
5999 Misc. retail stores, nec	26	8	7	87.5	1	12.5
6053 Check cash. & currency exch.	10	3	2	66.7	1	33.3
6151 Business credit institutions	1	0				
6161 Loan correspondents & brokers	1	0				
6411 Insurance agents, brokers, & serv.	30	2	2	100.0		
6513 Apartment building operators	1	1			1	100.0
6531 Agents, brokers, managers	87	19	11	57.9	8	42.1
6611 Combined real estate, ins.	9	4	4	100.0		
6711 Holding companies	1	0				
7211 Power laundries, fam. & com.	2	0				
7212 Laundries, exc. power	22	11	10	90.9	1	9.1
7213 Linen supply	2	1	1	100.0		
7215 Coin-op laundries & cleaning	17	9	6	66.7	3	33.3
7216 Dry cleaning plants, exc. rug	106	51	45	88.2	6	11.8
7218 Industrial launderers	1	1	1	100.0		
7221 Photographic studios	11	4	4	100.0		
7231 Beauty shops	287	61	59	96.7	2	3.3
7241 Barber shops	123	55	53	96.4	2	3.6
7251 Shoe repair & hat cleaning	23	8	8	100.0		
7261 Funeral service & crematories	47	18	7	38.9	11	61.1
7271 Garment press, alter, repair	11	4	4	100.0		
7299 Misc. personal services	8	4	3	75.0	1	25.0
7311 Advertising agencies	2	0				
7321 Credit reporting & collection	2	0				
7339 Steno & duplicating, nec	2	1	1	100.0		
7341 Window cleaning	1	1	1	100.0		
7342 Disinfecting & exterminating	2	2	1	50.0	1	50.0
7349 Misc. services to buildings	5	1	1	100.0		
7351 News syndicates	1	0				
7361 Private employment agencies	17	7	7	100.0		

Years in Present Location

Number Reporting	Mean Years	Age Distribution of Establishments			
		1-2	3-9	10-29	30 or more
3	27.7			1	2
4	19.2			3	1
24	17.0	7	4	10	3
1	23.0			1	
2	47.0				2
12	28.0		2	3	7
1	22.0			1	
12	26.6	1	3	4	4
4	12.5		3		1
1	1.0	1			
0					
1	15.0			1	
4	2.7	2	2		
8	12.6	2	2	2	2
3	10.7		1	2	
0					
0					
2	10.5		1	1	
0					
18	23.1	1	3	7	7
4	13.2		1	3	
0					
0					
10	19.4		2	6	2
1	15.0			1	
5	8.0		4	1	
48	14.5	6	10	26	6
1	5.0		1		
4	11.2		2	2	
57	15.4	6	14	30	7
55	15.7	6	15	27	7
8	5.9	1	5	2	
18	21.6	1	2	8	7
6	16.5	1		4	1
4	24.5		1	1	2
0					
0					
1	2.0	1			
1	32.0				1
2	19.0		1		1
2	10.0		1	1	
0					
7	15.1		1	5	1

(continued)

Standard Industrial Classification		Total Establish-ments	Number Report-ing	Ownership of Business Property			
				Rent Premises		Own Premises	
				No.	Pct.	No.	Pct.
7392	Business consulting services	2	0				
7393	Detective & protective service	14	1	1	100.0		
7398	Temp. help supply service	1	0				
7399	Business services, nec	7	3	3	100.0		
7512	Pass. car rental & leasing	1	0				
7516	Automobile rentals	1	1	1	100.0		
7523	Parking lots	3	2	2	100.0		
7525	Parking structures	10	7	5	71.4	2	28.6
7531	Top & body repair shops	3	1	1	100.0		
7538	Auto repair shops (general)	11	3	3	100.0		
7539	Auto repair shops, nec	1	1	1	100.0		
7549	Automobile services, nec	5	2	2	100.0		
7622	Radio & television repair	34	13	13	100.0		
7629	Electrical repair shops	4	0				
7631	Watch, clock, jewelry repair	2	0				
7641	Reupholstery & furn. repair	9	5	4	80.0	1	20.0
7694	Armature rewinding shops	1	0				
7699	Repair services, nec	11	6	6	100.0		
7821	Motion picture production serv.	1	0				
7911	Dance halls, studios, & schools	9	2	2	100.0		
7929	Entertainers & entertainment	2	1	1	100.0		
7932	Billiard & pool establishments	1	0				
7933	Bowling alleys	1	0				
7949	Amusement & recreation, nec	7	0				
8072	Dental laboratories	10	5	4	80.0	1	20.0
8211	Elementary & secondary schools	2	0				
8242	Vocational schools	1	1			1	100.0
8299	Schools & educational services	8	2	2	100.0		
8531	Botanical & zoological gardens	1	0				
8611	Business associations	1	0				
8621	Professional organizations	1	1	1	100.0		
8811	Private households	1	0				
8911	Engineering & arch. services	1	0				
8931	Account., auditing, bookkeeping	13	1	1	100.0		
	Totals	2,690	1,001	888	88.7	113	11.3

nec = not elsewhere classified.

Years in Present Location					
		Age Distribution of Establishments			
Number Reporting	Mean Years	1-2	3-9	10-29	30 or more
0					
2	16.0	1			1
0					
3	23.7		1		2
0					
1	5.0		1		
2	7.0	1		1	
7	18.6	1	1	4	1
1	6.0		1		
5	13.2	2		3	
1	10.0			1	
2	18.5		1		1
14	8.0	3	6	5	
0					
0					
5	7.6	1	3	1	
0					
4	9.2	1	2	1	
0					
2	23.5			1	1
1	30.0				1
0					
0					
0					
4	23.7			3	1
0					
1	37.0				1
1	8.0		1		
0					
0					
0					
0					
0					
1	15.0			1	
969	16.5	114	262	403	190

Source: Center for Economic Planning, The New School for Social
Research, Harlem Business Inventory.

APPENDIX TABLE 5

Race of Owners of Harlem Businesses, Winter 1967/68

Standard Industrial Classification	Total Establishments	Reporting Race	Race of Owner or Manager			
			Black	White	Spanish	Other
134 Poultry, exc. broiler chickens	1	0				
1511 General building contractors	37	11	5	6		
1711 Plumbing, heating, air conditioning	16	4	2	2		
1721 Painting, paper hanging, decorating	3	0				
1731 Electrical work	16	5	3	2		
1742 Plastering & lathing	1	0				
1743 Terrazzo, tile, marble, mosaic work	1	1		1		
1751 Carpentering	5	2	1	1		
1761 Roofing & sheet metal work	4	4		4		
1791 Structural steel erection	2	2		2		
1796 Installing building equip., nec	1	0				
1799 Special trade contractors, nec	2	1		1		
2011 Meat packing plants	2	2	2			
2024 Ice cream & frozen desserts	2	1		1		
2051 Bread, cake, & related products	1	1	1			
2086 Bottled & canned soft drinks	2	0				
2259 Knitting mills, nec	1	1		1		
2331 Women's blouses & waists	5	5		2	3	
2335 Women's & misses' dresses	5	3		1	2	
2337 Women's suits & coats	6	4		2	2	
2339 Women's & misses' outerwear	2	2			2	
2351 Millinery	1	0				
2355 Hats, caps, & millinery	2	1		1		
2369 Children's outerwear, nec	1	1				1
2381 Fabric dress & work gloves	1	0				
2512 Upholstered household furn.	4	4	2	2		
2515 Mattresses & bedsprings	1	0				
2541 Wood partitions & fixtures	1	1		1		
2711 Newspapers	3	0				
2731 Book publishing	1	0				
2741 Misc. publishing	2	0				
2751 Com. printing, exc. litho.	18	11	5	6		
2752 Com. printing, lithographic	3	2	2			

SIC	Description				
2834	Pharmaceutical preparations	1	1		1
2842	Polishes & sanitation goods	2	2	2	
2844	Toilet preparations	1	1	1	
2899	Chemical preparations, nec	1	0		1
3142	House slippers	1	1		
3161	Luggage	1	0		
3231	Products of purchased glass	1	1		1
3292	Asbestos products	1	1		1
3433	Heating equip. exc. electric	1	0		
3441	Fabricated structural steel	5	2		2
3443	Fabricated plate work	1	0		
3449	Misc. metal work	1	1		1
3561	Pumps & compressors	1	1		1
3574	Calculating & accounting mach.	1	0		
3585	Refrigeration machinery	1	2		
3599	Misc. machinery, exc. electrical	3	0	1	1
3652	Phonograph records	1	1		
3679	Electronic components, nec	1	0	1	
3711	Motor vehicles	1	1		
3941	Games and toys	3	3		1
3942	Dolls	2	1		3
3962	Artificial flowers	1	1		1
3993	Signs & advertising displays	1	1	1	1
3994	Morticians' goods	4	3		
3999	Manufactures, nec	3	0		3
4119	Local passenger transp., nec	3	0		
4121	Taxicabs	1	0		
4172	Bus service facilities	2	0		
4211	Trucking, local & long distance	11	9	9	
4214	Local trucking, w/o storage	10	5	4	1
4217	Trucking, exc. local	2	0		
4224	Household goods warehousing	3	1		1
4225	Gen. warehousing & storage	1	1		1
4226	Special warehousing & storage	1	0		
4412	International shipping	1	0		
4712	Freight forwarding	1	0		
4721	Arrangement of transportation	10	2	2	
4821	Telegraph communication	1	0		

(continued)

APPENDIX TABLE 5 (continued)

Standard Industrial Classification	Total Establishments	Reporting Race	Race of Owner or Manager			
			Black	White	Spanish	Other
5022 Drugs, proprietaries, sundries	1	0		1		
5033 Piece goods	1	1				
5048 Fresh fruits & vegetables	1	0				
5064 Electrical appliances, TV, & radio	1	1	1			
5065 Electronic parts & equipment	1	0				
5074 Plumbing & heating equipment	3	3		3		
5081 Com. mach. & equipment	1	1		1		
5082 Constr. & mining machinery	2	2		2		
5086 Professional equip. & supplies	2	1		1		
5091 Metals & minerals, exc. petroleum	3	0				
5092 Petroleum & petroleum products	1	1	1			
5096 Paper & its products	1	0				
5097 Furniture & home furnishings	1	0				
5098 Lumber & construction materials	1	0				
5099 Wholesalers, nec	8	4	3	1		
5113 Trade	1	1		1		
5211 Lumber & other building mtl.	2	2		2		
5231 Paint, glass, wallpaper stores	9	3	1	2		
5241 Electrical supply stores	3	1	1			
5251 Hardware stores	25	13	5	8		
5311 Department stores	3	1		1		
5321 Mail order houses	1	0				
5331 Variety stores	34	15	12	3		
5392 Misc. general mdse. stores	1	0				
5399 Misc. general mdse. stores	12	2		2		
5411 Grocery stores	201	97	48	36	10	3
5421 Meat & fish markets	63	39	7	30	2	
5422 Meat & fish markets	1	1		1		
5431 Fruit stores & vegetable mkts.	5	2		1	1	
5441 Candy, nut, & confectionary stores	38	13	10	3		
5451 Dairy products stores	3	2	1	1		
5462 Retail bakeries, baking & selling	11	3	3			
5463 Retail bakeries, selling only	2	0				
5499 Misc. food stores	1	0				
5531 Tire, battery, & accessory dealers	5	3	1	2		

SIC							
5541	Gasoline service stations	29	19	15	4		
5611	Men's clothing & furnishings	38	12	1	11		
5621	Women's ready-to-wear stores	33	13	7	5	1	
5631	Women's specialty stores	27	12	7	5		
5641	Children's & infants wear stores	5	3	3			
5651	Family clothing stores	2	0				
5661	Shoe stores	29	7	7	7		
5671	Custom tailors	16	7	6	1		
5681	Furriers & fur shops	3	1	1			
5691	Misc. apparel & accessories	4	1	1			
5699	Misc. apparel & accessories	4	1	1			
5712	Furniture stores	58	29	5	22	2	
5713	Floor covering stores	3	0				
5714	Drapery & upholstery stores	1	0				
5715	China, glassware, metalware stores	1	0				
5719	Misc. home furnishings stores	3	3	3			
5721	Household appliance stores	2	0				
5722	Household appliance stores	5	2	2			
5731	Radio, TV, & music stores	5	3	1	1	1	
5732	Radio & TV stores	8	3	3			
5733	Music stores	22	10	8	2	6	4
5812	Eating places	303	100	61	29	6	
5813	Drinking places	29	11	6	5		
5912	Drug & proprietary stores	51	28	11	17		
5921	Liquor stores	90	50	22	28		
5933	Secondhand stores	14	2	2	2		
5942	Book stores	8	2	1	1	1	
5943	Stationery stores	94	37	32	4	1	
5952	Sporting goods stores	2	1	1			
5953	Bicycle shops	2	2	2			
5971	Jewelry stores	29	14	6	8		
5982	Fuel & ice dealers, nec	3	1	1			
5992	Florists	22	13	9	3	1	
5993	Cigar stores & stands	7	4	2	2		
5994	News dealers & newsstands	1	1	1			
5995	Hobby, toy, & game shops	1	1	1			
5996	Camera & photo supply stores	1	1	1			
5997	Gift, novelty, & souvenir shops	7	3	2	1	1	
5999	Misc. retail stores, nec	26	9	6	3		
6053	Check cashing & currency exch.	10	4	4	4		

(continued)

APPENDIX TABLE 5 (continued)

Standard Industrial Classification	Total Establishments	Reporting Race	Race of Owner or Manager			
			Black	White	Spanish	Other
6151 Business credit institutions	1	0				
6161 Loan correspondents & brokers	1	0				
6411 Insurance agents, brokers & serv.	30	1		1		
6513 Apartment building operators	1	1		1		
6531 Agents, brokers, managers	87	21	13	8		
6611 Combined real estate, insurance	9	4	2	2		
6711 Holding companies	1	0				
7211 Power laundries, fam. & com.	2	0				
7212 Laundries, exc. power	22	11	4	5	1	1
7213 Linen supply	2	1		1		
7215 Coin-op laundries & cleaning	17	6	5	1		
7216 Dry cleaning plants, exc. rug	106	58	38	20		
7218 Industrial launderers	1	1		1		
7221 Photographic studios	11	4	4			
7231 Beauty shops	287	73	70	3		
7241 Barber shops	123	59	54		5	
7251 Shoe repair & hat cleaning	23	10	8		2	
7261 Funeral service & crematories	47	20	20			
7271 Garment press., alter., repair	11	6	5	1		
7299 Misc. personal services	8	4	3	1		
7311 Advertising agencies	2	0				
7321 Credit reporting & collection	2	0				
7339 Steno & duplicating, nec	2	0				
7341 Window cleaning	1	1		1		
7342 Disinfecting & exterminating	2	2		2		
7349 Misc. services to buildings	5	0				
7351 News syndicates	1	0				
7361 Private employment agencies	17	7	6	1		
7392 Business consulting services	2	0				
7393 Detective & protective services	14	0				
7398 Temp. help supply service	1	0				
7399 Business services, nec	7	3	2	1		
7512 Pass. car rental & leasing	1	0				

SIC							
7516	Automobile rentals	1	1	1			
7523	Parking lots	3	3	1	2		
7525	Parking structures	10	6	2	4		
7531	Top & body repair shops	3	1	1			
7538	General auto repair shops	11	5	4	1		
7539	Auto repair shops, nec	1	1	1			
7549	Automobile services, nec	5	1	1			
7622	Radio & television repair	34	12	11	1		
7629	Electrical repair shops	4	0		1		
7631	Watch, clocks, jewelry repair	2	1	1			
7641	Reupholstery & furn. repair	9	4	4			
7694	Armature rewinding shops	1	0				
7699	Repair services, nec	11	5	4	1		
7821	Motion picture production serv.	1	0				
7911	Dance halls, studios, schools	9	2	2			
7929	Entertainers & entertainment	2	1	1			
7932	Billiard & pool establishments	1	0				
7933	Bowling alleys	1	0				
7949	Amusement & recreation, nec	7	0				
8072	Dental laboratories	10	4	1	3		
8211	Elementary & secondary schools	2	1	1	1		
8242	Vocational schools	1	1		1		
8299	Schools & educational services	8	2	2			
8531	Botanical & zoological gardens	1	0				
8611	Business associations	1	0				
8621	Professional organizations	1	0				
8811	Private households	1	0				
8911	Engineering & arch. services	1	0				
8931	Accounting, auditing, bookkeeping	13	1	1			
	Totals	2,690	1,078	629	397	44	8

nec = not elsewhere classified.

Source: Center for Economic Planning, The New School for Social Research, Harlem Business Inventory.

APPENDIX B   A LIST OF LEADS FOR
             FURTHER WORK ON
             GOVERNMENT
             PROCUREMENT

PUBLICATIONS, GOVERNMENT PERIODICALS,
AND OTHER INFORMATION ON COMMODITIES
AND SERVICES PURCHASED BY THE
FEDERAL GOVERNMENT

Ammunition End Items and Components Normally Procured
by the U.S. Army Ammunition Procurement and Supply
Agency (Joliet, Illinois, September 1967)

An Identification of Commodities Purchased by the
Defense Supply Agency, Cameron Station, Alexandria,
Virginia (1966)

APPI (Advance Planning Procurement Information) U.S.
Army Material Command (June 1967)

Commerce Business Daily (Synopsis of U.S. Government
Proposed Procurement, Sales and Contract Awards,
Catalog No. C. 41.9)

Construction Work and Supplies Procured by the Department of the Army, Philadelphia District, Corps
of Engineers (August 1967)

Customer's Guide to Sources of Supply and Service,
Interim Issue Sections 1-4 (GSA Federal Supply
Service, July 1966)

Doing Business with AVCOM (U.S. Army Aviation Material Command, St. Louis)

Federal Item Identification Guides for Supply Cataloging, Section B-f (Government Periodical)

Federal Supply Classification (Government Periodical)
(Pt. 2, Numeric Index of Classes, Cataloging Handbook H2-2, Cat. No. D 7.6/2:2-2)

Federal Supply Classification (Government Periodical)
(Pt. 3, Alphabetical Index, Cataloging Handbook
H 2-3, Cat. No. D 7.6/2:2-3)

Federal Supply Code for Manufacturers, U.S. and
Canada (Government Periodical) (Handbook H 4-2,
Cat. No. D 7.6/2:4-2)

GSA Stock Catalog Part 1, General Supplies (Government Periodical) (Cat. No. GS 2.10/6 pt. 1/967)

List of Commodities, GSA Federal Supply Service (GSA Form 1382) (April 1967)

List of Materials Acceptable for Use on Systems of REA Electrification Borrowers (Government Periodical) (Catalog No. A 68.6/2:967)

List of Materials Acceptable for use on Telephone Systems of REA Borrowers (Government Periodicals) (Catalog No. A 68.6/5:967)

Military Prime Contract Awards and Subcontract Payments or Commitments (July 1966-June 1967) (Office of the Secretary of Defense)

Products Purchased by U.S. Army, New York Procurement Detachment (August 1967)

Selling to AEC, Procurement Program and Organization, Purchasing Offices, Products, Purchased, Private Industrial Participation (1966)

Selling to the Military
army, navy, air force, defense supply agency
General Information, Items Purchased, Location of
Military Purchasing Offices, Department of Defense,
Washington, D.C., 20301

U.S. Agency for International Development Architect-Engineer Questionnaire

U.S. Agency for International Development Construction Contractor Questionnaire

U.S. Agency for International Development Management Consultant Questionnaire

U.S. Army Weapons Command (U.S. Army Munitions Command)

U.S. Government Purchasing and Sales Directory (SBA, Washington, D.C., July 1965)

GOVERNMENT PERIODICALS, HANDBOOKS, AND
GUIDES DESCRIBING LEGAL CONDITIONS
AND THE ADMINISTRATIVE STRUCTURE
OF FEDERAL GOVERNMENT
PROCUREMENTS

An Introduction to the Defense Supply Agency, January 1967 (Cameron Station, Alexandria, Virginia 22314)

Armed Services Procurement Regulation (Government Periodical) (Catalog No. D 1.13:963/rep)

Bank-SBA Participation Loan Plans, A Guide for Banks (SBA, 1965)

Certificates of Competency (Their Purpose, Use, Benefits in Helping Small Business, 1962)

Contractor's Guide (U.S. Army Material Command) (February, 1967)

Defense Industry Bulletin (Department of Defense, monthly)

Defense Procurement Circular (1967, Department of Defense)

Defense Supply Procurement Regulation (Government Periodical) (Catalog No. D 7.615:966)

Department of Defense Prime Contract Awards in Areas of Substantial Unemployment (July 1966-June 1967) (Office of the Secretary of Defense Directorate for Statistical Services)

Department of Defense Single Stock Point for Specifications and Standards (U.S. Naval Supply Depot)

Doing Business with the Federal Government (GSA, Washington, D.C. 20405, 1966)

Doing Business with AVCOM (U.S. Army Aviation Material Command, St. Louis)

Federal Item Identification Guides for Supply Cataloging, Section B-J (Government Periodicals)

Federal Procurement Regulations (An Irregular Government Periodical, Catalog No. GS 1.6/5:964)

The Federal Supply Service (GSA, Washington, D.C.,
1964)

GSA, Business Opportunities (Information, Counseling
and Assistance) (GSA Washington)

GSA, Disposal of Surplus Real Property (Washington,
D.C. 1966)

GSA, Donation of Federal Surplus Personal Property
(Washington, D.C. 1966)

GSA, Selling New Products to the Federal Government
(Washington, D.C. 1967)

GSA, Washington, D.C. Federal Buying Directory
(Business Service Center, Counseling Guide) (August 1966)

Guide to Specifications and Standards of the Federal
Government (GSA, Washington, D.C., 20405, 1966)

Hearings Before Subcommittee No. 2 on Government
Procurement (Small Business Subcontracting and
Set-Aside Programs) (Washington, 1966)

How Small Business Can Obtain Government Contracts
and Subcontracts (List of SBA Field Offices, 1966)

Incentive Contracting Guide 1965 (Prepared by the
Office of Assistant Secretary of Defense)

Introduction to the United States Army Munitions
Command (Industry Orientation Brochure) (Dover,
New Jersey)

NASA Incentive Contracting Guide (NHB 5104.3) (August, 1967)

NASA Procurement Regulation (Government Periodical)
   (Catalog No. NAS 1.6/2:9641/rep)

Navy Procurement Directives (Government Periodical)
   (Catalog No. D 201.6/10:966)

Questions and Answers, The Defense Materials System
   and Priorities (U.S. Department of Commerce, 1967)

SBA Business Loans (1966)

SBA's Simplified Bank Participation Loan Plan with
   Early Maturity Feature (1963)

Selling to AEC, Procurement Programs and Organization, Purchasing Offices, Products Purchased,
   Private Industrial Participation (1966)

Selling to the Military (army, navy, Air Force De-
   fense Supply Agency) (General Information, Items
   Purchased, Location of Military Purchasing Offices)
   (Department of Defense, Washington, D.C., 20301)

Selling to Navy Prime Contractors, August 1967 (Navy
   Department, Washington, D.C., Navmat P-1030)

Small Business and Labor Surplus Area Specialists
   (Office of Assistant Secretary of Defense Instal-
   lations & Logistics, Washington, D.C., 20301)

Small Business Subcontracting and Set-Aside Programs
   (Hearings Before Subcommittee No. 2 of Government
   Procurement of the Select Committee on Small Busi-
   ness, House of Representatives)

U.S. Army Electronics Command, Fort Monmouth, New
   Jersey (U.S. Army Electronics Command)

U.S. Army Missile Command Plus Industry Equals Mis-
   siles

U.S. Army Weapons Command (U.S. Army Munitions Command)

U.S. Government Procurement Offices (For Each Region)
   (GSA, Business Service Center Washington, D.C.,
20407, June 1967)

APPENDIX   C   EMPLOYMENT AND WAGE
                 STATISTICS, BY
                 INDUSTRIES, FOR THE
                 UNITED STATES, THE
                 NEW YORK STANDARD
                 METROPOLITAN
                 STATISTICAL AREA, AND
                 NEW YORK CITY*

---

*We studied thirty-five industries with
multiple-digit Standard Industrial Classification
(SIC) codes; these industries represent between 50
and 60 per cent of total employment. This includes
all SIC 2-digit manufacturing industries, six 3-
and 4-digit wholesaling activities, and ten other
2-digit industries. This mix of aggregation levels
represents, we believe, the finest level of detail
for which reasonably complete and consistent time
series can be constructed from existing data sources.

APPENDIX TABLE 6

Distribution of Employment, United States, 1958-66
(in thousands)

Standard Industrial Classification	Employment							
	1958		1962		1965		1966a	
	No.	%	No.	%	No.	%	No.	%
(D) Manufacturing								
20 Food & kindred products	1,759	3	1,757	3	1,761	3	1,779	3
21 Tobacco products	93	–	90	–	88	–	84	–
22 Textiles	922	2	908	2	930	2	962	2
23 Apparel	1,158	2	1,259	2	1,345	2	1,399	2
24 Lumber & wood products	613	1	588	1	612	1	613	1
25 Furniture	634	1	384	1	429	1	462	1
26 Paper & allied products	558	1	615	1	640	1	668	1
27 Printing & publishing	871	2	926	2	982	2	1,022	2
28 Chemicals	795	2	850	2	910	2	958	2
29 Petroleum	227	–	196	–	184	–	186	–
30 Rubber & plastics products	345	1	408	1	467	1	510	1
31 Leather products	356	1	357	1	353	1	364	1
32 Stone, glass, clay & concrete products	563	1	589	1	630	1	645	1
33 Primary metals	1,159	2	1,173	2	1,302	2	1,345	2
34 Fabricated metal products	1,078	2	1,126	2	1,265	2	1,349	2
35 Machinery (except electrical)	1,359	3	1,493	3	1,749	3	1,911	3
36 Electrical machinery, equipment, supplies	1,232	2	1,573	3	1,656	3	1,896	3
37 Transportation equipment	1,148	2	1,127	2	1,138	2	1,912	3
38 Instruments: scientific, optical	327	1	356	1	384	1	433	1
(E) Infrastructure								
40-47 Transportation	2,532	5	2,475	5	2,537	5	2,548	5
48 Communications	858	2	825	2	881	2	900	2
49 Utilities	615	1	612	1	626	1	630	1

(continued)

APPENDIX TABLE 6 (continued)

Standard Industrial Classification	Employment							
	1958		1962		1965		1966ᵃ	
	No.	%	No.	%	No.	%	No.	%
(F1) Wholesale Tradeᵇ								
501 Motor vehicles, auto equipment	179	–	219	–	240	–	265	–
502 Drugs, chemicals	78	–	87	–	93	–	95	–
504 Groceries	174	–	198	–	216	–	221	–
507 Hardware, plumbing & heating goods	124	–	124	–	125	–	125	–
5096 Paper products & office supplies	65	–	80	–	91	–	102	–
5097 Furniture	51	–	57	–	60	–	61	–
(H) Services								
73 Miscellaneous business	637	1	883	2	1,118	2	1,216	2
75 Auto repair, service & garages	234	–	285	1	333	1	350	1
76 Miscellaneous repair	124	–	145	–	160	–	169	–
80 Medical & health	1,455	3	1,756	3	2,090	3	2,200	4
82 Education	663	1	306	2	917	2	941	2
(I) Government								
91 Federal	4,994	10	5,334	10	5,329	9	5,332	8
92-93 State & local	5,834	12	6,829	12	7,913	13	8,410	13
Total U.S. employment excluding mining and agriculture	50,622	100	54,946	100	60,201	100	63,358	100

ᵃ1966 manufacturing data are from the Survey of Current Business, January, 1968, p. S-13. All other 1966 data are linear extrapolations.

ᵇNational Industrial Conference Board, Economic Almanac, 1967/68, Section 13.

Source: U.S. Department of Commerce, Office of Business Economics, The National Income and Product Accounts of the United States, 1929-65, Table 6.3.

APPENDIX FIGURE I

Proportional Rates of Employment Growth, United States, 1958-66

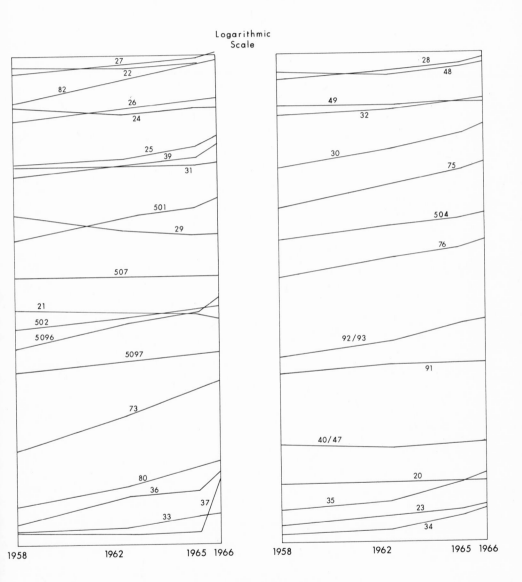

Logarithmic
Scale

LEGEND

Numbers refer to Standard Industrial Classification
codes as given in Appendix Table 6.

APPENDIX TABLE 7

Distribution of Employment, New York Standard Metropolitan Statistical Area, 1958-66
(in thousands)

Standard Industrial Classification	Employment							
	1958		1962		1965		1966	
	No.	%	No.	%	No.	%	No.	%
(D) Manufacturing								
20 Food & kindred products	96.9	2	90.9	2	80.4	2	76.7	2
21 Tobacco products	3.2	–	2.8	–	2.7	–	2.8	–
22 Textiles	36.8	1	37.9	1	39.5	1	41.0	1
23 Apparel	290.5	7	269.3	6	258.2	6	259.0	6
24 Lumber & wood products	6.9	–	6.8	–	6.9	–	6.9	–
25 Furniture	20.7	1	20.9	1	21.8	1	22.2	1
26 Paper and allied products	33.5	1	35.1	1	33.7	1	34.2	1
27 Printing & publishing	138.6	3	143.6	3	143.0	3	142.7	3
28 Chemicals	58.1	1	55.1	1	56.5	1	56.7	1
29 Petroleum	9.9	–	7.7	–	7.6	–	7.9	–
30 Rubber & plastics products	12.4	–	13.7	–	15.0	–	16.1	–
31 Leather products	32.0	1	32.4	1	30.5	1	32.1	1
32 Stone, glass, clay & concrete products	14.1	–	14.6	–	13.0	–	13.0	–
33 Primary metals	18.7	–	20.5	–	20.0	–	20.9	–
34 Fabricated metal products	56.5	1	54.9	1	52.6	1	55.0	1
35 Machinery (except electrical)	45.0	1	51.5	1	49.9	1	51.9	1
36 Electrical machinery, equipment, supplies	75.6	2	87.0	2	77.6	2	85.8	2
37 Transportation equipment	50.9	1	49.0	1	51.1	1	56.1	1
38 Instruments: scientific, optical	48.6	1	47.1	1	44.1	1	45.9	1
(E) Infrastructure								
40-47 Transportation	225.0	5	227.0	5	238.1	5	239.9	5
48 Communications	77.2	2	83.0	2	90.6	2	92.3	2
49 Utilities	36.4	1	36.1	1	34.9	1	34.3	1

(F₁) Wholesale Trade^a

501	Motor vehicles & automotive equipment	13.8	–	14.3	–	14.9	–	15.0	–
502	Drugs, Chemicals	23.6	1	22.2	1	20.6	–	20.4	–
504	Groceries	40.2	1	38.6	1	37.0	1	36.5	1
507	Hardware, plumbing & heating goods	10.2	–	10.6	–	11.0	–	11.1	–
5096	Paper products & office supplies	12.7	–	15.3	–	17.8	–	18.7	–
5097	Furniture	14.5	–	15.3	–	16.2	–	16.4	–

(H) Services^b

73	Miscellaneous business	134.7	3	160.0	4	187.0	4	194.0	4
75	Auto repair, service & garages	18.6	–	20.8	–	23.1	–	23.9	–
76	Miscellaneous repair	12.4	–	12.5	–	14.0	–	14.4	–
80	Medical & health	108.0	3	132.0	3	150.0	3	155.6	3
82	Education	66.2	2	77.0	2	85.0	2	88.0	2

(I) Government^c

91	Federal	128.6	3	129.0	3	129.4	3	129.7	3
92–93	State & local	316.0	8	420.0	10	482.8	11	512.2	11
	Total NYSMSA employment excluding mining and agriculture	4,131.0	100	4,335.0	100	4,458.0	100	4,565.0	100

a1958 data are from 1958 Census of Business, IV, Wholesale Trade–Area Statistics, Chapter 32. Data was obtained for 1963 from the 1963 Census of Business. From these two observations, 1962 data was interpolated and 1965–66 data extrapolated.

b1958 data are from 1958 Census of Business, VI, Selected Services–Area Statistics, Chapter 32.

cThe 1958 estimates are extrapolations.

Sources: U.S. Department of Labor, Bureau of Labor Statistics, Employment and Earnings Statistics for States and Areas, 1939–66, pp. 508–22; N.Y. State Department of Labor, Employment Review, August, 1967, pp. 17–22.

APPENDIX FIGURE 2

Proportional Rates of Employment Growth, New York Standard Metropolitan Statistical Area, 1958-66

Logarithmic
Scale

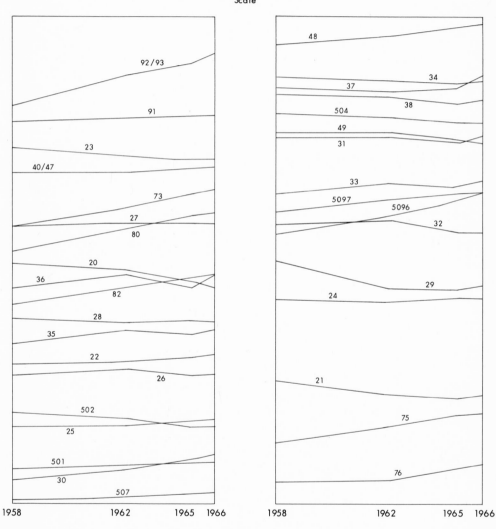

LEGEND

LEGEND

Numbers refer to Standard Industrial Classification codes
as given in Appendix Table 7.

APPENDIX TABLE 8

Distribution of Employment, New York City, 1958-66
(in thousands)

Standard Industrial Classification	1958		1962		1965		1966	
	No.	%	No.	%	No.	%	No.	%
(D) Manufacturing								
20 Food and kindred products	84.4	2	76.3	2	66.0	2	63.4	2
21 Tobacco products	3.1	–	3.0	–	2.8	–	2.8	–
22 Textiles	34.7	1	35.7	1	36.8	1	37.6	1
23 Apparel	276.9	8	253.6	7	244.0	7	241.4	7
24 Lumber and wood products	5.9	–	5.6	–	5.7	–	5.7	–
25 Furniture	18.2	1	17.8	1	17.9	1	18.0	1
26 Paper and allied products	29.4	1	28.0	1	28.0	1	28.1	1
27 Printing and publishing	125.9	4	125.5	4	124.8	3	125.1	3
28 Chemicals	47.7	1	44.8	1	42.9	1	42.5	1
29 Petroleum	9.6	–	7.1	–	7.5	–	7.6	–
30 Rubber & plastics products	10.6	–	10.6	–	11.2	–	11.9	–
31 Leather products	31.4	1	30.0	1	30.3	1	30.9	1
32 Stone, glass, clay & concrete products	11.0	–	11.0	–	9.8	–	9.5	–
33 Primary metals	13.5	–	14.6	–	14.0	–	14.3	–
34 Fabricated metal products	46.4	1	42.5	1	39.4	1	40.5	1
35 Machinery (except electrical)	35.1	1	34.8	1	30.5	1	30.4	1
36 Electrical machinery, equipment, supplies	53.8	2	55.6	2	49.4	1	52.6	1
37 Transportation equipment	13.6	–	11.5	–	10.3	–	10.3	–
38 Instruments: scientific, optical	23.4	1	22.0	1	22.9	1	24.5	1
(E) Infrastructure								
40-47 Transportation	217.6	6	213.5	6	218.0	6	219.7	6
48 Communications	75.0	2	72.1	2	74.7	2	76.2	2
49 Utilities	27.4	1	27.2	1	26.6	1	26.0	1

(continued)

APPENDIX TABLE 8 (continued)

Standard Industrial Classification	Employment							
	1958		1962		1965		1966	
	No.	%	No.	%	No.	%	No.	%
(F1) Wholesale Trade								
501 Motor vehicles & automotive equipment[a]	11.4	—	11.5	—	9.9	—	9.7	—
502 Drugs; chemicals[a]	22.1	1	19.8	1	20.1	1	20.1	1
504 Groceries[a]	25.4	1	32.4	1	31.8	1	31.4	1
507 Hardware, plumbing & heating goods[a]	8.4	—	8.0	—	9.4	—	9.0	—
5096 Paper products & office supplies[b]	12.0	—	14.0	—	15.9	—	16.6	—
5097 Furniture[b]	13.8	—	14.0	—	14.1	—	14.2	2
(H) Services								
73 Miscellaneous business	125.2	4	140.0	4	162.0	5	167.5	5
75 Auto repair, service & garages	14.5	—	16.0	—	17.6	—	18.0	—
76 Miscellaneous repair	8.9	—	9.9	—	10.8	—	11.1	—
80 Medical & health	86.1	3	101.0	3	113.0	3	117.9	3
82 Education	42.9	1	59.8	2	66.0	2	67.6	2
(I) Government								
91 Federal	117.5	3	115.8	3	112.5	3	111.1	3
92-93 State & local	287.3	8	313.1	9	349.5	10	372.4	10
Total N.Y.C. employment excluding mining and agriculture	3,478.0	100	3,557.0	100	3,575.0	100	3,630.0	100

a1958 data from Census of Business, IV, Wholesale Trade Area Statistics, Chapter 32.

b1958 data from Census of Business; data for 1963 from the 1963 Census of Business. From these two observations, 1962 data was interpolated and 1965-66 data extrapolated.

Sources: U.S. Dept. of Commerce, Office of Business Economics, The National Income and Product Accounts of the U.S., 1929-65, Table 6.3; Abraham Burstein, "The City Economy," The Commerce News (11 installments; N.Y.C. Department of Commerce and Industrial Development, 1965).

APPENDIX FIGURE 3

Proportional Rates of Employment Growth, New York City, 1958-66

Ratio
Scale

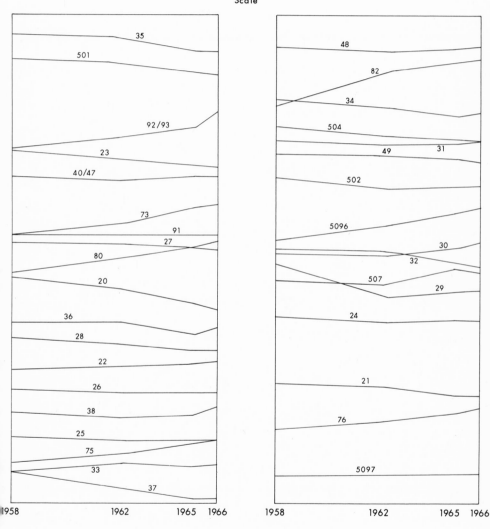

LEGEND

Numbers refer to Standard Industrial Classification codes
as given in Appendix Table 8.

APPENDIX TABLE 9

Weekly Wage Rates, United States, New York Standard Metropolitan Statistical Area, and New York City, 1958 and 1966

Standard Industrial Classification	Current Dollars					
	Wages, U.S.a		Wages, N.Y.C.b		Wages, SMSAC	
	1958	1965	1958	1965	1958	1965
20 Food & kindred products	$ 91	$116	$ 89	$120	$103	$137
21 Tobacco products	74	96	92	137	59	59
22 Textiles	68	91	74	91	81	86
23 Apparel	63	78	70	83	74	88
24 Lumber & wood products	71	94	83	107	85	106
25 Furniture	83	102	83	98	90	110
26 Paper & allied products	103	113	78	102	90	113
27 Printing & publishing	105	130	104	138	117	148
28 Chemicals	118	151	91	118	108	135
29 Petroleum	135	165	155	190	136	167
30 Rubber & plastic products	101	125	63	80	79	94
31 Leather products	68	85	65	75	69	81
32 Stone, clay, glass, concrete	98	126	98	116	97	135
33 Primary metal products	117	151	95	125	105	127
34 Fabricated metal products	106	134	86	107	96	118
35 Machinery (except electrical)	112	146	93	121	100	141
36 Electric machinery, equipment	105	133	74	94	92	144
37 Transportation equipment	121	161	87	115	122	174
38 Instruments (scientific)	109	140	85	105	111	126
40-47 Transportation	114	149	n.a.	n.a.	n.a.	n.a.

Code							
49	Utilities	109	146	102	152	n.a.	n.a.
501	Motor vehicles; auto equipment	77	110	60	164	105	137
502	Drugs, chemicals	90	113	117	172	117	166
504	Groceries	116	145	91	149	105	133
507	Hardware, plumbing, heating	96	130	119	136	103	128
5096	Paper products; office supplies	98	120	111	137	111	136
5097	Furniture	92	128	106	137	105	136
73	Miscellaneous business	101	124	108	118	88	115
75	Auto repair, services	77	99	87	94	69	98
76	Miscellaneous repair	98	131	103	111	76	111
80	Medical and health	56	74	51	82	n.a.	n.a.
82	Education	54	78	77	104	n.a.	n.a.
91	Federal government	89	117	n.a.	n.a.	n.a.	n.a.
92-93	State & local government	83	112	n.a.	n.a.	n.a.	n.a.

aBasic source is U.S. Department of Commerce, Office of Business Economics, The National Income and Product Accounts of the U.S., 1929-65, Table 6.5. The wholesaling activities (SIC 50) are estimated from employment and wage bill statistics in National Industrial Conference Board, Economic Almanac 1967/68, p. 246 (hereafter cited as N.I.C.B.)

bBasic source is U.S. Department of Labor, Bureau of Labor Statistics, Employment and Earnings Statistics for States and Areas, 1939-66, pp. 508-23. The 1958 statistics for SIC 21, 29, 40-47, 48, 501, and 92-93 are estimated from statistics in N.I.C.B., op.cit., pp. 216-24, 232. The 1958 statistics for SIC 502, 5096, and 5097 are from 1958 Census of Business, IV, Wholesale Trade-Area Statistics, Chapter 32; 1965 statistics for the same SIC's are linear extrapolations of the 1958, 1963 census data.

c1958 manufacturing data is from 1958 Census of Manufacturers, III, Area Statistics, Chapter 31; 1965 statistics are extrapolated from the 1958 and 1963 censuses. The same technique was used for wholesaling (Census of Business, Wholesale Trade-Area Statistics-N.Y.) and for services (Census of Business-Selected Services-Area Statistics-N.Y.).

ABOUT THE AUTHORS

THOMAS VIETORISZ is Professor of Economics at
the Graduate Faculty of the New School for Social
Research and Director of the School's Center for
Economic Planning. He has served as Associate
Director of the United Nations Economic Development
Training Program in Santiago, Chile, and as a re-
search staff member of the IBM Corporation in York-
town Heights, N.Y. He has also been a consultant
in development planning to the Economic Development
Administration in San Juan, Puerto Rico; the Ente
Nazionale Idrocarburi, Rome; and to the United Na-
tions Industrial Development Organization and the
World Bank.

In 1967-68, Dr. Vietorisz directed the Demonstration Economic Development Program for Harlem
for the United States Office of Economic Opportunity (OEO). This project forms the basis of this
volume.

Dr. Vietorisz is co-author of Industrial Complex Analysis and Regional Development and the
author of Techniques of Sectoral Economic Planning:
The Chemical Industries and several forthcoming
United Nations monographs: The Engineering Industries, The Chemical Industries, and Planning and
Programming of Metalworking Industries with a Special View to Exports. He has also written numerous
articles and technical papers, including contributions to the fields of housing economics, location
and regional development, and urbanization.

Mr. Vietorisz received his master's degree in
chemical engineering and his doctorate in economics,
both from the Massachusetts Institute of Technology.

BENNETT HARRISON teaches urban economics and economic development at the University of Maryland in College Park. During the academic year 1967/68, he served as Principal Investigator for the OEO study that culminated in this book. Previously, Mr. Harrison engaged in program budgeting and foreign agricultural assistance planning with the Program Evaluation Staff of the United States Bureau of the Budget. He has written technical papers on agricultural development and agro-industrial planning for the Office of Program and Policy Coordination, United States Agency for International Development. In addition, he has served as a Senior Urban Economics Specialist for the Development and Resources Corporation in New York and is currently a consultant to the Economic Development Department of the New York City Planning Commission and to the National Civil Service League.

Mr. Harrison received his bachelor's degree in political science from Brandeis University and his master's degree in economics from the University of Pennsylvania. He expects to receive his doctorate in economics, also from Pennsylvania, in 1970.